DAYS IN THE LIVES
OF COUNSELORS

DAYS IN THE LIVES
OF COUNSELORS

Editors

ROBERT L. DINGMAN
Professor Emeritus, Marshall University

JOHN D. WEAVER
Eye of the Storm, Inc.

Boston   New York   San Francisco
Mexico City   Montreal   Toronto   London   Madrid   Munich   Paris
Hong Kong   Singapore   Tokyo   Cape Town   Sydney

Executive Editor: *Virginia Lanigan*
Series Editorial Assistant: *Robert Champagne*
Marketing Manager: *Taryn Wahlquist*
Composition Buyer: *Linda Cox*
Manufacturing Buyer: *JoAnne Sweeney*
Editorial-Production Administrator: *Karen Mason*
Editorial-Production Service: *Walsh & Associates, Inc.*
Electronic Composition: *Galley Graphics, Ltd.*
Cover Administrator: *Kristina Mose-Libon*
Cover Designer: *Jennifer Hart*

For related titles and support materials, visit our online catalog at www.ablongman.com.

Between the time Website information is gathered and then published, it is not unusual for some sites to have closed. Also, the transcription of URLs can result in unintended typographical errors. The publisher would appreciate notification where these errors occur so that they may be corrected in subsequent editions.

Library of Congress Cataloging-in-Publication Data

Days in the lives of counselors / Robert L. Dingman and John D. Weaver, editors.
    p. cm.
   Includes bibliographical references.
   ISBN 0-205-35192-1
   1. Counseling. 2. Psychotherapy. 3. Educational counseling. 4. Clinical psychology. I. Dingman. Robert L. II. Weaver, John D.

  BF637.C6 D365 2002
  361'.06—dc21

                                    2002071172

Printed in the United States of America

10 9 8 7 6 5 4 3 2 1   VHG 08 07 06 05 04 03 02

CONTENTS

For many years, one of the most popular units I taught in my introductory classes was what I titled *A day in the life of a counselor in* _____ , illustrated by one of the following: an elementary school, a middle school, a high school, a private practice, or a mental health agency. I excerpted from my own experiences in those roles, or from those of interns I had supervised. I felt it was a realistic way to help the neophyte get a feel for the realities of work in the field. Some illustrations I changed over and over, but one became old and worn because students liked it so well.

As an intern supervisor having students in a multitude of settings, I had many opportunities to expand my knowledge of what it was like in each of the placements my students selected. I found these experiences valuable in responding to questions about what kinds of jobs my students might expect when they receive their degrees. When I retired, I thought all those experiences were over and just fond memories of my university teaching days.

Then, in 1996, John Weaver answered an advertisement that ran in a National Association of Social Workers newsletter calling for authors to submit chapters for *Days in the Lives of Social Workers,* an edited book that was being developed by Linda Grobman. Her vision was to gather the first-person stories from many different social workers about the kinds of things they typically would do in their everyday practices. Once completed, the book would offer undergraduate and graduate social work students a glimpse inside the hearts and minds of many real-life people who pursued careers in social work and who now spent their days helping others.

While serving as a disaster mental health volunteer on assignment for the American Red Cross (ARC), John wrote a chapter describing his experiences as he helped out at the recovery site following the crash of a large passenger airliner in the Everglades, near Miami. In the chapter, he compared his work at that crash site with his previous ARC disaster relief assignments, including his work as the morgue coordinator for a similar airline crash near Pittsburgh. He also described some of his regular duties as a casework supervisor in a community mental health clinic—his regular, full-time, paid employment position back home. He submitted the chapter electronically, and it soon became part of the original Grobman book.

The book became an immediate success as an inexpensive, extremely interesting, and easily readable textbook. John recently learned firsthand how well received that book had become, when he used it as a text for an undergraduate seminar class he taught as one of his current work assignments, moonlighting at a local college. Knowing a good concept when he saw it, he soon began pestering me to work with him on a similar book for counselors.

The book began to move toward a reality when I talked to several friends at an ACA conference, all of whom indicated great interest in writing about their lives as counselors. They also indicated that they felt such a book would be a valuable addition to the literature. I talked to several university professors who indicated that they would be eager to have such a book for their introduction to counseling or internship classes. We put out a call for papers and, pretty soon, the draft chapters began arriving.

As the project has progressed, we discovered much more variety than we had expected. The richness of counselors' experiences and the variety of settings in which they work has been inspiring. We believe you will find it enriching too. The richness and diversity of the counseling field is amazing.

ACKNOWLEDGMENTS

Many people helped us move this book from a dream to a reality. Our friends have written chapters and provided other suggestions and support—their fine work comprises the body of this text. The following reviewers provided valuable guidance in our writing of this book:

Charlotte Daughhetee, University of Montevallo
James Hanson, Grand View College
Robert E. Hayes, Ball State University
Michael LeBlanc, State University of New York, Oswego
Wanda L. Staley, Morehead State University

We gratefully thank all of them for all of their help.

We also cannot forget to acknowledge the members of our own families, who allowed us the time needed to complete this project and, all the while, supported us in our efforts. We proudly dedicate this book to them.

SUPPLEMENTAL MATERIALS FOR INSTRUCTORS

We have developed an instructor's guide to assist anyone who adopts this book as a supplemental text. This guide is posted on the Allyn and Bacon Web site: www.ablongman.com/dingman.

INTRODUCTION

This book is for counselors, or would-be counselors, who wonder what is out there in the job market for persons with a graduate degree in counseling. Whether you are just starting your course work in counseling, beginning your career just after completing your degree, or working in a counseling position and considering a change of setting, we know this book will help you to explore and consider the many options available to you.

Thirty-three individuals have written the stories of their unique and rewarding counseling positions. Many did not set out to enter counseling careers and share how they eventually entered the field. Each offers descriptions of his or her typical activities, including the challenges, the paperwork, the meetings, the successes, and even the frustrations. Most also share their hints on surviving the stresses that are inherent in their work.

We did not intend that each chapter would document a day. We wanted a variety of approaches about how counselors spend their time. Days, projects, part-time work, unusual settings, variety of tasks—all were intended as part of this book. Our authors responded well. Some of the chapters are clinical, while others are administrative. One looks back on a lifetime of counseling work. All approached the task of writing about their work in a unique manner. We believe you will enjoy the variety, and we know it will inspire discussion. We hope it encourages exploration of the profession; we anticipate many will find it inspirational.

The chapters are clustered in categories within similar settings, but, as you will see, each person's experience is unique and different. Counseling degrees are the beginning of opportunities well beyond what most of us imagine. In addition to stories about school and college counselors, counselor educators, and mental health counselors, there are also stories from a sexologist, an editor, a gerontologist, an addictions specialist, a counselor who is a part-time deputy sheriff, a professional association manager, and many others. Also included are two international stories, one by a school counselor working in Guam and another by a school counselor who worked in Africa. All of these stories are written by counselors who love their work.

We hope that this volume will make interesting reading for everyone in the counseling field. We anticipate it will initiate many discussions among counselors who have no intention of changing their positions, and we anticipate it will inspire many persons to begin thinking creatively about what to do with the rest of their lives. If it does any of these things for you, our efforts—and the efforts of the many counselors represented here—have been well worth it.

ABOUT THE EDITORS

Robert L. Dingman, Ed.D, LPC (WV), CCMHC, NCC, is Professor Emeritus at Marshall University, having retired in 1996 after twenty-eight years teaching in the counseling department. He was also in private practice as a counselor for twenty-six years.

He has served as a volunteer for the American Red Cross since 1981 and has been instrumental in the development of their disaster mental health services program. He has served in more than seventy disasters all over the United States and has taught many, many classes related to disaster mental health. Among the many disasters in which he has served are Hurricanes Hugo, Andrew, Hortense, and Georges; the great Mississippi floods; Alaska Airlines crash; and the 9/11 terrorist attack on the World Trade Center.

He is the author of dozens of articles in professional newsletters and journals. He also served as associate editor of the *Mental Health Counseling Journal* and as special issue editor of the *Mental Health Counseling Journal* titled "Disasters and Crises: A Mental Health Counseling Perspective," and as editor of a monograph titled *Licensure for Mental Health Counselors.*

Dr. Dingman has been very active in the professional organizations related to counseling on the local, state, regional, and national levels. He served as chairperson for ACA's Public Awareness and Support Committee, President of the American Association of State Counseling Boards, and a founding member of the West Virginia Counselor Licensure Board.

For his years of service to the profession, he has received many awards. Among them are Counselor of the Year, Counselor Educator of the Year, and Services to the Counseling Profession from the West Virginia Counselors Association; Counselor Educator of the Year and Researcher of the Year from the American Mental Health Counselors Association; the Gilbert & Kathleen Wrenn Humanitarian and Caring Person Award from the American Counseling Association; and the Distinguished Service Award from Marshall University.

Robert L. Dingman
2480 Smokehouse Road
Virginia Beach, VA 23456
e-mail: rldvabva@aol.com

John D. Weaver, LCSW, BCD, ACSW, CBHE, is a Casework Supervisor (and the Mental Health Disaster Response Coordinator) for Northampton County Mental Health and works as a part-time therapist for Concern, both in Bethlehem, PA. He is a member of the Adjunct Faculty of DeSales University (teaching undergraduate social work courses) and is a former member of the Adjunct Faculty for Marywood University's Graduate School of Social Work and the Psychology Department of Northampton Community College, all in the Lehigh Valley, PA. In addition to his direct-service work, noted above, Weaver is a founding partner of Eye of the Storm, Inc., a private consultation and education group practice specializing in disaster mental health (DMH), crisis intervention, and risk management–related training and support. He served as a DMH consultant to Operation Help (the FEMA crisis counseling grant program in PA resulting from the January 1996 blizzard and subsequent flooding, FEMA-1093-DR).

Weaver received his undergraduate degree in Psychology from Moravian College, Bethlehem, PA and his master's degree in Social Work from the University of Pennsylvania, Philadelphia, PA. Throughout his career he has written several articles and two other books. He has served as an expert reviewer for crisis management guide for schools. Weaver is frequently invited to present seminars and papers at national conferences in social work (including NASW 1990 in Boston, 1995 in Philadelphia, and 1996 in Cleveland), psychology (APA 1995 in New York), counseling (ACA 1996 in Pittsburgh and 1997 in Orlando), and nursing (ACAPN 1997 in Philadelphia).

He has been an active volunteer with several organizations, including the Mental Health Association and the American Red Cross (ARC). Weaver has assisted at several local and national disasters including service during the great Mississippi River/Midwest floods of 1993, coordinating Department of Mental Health services for morgue volunteers following the 1994 airline crash in Pittsburgh, and service with the ARC team at the 1996 plane crash in the Everglades, near Miami. He served as Coordinator of the ARC AIR Team's Family Assistance Center following the 9/11/01 terrorist incident that led to the crash of United Flight 93 in Shanksville, PA. He then served as an Assistant Officer helping manage the larger World Trade Center relief operation in New York City. He is also a volunteer DMH instructor for ARC and travels the country several times each year to help teach their two-day classes and expand the level of preparedness. In recognition of his service to the organization, ARC has presented him the Clara Barton Honor Award for Meritorious Volunteer Leadership. Weaver is donating half of his royalties from *Disasters: Mental Health Interventions* (1995, Sarasota, FL, Professional Resource Press; phone 1-800-443-3364) to the American Red Cross National Disaster Relief Fund and his publisher, Larry Ritt of Professional Resource Press, is matching his donation.

John Weaver
4635 Hillview Drive
Nazareth, PA 18064-8531
e-mail: johndweaver@compuserve.com

To view more information about DMH and disaster preparedness, see Weaver's Internet Web site: http://ourworld.compuserve.com/homepages/johndweaver

DAYS IN THE LIVES
OF COUNSELORS

1

COUNSELING IN RURAL AMERICA
DANIEL J. WEIGEL

Throughout my master's program, I had heard repeatedly that if you want to get a well-rounded counseling experience, you should venture into rural America and practice your trade. There is a poignant truth to this statement. The information shared here is based on my experiences working three years in a community mental health center serving a two-county area in an extremely rural portion of eastern Colorado. This was indeed a unique practice setting, in a remote area with 9,500 people scattered across nearly 4,000 square miles of rolling plains.

I accepted this rural counseling position directly out of graduate school. From the moment I parked my moving van, my education and professional growth in the field of counseling truly began. When I first walked in the door of my new office, I was given a five-minute orientation that I remember well. I was told that in this type of setting I would have to don the cap of the *generalist counselor* and see how well it fit. For those who are unfamiliar with this term, a generalist counselor is a mental health professional who is expected to handle any and all of the mental health needs in an often-isolated area, with no focused areas of specialization and limited referral options.

In many ways, the generalist counseling philosophy parallels the general practitioner model used in medicine. Conveniently and succinctly, the generalist philosophy incorporates both the positive and negative aspects of working as a rural counselor. On the positive side, there is no boredom or monotony in a job that changes every day. On the negative, there is very little time for comfort or familiarity in a job that is always changing.

On and off during my three-year tenure at this agency, I was the only full-time mental health counselor in this two-county area. At times there were two of us, but the turnover rate is high. Once you dive in, you quickly learn if you are comfortable with this kind of work. The salary in this type of position is usually about the same as other mental health centers; however, the cost of living in rural communities tends to be much cheaper. As a bonus, like their medical counterparts, some rural mental health centers offer grant money to pay back school loans for those willing to commit specified amounts of time to these settings. As I will attempt to describe, there are many unique benefits and challenges to this type of practice and, like other areas of specialty, not all counselors are cut out for this.

OVERVIEW

When I try to summarize my rural counseling experiences, three key words come to mind: isolation, ambiguity, and responsibility. Unlike their urban counterparts, rural counselors have few resources from which to draw and therefore must shoulder numerous responsibilities on their own. Where I was located, there were no private agencies taking referrals. There were no other counselors, social workers, psychologists, or psychiatrists for hundreds of miles. Even the local social services agency did not have professional counselors on staff to assist with family needs once they were identified. Therefore, *all* local agencies immediately turned to me with their mental health needs. This included law enforcement, school systems, local physicians, social services, and local group homes serving the developmentally disabled members of the community.

The agency I worked for provided services for a variety of needs. We were contracted by the state to provide all substance abuse counseling (mandated or voluntary) and all mental health counseling for the two-county area being served by my office. In addition, the agency was the state-contracted emergency mental health responder for all mental health crises that arose in these counties, 24 hours a day, 7 days a week. As the only mental health provider in the two-county area, we also had contracts with numerous third-party and managed care organizations along with Medicare and Medicaid clientele. Last, we provided sliding fee and *pro bono* services for low-income clients with mental health needs as a public service to the community in which we served.

TYPICAL ACTIVITIES OF A RURAL COUNSELOR

A typical day in this setting was atypical. Nonetheless, I will attempt to describe some of the activities I participated in as a rural counselor. The descriptions that follow are simply a smattering of my experiences—a minimally comprehensive summary, leaving many experiences untold. There really is no way to completely describe such a broad spectrum of activity in such a short amount of space. From the moment I started, my schedule was full. Until I set firm boundaries, I would easily see thirty to forty individual clients each week. I saw clients with a variety of presenting issues referred by the local physicians. I worked with families (often in their homes) at risk of having a child removed from the home due to abuse or neglect. I counseled clients with severe and persistent mental illness who were in and out of inpatient care. I met with court-ordered referrals and inmates, often right in their cells. I provided services to several persons with developmental disabilities in their group homes. I consulted with teachers and principals in the schools.

My clients cut across socioeconomic boundaries; some were wealthy, some were poor. The age range of my clients went from preschool to geriatric. The issues presented by these clients spanned the entire DSM range. I can say with some confidence that in my entire time at this agency, I did not provide the same type or nature of service twice. My role often fluctuated between being counselor, case manager, consultant, teacher, and professional colleague.

Emergency services were the most taxing part of this job. Many late nights, I was awakened by law enforcement or emergency room personnel to intervene on mental health crisis situations. Often I would drive for miles down desolate highways to arrive at the scene of a crisis. On many occasions I provided counseling services in a cold emergency room at night with a client who had just attempted suicide. I was also brought face to face with many clients who were actively psychotic and occasionally less than friendly or safe. Many times I had to move my head to gain eye contact with a client through the bars at the local jail, while also assessing my surroundings for safety. Because of these situations, I became very close to local law enforcement personnel, judges, doctors/nurses, and child protection workers. I also became the focal point of many curious glances of uncertainty as I established my role as a professional while assisting with these situations.

My two main roles in these emergency situations were de-escalation and critical decision making. Since I was often the only mental health provider in the county, I was faced with making final decisions regarding the involuntary hospitalization of clients who were a danger to themselves/others or were gravely disabled due to mental illness in the midst of these crisis situations. This was the hardest part of my work. If the legal papers were signed, the person's civil rights would be taken away for at least 72 hours. These decisions were not made lightly and clients (or their families) often disagreed with me. It was at these times that I felt most alone. However, I vigilantly kept in mind that the purpose of these interventions was to keep my clients alive, even if they were unwilling or unable to do it for themselves. These decisions were never easy to make.

BENEFITS AND CHALLENGES OF RURAL PRACTICE

There are many benefits to practicing counseling in rural America. The most apparent for me was the incomparable professional experience I received in this environment. During my rural tenure, I learned as much about myself as I did my clients and the profession. Closely paired to my professional experience was the amount of professional autonomy and independence afforded in this type of practice. My employer and my supervisor were not two doors down the hall as is the case in many agencies. There were hours of highway between us. This led to more independence in my work, coupled with greater professional responsibility. A rural counselor must learn to be comfortable with this arrangement and so must the employing agency.

Another benefit of this setting was the opportunity for me to explore future areas of specialty. With the opportunity to work with such diverse populations and issues, I was able to discover what type of work I most enjoyed. This is a serendipitous side effect of the generalist model of mental health counseling practice.

A further benefit is the close-knit nature of a rural community. When community members see that you are committed to working within the special fabric of their communities, you can feel quite welcome. On the other hand, if a person barges into a rural community and tries to change it or take advantage of it in any way, a rather unpleasant experience tends to result for everyone. Humility and open-mindedness are the keys to joining these community systems, and the rewards of these peaceful settings are immeasurable.

Along with the benefits of rural practice come many unique challenges. As mentioned earlier, frequently rural counselors face both personal and professional isolation. On the personal level, it can be difficult to *join* a closely knit rural community. Compared to the other professions in rural communities, counseling is young and often mysterious and misunderstood. Many people are leery about associating with the new professional in town. The counselor has to be careful not to push too hard or too fast. The community has subtle and unique ways of letting you know when you fit in. For example, when I first began shopping at the local grocery store, I found myself receiving many skeptical glances and an excessive buffer of personal space. However, as time passed, many people began approaching me and calling me by my first name before I had an opportunity to introduce myself.

Professional isolation carries a different meaning. Specifically, a counselor in a rural community is *always* a counselor, even when not at work. Due to the intricately established rural grapevine, everyone in town immediately knows who you are and what you do. Often your actions are being scrutinized in detail when you might least expect it. Privacy is rare and reputation is everything when trying to assimilate into a culture of this nature. In summary, by the very nature of the rural community, upon entry into the system, the rural counselor is often viewed as a mysterious outsider with questionable motives, frequently leading to feelings of isolation and alienation. Unfortunately, rural counselors tend to have few, if any, local colleagues with whom to discuss this uncomfortable initiation and transition.

Not surprisingly, another challenge facing the rural counselor is the heightened risk of professional burnout. The ambiguous nature of this type of practice opens the counselor up to a great deal of stress and uncertainty. Paired with high levels of individual accountability, critical decision making can also be particularly draining. Distances between the rural counselor and his or her colleagues, supervisors, continuing education (and other training opportunities), and professional literature resources may further feed the ambiguities.

Therefore, it is crucial that rural counselors take extra precautions in ensuring that their own mental health needs are being met. Two key methods of accomplishing this task include boundary setting and regularly scheduled consultation/supervision. The truth is, although rural counselors are often expected to do everything, they must accept the reality that they simply cannot. As with all mental health professionals, rural counselors must remain attentive to their personal needs and take care of themselves before attempting to provide care to others.

A final challenge facing the rural counselor is the fact that current professional ethics codes across the mental health professions have been written for and by urban practitioners. These codes often do not fit smoothly in rural mental health systems. For example, dual relationships in close-knit rural environments are nearly inevitable. Rural counselors cross paths with their clients everywhere they go. This is the nature of the setting and is simply unavoidable.

Small communities also provide unique challenges to client privacy. For example, due to the previously described community grapevine, people immediately know who is seeing the local counselor and at what time. Rumors blossom quickly from there. On many occasions, my clients expressed hesitancy with participating in much needed longer-term therapies due to fears that being seen as a regular at the mental health center might negatively affect their reputations in the community and ultimately affect their community and/or employment status.

Another challenge involves professional competency issues and a newcomer's lack of experience. Due to the lack of referral sources and vast distances to other professionals, rural counselors are often faced with treating issues with which they may not be overly familiar. Considering the fact that the alternative is often no treatment at all, rural counselors must do the best they can with whatever resources are at their disposal. An entirely different course of action would likely take place with the expanded resources available in an urban community. Awareness of these issues is vital, and extra precautions must often be taken in the interest of one's clients and one's own professional credibility.

LESSONS LEARNED IN THE RURAL TRENCHES

The primary survival tip I can offer to those working in this type of environment is to remain flexible, creative, and, at times, take a moment to laugh at everything. Rural communities have a unique kind of homeostasis and things seem to always return to balance with or without one's greatest efforts. Rural counselors must do what they can to assist the community. The best way to accomplish this is by becoming a community member and joining the culture while providing your services.

Another key to survival is to maintain close contact with colleagues in any way possible. A rural counselor must actively seek supervision and consultation from others in the field for rejuvenation. I believe it is nearly as important to regularly attend professional trainings and stay current with literature in the counseling field to avoid stagnation amid the fast-paced ambiguity of rural practice. Training refills your energy and compassion tanks and allows you to seek support from others who participate in the same type of work. Last (and I believe most important), when not on the clock *find a healthy escape* from being a counselor and use it often. My method was humor. Without humor, I would have been driven out of this type of setting within days.

SUMMARY

Although it is rarely discussed, rural counseling is a unique and challenging environment for the professional counselor. Few work environments compare to the diversity and excitement of this type of counseling practice. It takes a special type of person to practice successfully in this setting, and it generally does not take long to find out if rural counseling is a match for you. Personally speaking, I have never had a more rewarding experience or opportunity in my life.

Daniel J. Weigel, Ph.D., LPCP, CCMHC, ACS, is an Assistant Professor at Southeastern Oklahoma State University. He received his bachelor's degree in psychology and alcohol and drug abuse counseling along with his master's degree in community/agency counseling from the University of South Dakota. He attained his doctorate in counselor education and counseling from Idaho State University. His dissertation research focused upon examining the differences between rural and urban counseling practices. He is a licensed professional counselor in both Colorado and Idaho and is a certified addictions counselor in Colorado.

SUGGESTED READINGS

Murray, J. D., & Keller, P. A. (Eds.). (1986). *Innovations in rural community mental health.* Mansfield, PA: Rural Services Institute, Mansfield University.
This book presents a practical and updated approach to addressing many of the issues previously discussed by the authors in a groundbreaking earlier publication (Keller, P. A., & Murray, J. D. [Eds.]. [1982]. *Handbook of rural community mental health.* New York: Human Services Press) and provides an invaluable overview of many issues facing the field of rural mental health.

Sawyer, D. L., & Beeson, P. G. (1998). *Rural mental health: 2000 and beyond.* St. Cloud, MN: National Association for Rural Mental Health.
The National Association of Rural Mental Health (www.narmh.org), an exceptional organization devoted to addressing unique issues facing rural mental health professionals, developed this report, which examines current issues and future needs with a proactive focus.

Wagenfeld, M. O., Murray, J. D., Mohatt, D. F., & DeBruyn, J. C. (1994). *Mental health and rural America: 1980–1993* (NIH Publication No. 94-3500). Rockville, MD: U. S. Department of Health and Human Services.
This publication presents a remarkably thorough overview and annotated bibliography discussing numerous issues facing the rural mental health professional. It is an extremely useful resource that examines a wide range of rural mental health issues.

Weitz, R. D. (Ed.). (1992). *Psychological practice in small towns and rural areas.* New York: The Haworth Press.
This book, concurrently published as special issues in a journal (*Psychology in Private Practice, 10* [3], 1992), examines numerous challenges facing the mental health professional working in a rural private practice. A reasonably comprehensive examination of many issues involved in rural private practice.

Wodarski, J. S. (1983). *Rural community mental health practice.* Baltimore, MD: University Park Press.
This book examines numerous educational and administrative issues involved in rural mental health practice. An excellent resource for those working as administrators of rural mental health centers.

2

A FEW PILLS HERE, A LITTLE LSD THERE, SOME ALCOHOL, AND HEY, IF A NEW DRUG HITS TOWN, WHY NOT?

MIKE GRABILL

Most of my working days are the same, but sometimes the clients seem to be the same with only different faces and names—which, I think for me, is a shame, because of the reason I began this journey in the addictions field. It is probably the same reason that anyone gets into helping people. It is because we feel a "reason" to help someone, whatever that personally may be. But I enjoy what I do and I try to make sure my own house is in order.

Let me say a few words here in the beginning in regard to who makes a good addictions counselor. There is a myth, at times, that says *the good ones are the ones in recovery from their own addictions.* Some of the best addictions counselors I've seen were not in recovery. They certainly have known about addictions, and they have all been personally touched by the problem. They are extremely dedicated to helping folks who suffer. The recovering counselors, at times, do seem to be able to *connect* with an addicted client, which is a therapeutic plus. Both the recovering and nonrecovering, if they are going to be effective, usually work a program that is based on the Twelve Steps. These are also used in helping clients in their recovery process, and they are vital.

My typical day begins at 7:30 A.M. with my arrival at the office. Before I was primarily a director, I would start off my day looking at my schedule. Not that directors don't look at their schedules—it's just that when you are seeing people, and it is your primary responsibility, you check it so you don't forget who is coming in (and you don't forget their names), which can happen. It is similar to when you are doing the eighth session that day, it is 6:00 in the evening, and you have to yawn. You don't want to offend the client so you develop a *secret-yawn* skill. This is the ability to yawn without the client having any idea whatsoever that you are yawning. It has to be perfected, but only with practice. The more sessions you do,

7

the better you get at it. It's not necessarily the years of service. And believe me, you share this secret-yawn skill with your cohorts. Especially when it's a close call and you have had to do multiple secret yawns in a row.

Oh well, on with the day. So my schedule is checked, I've got the names in order for the morning so I don't forget who is who and my first client arrives at 8:10 A.M., just 10 minutes off schedule. Not bad for the first client, huh? But, he's rarely late and he has been clean and sober for a while. Notice I said clean and sober. It's been quite a while since I've seen a real live alcoholic. Most folks are polydrug users—booze, weed, coke, and heroin. A few pills here, a little LSD there, and hey, if a so-called new drug like ecstasy hits town, why not? So, times have changed since 1983 when I officially started counseling alcoholics and addicts. Usually, back then a person was either an addict or an alcoholic, but there were a few of us around who imbibed in the vast pleasure and demise of mood-altering substances.

As with any clinical practice, my time with the client involves strengthening the counseling relationship by showing genuineness and positive regard and using reflective listening skills. One thing about working with addictions is that clients have an acute sense of knowing if you are sincere. Being nonjudgmental is essential in the therapeutic relationship in order to develop trustworthiness. What is the best treatment goal that is mutually developed with the client to address a specific problem area? Trustworthiness within the counseling setting is paramount on the therapist's part in order to develop the best treatment goal.

I would like to elaborate further on the Twelve Steps and their significance with the addictions counselor. It is imperative, regardless if one is recovering or nonrecovering, that the addictions counselor have a working understanding of the Twelve Steps. How will a counselor ask a client to make application of the Steps to a particular issue if the counselor has a limited understanding of the Steps? It will have an effect upon treatment planning as well as the therapeutic relationship. Remember, the addicted client is very perceptive and will probably confront the counselor if the client suspects the counselor, recovering or not, is limited in his or her understanding of the Steps.

As I stated earlier, working a program is beneficial for the counselor for a number of reasons. First, and at a deeper level, the counselor who "works a program," will probably use the Twelve Steps in his or her daily life. The addictions field is not any easier to work in than any of the other human service fields. Honestly, it appears that many of us don't last very long. So using the Steps can only help. Secondly, Glasser (1989) talks about not asking our clients to do something we would not be willing to do ourselves. Imagine the "connectedness" that could potentially happen when the client realizes the counselor practices a program that incorporates the Steps. The Steps help one deal with the rigors of daily living. This is the area—the rigors of daily living—that the client has to handle once he or she begins to abstain from drugs and alcohol. Those daily living issues are what we all have to handle; some of us manage them in a self-destructive manner and become addicted. So, regardless if one is a recovering counselor or not, the ability to connect with the client is nestled in recovery and the application of the "tools" or Twelve Steps to achieve that recovery. And if the counselor works a program, helping the client is intensified.

Although paramount, there is more to being an addictions counselor than practicing the Steps. One rigorous credential that is helpful in working with addictions is the Certified Addiction Counselor (CAC). Requirements for the CAC are:

- Three years of providing primary alcohol and other drug abuse counseling 51 percent of the time
- Documentation of at least 300 clock hours of on-the-job supervision in the twelve core skill areas of counseling (screening, intake, orientation, assessment, treatment planning, counseling, case management, crisis intervention, client education, referral, reports and record keeping, consultation)
- A bachelor's degree in the human service field, with specific drug and alcohol, ethics, and HIV/AIDS education course work
- A case study and written and oral examinations

The recently legislated Pennsylvania Licensed Professional Counselor is another worthwhile credential for reimbursement purposes, but it does not have the needed specificity to work with the addicted client.

My 8:00 A.M. client was dealing with developing a daily program so he could maintain a drug-free lifestyle. Our main goal this day was to design a functional program he could apply by incorporating the Twelve Steps. We looked at what he had been doing the past month to remain abstinent. Besides sharing about frustrations with co-workers and feelings of guilt and shame over past using behaviors during sessions, the client had been staying clean and sober by what appeared to be luck and will power. He had identified substance abuse as a problem, yet he had not begun to internalize the fact that if he continued to drink and use drugs, he would have problems.

The client was familiar with the book *Alcoholics Anonymous* and the suggested Twelve Steps, so our treatment plan included readings to develop a daily program from this text. The task of writing out a daily program was undertaken in session, taking note where and when frustrations and negative feelings would or could be a problem throughout a typical day. By the end of the session, the client expressed confidence with practicing his daily program until our next time together. We also discussed the practicality for him to become involved in the weekly recovery group that I facilitated. Although he was hesitant at first, after we discussed the potential benefits he was eager to begin, especially after learning that other folks who had been in recovery for over a year would be participating.

Groups with addicts are exciting to lead once trust has been established among the members and the facilitator. Prior to that, they are a lot of work for the leader because of the need to exercise much direction and facilitation. My training took place on the job in the first inpatient unit where I worked. I was fortunate to have a clinical director who provided the time for me to use him as a role model and mentor. I also took group-specific training courses over the years and trained staff members in our agency. The best way to learn about groups is to co-facilitate with someone who has been doing them for a while. There is a magic that takes place when the group members act like group members. As a facilitator, you know when that magic has happened. When the group concludes, you run out of the room, find your colleagues, and say "*Wow, man, that was the greatest group and I didn't have to do much of anything*!"

Well, back to my session. Following the closing, I hurriedly wrote a DAP (Discussion, Assessment, and Plan) progress note, placed the client's chart in the file cabinet, retrieved my next client's chart, and proceeded into my 9:00 A.M. session at 9:04 A.M. That's not bad after doing this for seventeen years now. I'm glad I'm a director and have a very limited caseload. But, the reality is that I enjoy counseling people who have addictions issues, even though I do other types of therapy as well.

My second session is with a self-referred 19-year-old female with a heroin problem. This is her first session, even though she has a long history of substance abuse and had been seen in the local Student Assistance Program in the past. She reports that she is tired of the heroin lifestyle. She and her boyfriend had been traveling to the city the past few months, and she had to get away. Most of the session was used encouraging the client that she had made the right decision to do something for herself and her potential need for detoxification. Another issue, besides her identification of heroin as a problem, was her lack of insight into the effects her use of other substances such as marijuana, alcohol, and Xanax were having on her life.

Assessing her potential for withdrawal came next. She did appear to be in Grade I withdrawal, so the next move in the session was to check the possibility of her being detoxed and hopefully placed in an inpatient D&A rehabilitation facility. Whenever one deals with the D&A funding, it is always a tricky situation, since funding is always at a premium. You'd better make absolutely sure you know what you're doing, especially with the required placement criteria such as ASAM and the PCPC. Well, the client was authorized for detoxification and was scheduled for admission that afternoon. She was grateful and saw it as a new start.

Some brief explanation of ASAM and PCPC is in order. Both ASAM and PCPC are addictions level-of-care placement tools. ASAM is the American Society of Addiction Medicine, which was developed in the early 1990s. It is recognized nationally. The PCPC is the Pennsylvania Client Placement Criteria developed in the mid 1990s; it uses ASAM as a base. It was developed specifically for Pennsylvania's publicly funded clients. Both ASAM and the PCPC are essentially the same as far as their utility.

It is 10:30 A.M. and I have completed all of the phone calls and paperwork, faxed that paperwork to the respective locations, and begun to complete my 9:00 A.M. client's chart, writing the DAP note and treatment plan. I check my interoffice mailbox and find it loaded with messages: Call the county chief probation officer, call the D&A commission about reauthorizations, call such-and-such managed care organization, call the other office in regard to a supervision issue. Where to begin?

Well, first things first. So I start with the probation office—it's concerning the treatment progress of a client. I inform the P.O. that I can release information in the following areas: whether the client is in counseling, if the client has relapsed and the frequency of the substance use, the client's prognosis, a description of the client's progress, and the nature of the agency. She is satisfied with the information I provide her and she says she won't bother me any more. We've known each other for a long time. It pays to have a good relationship with the courts. You can get a lot of referrals from them if you treat them respectfully.

My next two phone calls are somewhat more tense. There is always this issue of who controls the destiny of the client. I see my role as one of an advocate for the client—if the client requires more sessions because of clinical necessity, I should know, not someone who has seen the client one time or not at all. We are all professionals and we try to do quality, cost-effective work. Therapists do not have time to be on the phone arguing a point. So I treat the people on the other end of the phone with dignity, realizing they have a job to do. I want to make their job as easy as possible, just like I want my job to be, and at the same time not compromise the standards I've established in trying to help people.

The final call concerning a supervision issue related to how a therapist views information he read recently in Zimberg's *The Clinical Management of Alcoholism*. The therapist was encouraged to discuss the issue with colleagues and to bring it up as a discussion in the next staff meeting. Brown's *Treating the Alcoholic: A Developmental Model of Recovery* was also cited as a helpful addition to Zimberg's, especially since Brown's work was assisted by Yalom (1995).

Ah, lunchtime. Even though I sometimes stay around the office and shag phone calls, it's still important to use it as a time to make fun of the staff and myself. Oh, they make fun of me too. It's good for the counseling soul to do this—laugh!

Most of the afternoon is spent taking calls from referrals, trying to answer supervision questions, and preparing for the next staff meeting. But, as is typical in addictions counseling, a crisis client walks in at 3:00 P.M. A 25-year-old single white male, crying, yet apparently clean and sober, states he is headed for jail and he is scared. He begins his story by stating he had been out drinking with his friends and arrived home to his 6-year-old daughter and her 12-year-old babysitter. He states he retired to his room, ingested an ecstasy tablet, and the next thing he knew, he was on the floor with the 12-year-old babysitter, performing a sexual act with her. The next day, he is arrested by the police for sexual charges against a minor, thus his potential to go to jail and the basis of his very real fear.

The first issue to address is the client's present fear of jail and to try to look at the situation from a different point of view. The client calmed down following a review of the potential outcomes concerning his legal status. Next, we review the client's use of substances and the role they play in his present predicament. He acknowledges there is a substance abuse problem and that there may be a sexual issue that needs to be addressed. Finally, after exploring the potential scenarios and making a commitment to further treatment, the client states he will continue to abstain and maintain a regular schedule in his life. He is also told that if he has any further anxiety, he can call the crisis number any time, day or night, and someone will talk to him. After closure in the session, he is directed to meet with the office personnel and his method of payment is agreed upon. He schedules an appointment for the next day and I complete his chart.

Let's take a moment to talk about on-call duties for the outpatient staff. Historically, the agency has had an on-call service with each of the staff taking turns on a weekly, rotating basis. When we looked at the use of the service, we found it was not well utilized by our clients, so we discontinued the service through our office. There was some concern that our managed care contracts would be uneasy with the agency utilizing the community crisis line. Fortunately, the relationship with the community crisis line has worked out well and is acceptable to managed care. It has also been a favorable move for our therapists, since their jobs are tough enough without having to worry about being on call. We have had no complaints with our present setup and, as anticipated, client utilization has remained low.

As a manager, I am often dealing with administrative and organizational duties. What is the best way to serve the clients? How can we keep the workplace tolerable for the staff? The on-call issue is an excellent case in point. There are always issues that need to be handled. Also, being a co-owner of the agency brings in other aspects that are difficult for someone who was trained as a therapist. Thank goodness a person can still learn after being trained as a therapist. That is the only way my partner and I have been able to still be viable after seven years—we can continue to learn! Owning a human service agency is not easy, and you will not get rich at it, especially if you are trained as a helping professional. You want to help people too much and be a servant to them. But, as owners, we understand that creativity is part of the formula for being a good therapist. This is why we try to encourage our staff to also be creative in their search for positive treatment approaches.

Well, it's 4:30 P.M.—do you know where your addictions counselor is? For me, it means I'm off to the country to relax with my family and listen to what my wife and kids tell me to do. And, just maybe, I'll do them! You know, sometimes it's nice to have people ask you to do something for them. It's a welcome change at the end of a long day. That's a day in the life.

Mike Grabill, M.Ed., CAC grew up in Dayton, OH and graduated from Eastern Mennonite University with a bachelor's degree in Social Work in 1983 and a master's degree in Counseling from The Pennsylvania State University in 1988. He received his certification as an addictions counselor in 1990. Mike has served on local and state D&A and MH boards and work groups in the past. He has worked with adolescents in inpatient and outpatient D&A settings and in MH partial hospitalization settings. His work with adults has been in both inpatient and outpatient D&A settings as a therapist, supervisor, and clinical director. Mike currently co-owns Clear Concepts Counseling, an outpatient counseling agency in Central Pennsylvania. He also maintains a consulting practice specializing in addictions and healthy lifestyle development.

SUGGESTED READINGS

Alcoholics Anonymous. (1976). New York: AA World Services, Inc.
   This is must reading for any counselor who wishes to work in the addictions field. It provides the foundation for the Twelve Steps of recovery as well as an understanding of the alcoholic; it is written by recovered alcoholics and is the basic text of the Alcoholics Anonymous program, the model of all Twelve Steps programs.

Brown, S. (1985). *Treating the alcoholic: A developmental model of recovery.* New York: John Wiley & Sons.
   Brown spent much time interviewing and studying alcoholics and their perceptions of the counseling field and its ability to help in their recovery. Her conclusion, echoing her subjects, is that therapists need to learn from the addict who seeks counseling. This information is vital for the therapist to be of benefit in the helping relationship.

Glaser, W. (1989). *Reality therapy.* New York: HarperCollins.
   This is a very helpful text in working with the addictions. Glasser stresses the importance of allowing clients to be accountable and responsible for their behaviors while also asking clinicians to assess their own involvement in the therapeutic process.

Yalom, I. (1995). *The theory and practice of group psychotherapy.* New York: Basic Books.
   This is a book for all therapists who do group work, regardless if it is with addiction groups or not. Yalom was involved in Brown's research for her book, *Treating the alcoholic: A developmental model of recovery.*

Zimberg, S. (1982). *The clinical management of alcoholism.* New York: Brunner/Mazel.
   The text is written to help clinicians in the understanding, diagnosis, and treatment of alcoholism. It is a practical guide, written by a psychiatrist, in which the information represents what the therapist needs to know in the day-to-day diagnosis, differential diagnosis, and treatment of alcoholism in its various manifestations and degrees of severity.

3

PRIMING THE PUMP: PROVIDING NECESSARY SKILLS FOR POSITIVE MENTAL HEALTH

ELAINE ADAMS

P riming the pump. My activities provide the start in learning and living for the children with whom I work. My career is truly rewarding because, working with the very young, I am able to experience tremendous growth with each troubled youngster. A rather strong drawback to my chosen work is the ethical issue of touch. Perhaps hugs, or restraining a child in danger of harming himself or herself or another child, might be questioned differently than might have been the case years ago—a sad statement on our times. I usually follow my heart. There appear to be more children in need of mental health services than ever before. My heart yearns to be a part of their healing.

It is 7:30 Monday morning. My week has opened with a blast. The special education youngsters are getting off the bus after their morning trek from home and settling down in the hallways as they await their teachers. Lonnie is crying. It is only her second day and she is somewhat fearful of the unknown. Bubba sits shivering, improperly dressed for the 40-degree weather and still caked with the dirt from yesterday's crawl about the floors. Mark announces he has soiled his pull-ups and wants to be changed. Rosie carefully scans the other children with her eyes. She has not yet begun to speak, although she is almost 4.

My day unravels with the special education youngsters, totaling over fifty, their adult teachers and caretakers: It seems that two assistants have called in ill and strangers (to the children) have come to take their places. I show them where to sign in and take them to their respective classrooms. There are not enough hands to take care of immediate needs, so I assist in the classrooms until others arrive.

My office doubles as an office and playroom for therapy. I am a school educational counselor, a licensed professional counselor, and a certified play therapist. The early childhood program in Abilene consists of two sites: Locust and Woodson. Since I am the mental health professional for the federal government

Head Start program, I work with the Head Start students on both campuses. The Woodson campus has 230 Head Start students currently enrolled. My office is located on the Locust campus, where I function as the school counselor for all of the students, their families, the staff and their families. The children enrolled at Locust including the Head Start students total 373.

It is time to roll Rosie in her wheelchair down to my office to spend some much-needed therapy time. Even though Rosie has chosen not to speak, she has learned to communicate by biting and by collecting big gobs of spit in her mouth and then shooting them through the air and onto whoever vexes her at the moment. She also shuts her eyes, tilts her head to her chest, and completely closes down when the activities of the day become too frustrating. Rosie has not acknowledged me as we rolled down the hallway but does make a mumbling sound as we near the door with the big happy face mounted on the outside. She sits quietly while I set the hands of the clock face attached to the door, so that the outside traffic will know not to bother us until our session is over. When we get inside the room, I also set a timer that will ring with a bell and alert us when the session has come to a close. Now we are ready to get started.

Once we are in the room, Rosie lifts her head and scans the shelves with her eyes. She looks at a book, then back to me, again at the book, then back to me. *Oh, you would like to read a book,* I comment. Rosie smiles. I assist her down from her chair and she swiftly makes her way on all fours toward her target. Our session progresses and, before you know it, the bell rings and I am escorting Rosie back to her classroom for her day's activities. It is now time for the other 320 children to surface. They have been arriving by bus, or they have been brought into the school by their parents and left in the cafeteria for breakfast. The boys and girls are entering into the hallways with the adult assistants and being deposited at their classrooms for the day.

Our school is connected with the school district and we follow district guidelines, policies, and holidays. Our children are ages 3 and 4. We house the federal government Head Start children, the state prekindergarten students, and the preschool program for disabled youngsters and the young children with hearing impairments. We offer a multitude of services, including parent training, parent higher education courses, medical and dental care, mental health services, social services (clothes, jobs, etc.), and a state educational program.

As children flooded the hallways for the day, I received and gave hugs, encouragement, and behavior management assistance. I spoke with concerned parents and set up appointments. As the classroom activities got underway, I began my morning sessions with scheduled children.

I feel a great need for the therapy I offer to children. All children need a place and a vehicle where they can express themselves more fully. Play provides a medium through which conflicts can be resolved and feelings can be understood. Through play, the child is saying: *Do you want to know my thoughts and feelings? Watch and listen. I say them through play.* In return, I as the play therapist respond to the child. *I am here. I understand. I hear you. I care. We will work together.* My goal is to get into the child's world—to think as the child thinks, to see as the child sees, to understand as the child understands, to feel as the child feels. I watch the child's facial expressions, the body language, notice the choice of play materials, see how the materials are being used, match the child's breathing, and gently guide the child to a better way.

These children come from very problematic backgrounds and exhibit a wide variety of behaviors. Children who fit the guidelines for therapy are scheduled with me for 30- to 45-minute segments on a weekly basis. Tony has been tossed about among family members and, at the moment, is living with a grandmother. Tony witnessed his dad beating up his mom and the police taking his dad away. Leslie's mom died while Leslie lay in the bed beside her and the death was not discovered for several days. This little girl was found in the house alone with her dead mother. C.W. is a very angry young lad. He does not seem to have an attachment with any family member. He has been in day care since he was born and does not understand the meaning of family. He speaks a lot about hurting others. Roger's mom and dad just got a divorce and Roger was sent to live with an extended family member for a while. He has decided to close down and, for now, he will not speak. Dee Dee's mom is in a homosexual relationship and Dee Dee is responding to the other girls in her classroom in the only manner she knows, the relationship that has been modeled.

My morning is spent in sessions with our hurting youngsters. About mid-morning I am called to a classroom for crisis intervention. Joey had decided to solve his conflict by threatening to cut Jose. He indeed pulled a knife from his pants pocket when Jose refused to give him a chosen toy. The knife was removed. Joey and Jose talked through their conflict. Joey's parents were called and asked to take Joey home for the remainder of the day. The police department followed up with a legal intervention.

Sometimes I get a quick lunch, and then the parent conferences begin. This is the time when the paperwork, the interviews, and the assessments that enable other children to begin their time in therapy are completed. It is also the time when an ongoing progress report might be shared with the parents or caretakers of a child I'm seeing.

I am on call at all times for crisis interventions in the classrooms. This may entail calming an anxious child, controlling a child in rage, or working with the teacher on behavior management. The students leave our campus for home at 2 P.M., when my door is opened to our staff members. Teachers, other professionals, and coordinators begin to move in and out with their individual concerns. Some-times their issues are personal, but the majority are concerns for individual students in their classrooms. They are interested in current resources on school violence, new and intriguing behavior techniques, and any mental health tips that will assist them in the classroom.

Our school also *staffs* each one of our Head Start students twice a year. These staffings include reports from all the component areas (education, administration, mental health, parent involvement, social services, and disabilities). When the reports are complete, an individual plan is made for the student and family. This helps us equip the children with skills to assure success in their educational settings.

The mental health offices at our school assess each of our students twice a year. The first assessment is done within forty-five working days of their entrance into school. Upon completion of the first assessment, a plan is made for all of those children who show any evidence of mental health concerns. The plan may include formal observation, classroom intervention plans, individual behavior charts/ contracts, parent conferences, individual/group guidance, and/or play therapy sessions. The second assessment, which is subjective, is done in February and follow-up is done on an as-needed basis. This assessment also gives us a great longitudinal view of mental health progress for our students. I have also noticed that the subjective assessments give me a fairly accurate picture of how teachers view their students and their students' general mental health.

Additional responsibilities as a mental health professional include consulting with other professionals, visiting both students and staff in the hospital, offering training/workshops for parents and staff, writing progress notes, and recording updates in student files. I also provide spirit lifters (moral boosters) on a regular basis to all staff and am generally on call for a multitude of other related duties and responsibilities.

In our country there has been an increase in violence affecting our children. The Oklahoma bombing alerted us to the knowledge that, as much as we would like to, we are not always capable of keeping our children safe. Then came the school shootings. I did not hear or feel that the violence hit home until the Columbine incident. It was then that Abilene sat up and took notice. A public survey was taken to establish how parents viewed school uniforms, and if they felt there was a relationship between a dress code and violence. Also, additional security personnel were placed on our high school campuses. Each campus implemented a visitor identification system and the staff's knowledge and training about *stranger danger* increased.

Once in a while we have an incident that alerts our senses and increases our vigilance. One such incident happened in our school this week. A man entered our school office identifying himself as a child protective caseworker; however, he was unable to show identification. When the office worker questioned him, he stated that he had left the requested identification in his vehicle. She asked him to leave and return with the information. The man apparently left—no one really saw him leave the building—but he did not immediately return. All upper management staff was put on alert, and all classrooms and closets were scanned. It seems the fellow had left in his car, going back to his office to retrieve his identification badge, and then returned to our school. All ended well; however, it was good to know that our staff is alert and ready to act in the event of turmoil.

My workday at the public school ends at 4:00 P.M. At 4:15 my first client arrives at my private office. I work three evenings a week in private practice, serving a variety of clients. My clients are composed mainly of children ages 3 to 10; however, I also work with a few adults, offer training to parents, and have a third job as a consultant and trainer for a university.

My expertise in early childhood development and behavior management offers me many opportunities to assist counselors who are just getting started. The focus is to help them develop a top-rate mental health program for their own groups of youngsters.

My day ends in the mid-evening hours and not much time is left for relaxing. A good soak in the tub, perhaps a movie or good reading material, refreshes my soul and we begin again. Okay, off to bed. It won't be long before the sun will peek over the horizon. I will be up and out and touching young lives once again.

Elaine Adams, M.Ed., LPC, RPT, CPT-S earned her Bachelor of Science degree in education from West Texas State University in Canyon (now known as West Texas A & M University in Canyon) and her Master's in Education from Sul Ross University in Alpine, Texas. She currently works for the government Head Start program in Abilene, Texas as a counselor and play therapist and also has a private practice that focuses on positive mental health changes for children and their families. Elaine's expertise is in behavior management, and she conducts a variety of workshops offered to educators and parents. She also serves as a consultant for Texas Tech University in Lubbock, assisting counselors in establishing mental health practices in early childhood classrooms. Elaine is currently writing a book about her experiences with troubled youngsters.

SUGGESTED READINGS

Bodiford-McNeil, C., Hembree-Kigin, T. L., & Eyberg, S. M. (1996). *Short-term play therapy for disruptive children.* King of Prussia, PA: Center for Applied Psychology.
This book addresses a short-term therapy approach for children that integrates both traditional and behavioral concerns and offers a variety of strategies and skills for managing disruptive behavior. It also has some helpful techniques for involving parents into the therapy process.

Landreth, G. L. (1991). *Play therapy: The art of the relationship.* Muncie, IN: Accelerated Development.
This is a great training manual for play therapists. In particular, it assists new therapists in establishing a therapeutic environment for play.

Norton, C. C., & Norton, B. E. (1997). *Reaching children through play therapy.* Denver, CO: The Publishing Cooperative.
The stages of play therapy are described in depth, with the purpose of each stage identified. A good, useful description of the symbolic meanings of the toys and the environment is provided.

Rogers, A. G. (1995). *A shining affliction.* New York: Penguin Books.
A true account of healing through psychotherapy. This reading shows how play therapy sessions work as the young client begins to explore the trauma of his or her past. It also alerts the therapist to the possibility that close bonds may be established with their young clients, and this attachment can, and often does, overlap into the therapist's own personal life.

PLAY THERAPY
TRICIA BROWN

I have the privilege of working with children—play therapy is my method of choice. Play therapy is a way of working with people that involves the use of chosen toys and materials in the counseling process. It requires specific training: Workshops, training, and classes are offered from different theoretical approaches and include information on how play is used to help clients prevent or resolve psychosocial difficulties and well as move toward continued growth.

Play therapy may be provided in many settings, including hospitals, homeless shelters, victim support shelters, schools, preschools, traditional counseling offices, and nonprofit agencies. Personally, I have provided play therapy in both educational and nonprofit agency settings, and I have also supervised many who were using play therapy in elementary schools. I will focus on my work with children in a nonprofit setting.

I typically see clients once per week for a 45- to 50-minute session. The client's situation and the response to our work together dictate the total number of sessions. Some clients, those dealing with less severe issues, seem to progress quickly, coming for four sessions of play therapy. I get referrals from caseworkers for family services, from physicians, from pastors, teachers, school counselors, individuals, and other clinicians who know I work with children. Because I care about the clients I am currently seeing, they will often refer others to me. Children are connected to a lot of adults. Some of those adults will know of another child who could benefit from therapy.

I am nondirective in my work; however, play therapy can be used with a variety of theories. I believe that there are times to use more structure, such as when a child is acting out a traumatic event in a way that is retraumatizing. My play therapy clients are typically between the ages of 3 and 12, are referred for many different reasons, and present a variety of problems. Clients are referred for help dealing with developmental transitions, soiling self, sleeplessness, excessive anxiety, violent behavior, crying spells, complaints of friendlessness, homelessness, and history of traumatic events including sexual abuse or witnessing violent crimes. In addition to these types of problems, many clients referred have been previously diagnosed with Attention Deficit Hyperactive Disorder, Asperger's disorder, bipolar disorder, obsessive-compulsive disorder, oppositional defiant disorder, depression, and posttraumatic stress disorder. This variety is an important part of my work.

ABOUT THE PLAYROOM

I have done play therapy in counseling rooms sometimes referred to as *playrooms* as well as in traditional offices. A playroom is a space set up specifically for play therapy. One nonprofit organization I worked for was equipped with two such rooms. Part of my responsibilities was to see to the upkeep of these special counseling facilities, which entails choosing, finding, buying, cleaning, organizing, and replacing appropriate toys. These tasks take time and commitment.

I counsel children in a traditional office setting when a playroom is not available. This requires planning and creativity. I want to have materials available for children to work with regardless of the setting. I have ended up with a small portable version of a playroom that I can transport to any office.

The toys selected for use in therapy are important, and the playroom should be planned with care. Toys should be selected purposefully; it is not necessary that they are new, but they must be sturdy, replaceable, and easily cleaned. When toys get broken in the playroom, they should be replaced as soon as possible. When choosing toys, the clinician is guided by theory. Some basic categories of toys should be represented to facilitate expression. Children use toys in the communication, aggression, make-believe, and real-life categories. Examples of communication toys would be telephones, walkie-talkies, markers, and crayons. Example of toys in the aggression category might be dart gun, plastic knifes and sword, bop bags, and snakes. Make-believe toys may be masks, hats, magic wands, medical kits, and similar things. Real-life toys include a dollhouse, baby dolls, cars, trucks, play money, trees, animals, fences, books, and similar tools. Looking for toys and building a playroom can be an ongoing process.

The playroom itself should be designed purposefully as well. The ideal playroom has several components: The room should be far enough from the waiting area that others do not hear clients, and it should be child safe and easy to clean. It is very nice to have a sink and easy access to a bathroom. The playroom should be large enough for choices in play and open enough to keep the client in the therapist's range of vision.

The playroom is a counseling office for play therapy. It is not used for other purposes. In my office I devised a signal so other clinicians know when a room is being used, since several of us use the same two rooms. A stoplight hangs on the door to the playroom. Each child can turn it to red when he or she enters and to green when he or she leaves. This has worked to provide the information clinicians need as well as to provide children a concrete way to claim their time and to put closure on their sessions.

In addition to preparing the playroom or converting a room to a playroom, my days include meeting with parents, guardians, caseworkers, physicians, teachers, and other clinicians; writing case notes, reports for insurance, and reports to absent parents; reading new material; planning the next sessions, cleaning between clients; and seeing the clients themselves. Many of these components are part of any counselor's day. Each day is different. Each child is different. Each family is different. Each story is different. A typical day, then, is given in outline.

The first session begins as soon as the child comes to the office. I have three initial objectives: to build a relationship with the child, to build a relationship with the parent or guardian, and to exchange information. All of these objectives are best begun the first session.

To begin building a relationship with the child, I go to the waiting room and speak with the child and parent. I begin to make it clear that I see myself as the child's counselor. Speaking to the child, making eye contact, and introducing myself accomplish this. I do not assume the child knows why he or she is in the office or who I am. I explain that I would like the parent or guardian to come with us for a few minutes this time so we can meet each other and talk. This begins to place a boundary around our time and lets adults know that the therapy time usually will not involve presession meetings with them.

To begin the relationship with the parent or guardian, I introduce myself in the waiting room after having spoken to the child and explain my expectations for the prior session. Sometimes I will have had the opportunity to speak with the adult on the phone prior to the meeting. I invite the parent/guardian to come to my office. I go over limits of confidentiality, how that works with children, and how I approach therapy with both the adult and the child. In my office I will also ask some questions about history and the presenting issue, being mindful of the fact that the child is present. I may ask the child if this is how he or she sees the problem also. Again, my objectives to build relationship and exchange information need to work together. After I explain play therapy, how I work, and gather some history, I ask if either or both have any questions for me. Sometimes the adults ask if I have children; sometimes they ask if I see adults; sometimes they do not ask anything. I value the opportunity to see the child and adult together as part of the information exchange. This allows the relationships with both the child and parent/guardian to be strengthened because the child sees the adult and I working together and including him or her in the conversation. After this brief exchange of information however, the child is usually done with so much talking and ready to see the playroom. I then ask the parents/guardians if they would like to see the playroom on their way out. I tell them when their child will be done, and we go to the playroom. This is the end of most of the contact with the parent/guardian for the first session. I will, at the conclusion of the time with the child, let the parent know when I would like to see the child again and have the adult schedule that next meeting.

MY INTEREST IN PLAY THERAPY

I always intended to work with children. My interest in play therapy grew out of experience. Early in my career as a counselor I discovered that many people choose not to work with young children. In addition to this, I discovered that there are many young children in need of services. I had a wonderful practicum site and a great supervisor. Both encouraged me to try things out and find what I liked. I was allowed to see a young child (under 10), even though my site had not done this before. My faculty supervisor encouraged me to use toys with this child and gave me direction. This first child I saw as a counselor was very bright (now I know that if you look in the right way, they all are). The situation in her life convinced me that children do need counselors who will listen in their language—not require they learn to speak ours before they can be heard. Their first language is the language of play, not words.

An Example Client

A child named May was referred to me by a clinician who was seeing her older siblings. May was 6 years old, had moved many times, was currently living in a shelter for homeless women and children, and had witnessed repeated family violence. Her presenting problems included bed wetting and little interaction with other children. After the typical introductions and information gathering, I took May to the playroom. She stood and looked at the various containers of small toys, the bop bag, the dollhouse, and the dress-up things. She looked at me. I responded as I usually do—*You can play with any of the toys in the playroom almost any way you want. The rules are no breaking the toys on purpose and no hurting you or me with them.* May looked back at the toys. She gradually began to explore different things. Our session ended with my giving her notice that our session for today would be over in five minutes, and then with my telling her our time for today was over.

The next several sessions May played out the same theme with different toys: Each time some enemy or dangerous animal would be coming to hurt us, she would ask me to kill it, and then she would pretend we were moving away. One time May played that she killed the threatening thing herself. The next session she played that the dangerous thing was close but could not hurt us, because we would tell and the police would come. In each session we would move toward the end, with less emotion, energy, and time involved as time went by, moving on to more creative and original play each week. When her play no longer contained a prevalent theme, her symptoms of bedwetting had ended, and she was playing with other children at school, we discontinued therapy.

PREPARATION

I have had the privilege of working with children for a good part of my career. While these experiences do not count as formal training for any licensure, they have been crucial preparation for my work. I taught in a therapeutic child-care center for children at risk or identified as abused and neglected. I saw children and parents from infancy to 6 years of age and was responsible for those in the 2-year-old stage of development. I learned that children play what they know. I ran an in-home child care for infants through 9-year-olds. I saw parents care for and worry about their children as they worked to provide the best they could for them. I learned that parents have questions about their children and work very hard to protect them. I learned that children play with what they are given, and if they are allowed creativity they play that way. I was a supervisor for a play therapy program in an early childhood center. I learned many people work well with children when they sit down and try to learn from them. I have learned important things from classes and workshops as well.

Course work that was of great importance in my training included the study of human development from prenatal concerns through the lifespan. The knowledge of lifespan beyond childhood has been important as I work with those in the child's life. No child comes in without an adult connected in some way. Both individual and family counseling theory classes have been useful. Working with children as both a teacher and counselor has been helpful training. Supervision is, of course, invaluable. Workshops, books, and colleges have all brought freshness of ideas and stability of practice to my work with children. I have learned a great deal at workshops about what I believe and how to work with children. Books on child development, play therapy, and other child therapy approaches have encouraged me to use theory and structure in my work. Having the opportunity and freedom to work in a playroom, to choose toys, to arrange equipment, and to decorate in ways that indicated a purpose behind the choices rather than a collection of things was an important part of my training because it caused me to value that process more.

GOOD AND BAD DAYS

There are a few unpleasant things about play therapy with children. Occasionally clients vomit or wet themselves in session. Toys need to be cleaned frequently. The floors and therapist's clothes and shoes need to be washed and scrubbed often. The worst part of play therapy with children is wishing you could see a happy ending in each case, but sometimes no closure is possible with a child. Sometimes a parent moves with a child without telling you or anyone. Sometimes it is hard to trust in the benefit of a few sessions with a child when you have only been given a glimpse into his or her world. The child has begun to trust you, and children do not have much power in their lives. Those are the hard days.

The best part of play therapy is knowing that change in a child has an important impact. Listening to and working with children is exciting. Each day is different. Each child is growing and changing constantly. At the end of each day I know that several children have been listened to well. I am hopeful that work with children will bring change for them now and into the future and even as they someday parent. I believe that working with children is valuable because they are valuable. I have the opportunity to communicate that to them daily. That is the best part.

I continue to learn from each session. I learn that I may not understand but must respect their play. I learn that afternoons and evenings are the easiest times for school-aged children to come to appointments. I learn that custody issues are important to pay attention to. I learn that watching a child play will elicit the full range of emotions in me, from excitement and great joy to terrible pain as the child shares through play what he or she knows.

Tricia Brown, Ph.D., NCC, LPC is Assistant Professor of Counseling and Coordinator of the School Counseling Program at Truman State University. She received her doctoral degree in Counselor Education and Counseling from Idaho State University. She also holds a Master's of Education in Guidance and Counseling from Whitworth College and a bachelor's degree in psychology from Central Washington University. She has researched and presented on the topics play therapy and supervision, families and ill members, the process of becoming a caregiver to an aging parent, and suicide and the elderly. She is a member of the American Play Therapy Association, American School Counselor Association, American Counseling Association, Association of Counselor Education and Supervision, and Chi Sigma Iota. She is a Nationally Certified Counselor, a Licensed Professional Counselor in Idaho and Missouri, and a Registered Play Therapist. She has three tremendous boys ages 15, 8, and 8 months. They encourage her to dance and remind her to smile while pointing out daily how much she has left to discover about children and how much fun it is to learn.

SUGGESTED READINGS

Axline, V. M. (1969). *Play therapy.* New York: Ballatine Books.
    This book is a foundational work on play therapy. It offers a historical perspective as well as case studies.

Gil, E. (1991). *The healing power of play: Working with abused children.* New York: Guilford.
    I encourage students to read this book as preparation for some of the issues they may face if they are planning to work with children. Case studies and information specifically related to working with children who have been abused are presented in this book.

Landreth, G. L. (1991). *Play therapy: The art of the relationship.* Bristol, PA: Accelerated Development.
    Counselors interested in a client-centered approach to play therapy benefit from this book. I have students and supervisees start with this one.

Orton, G. L. (1997). *Strategies for counseling with children and their parents.* Pacific Grove, CA: Brooks/Cole Publishing Company.
    This book offers many ideas on work with children. Play therapy is included in this book but not the main focus of this book.

VanFleet, R. (1994). *Filial therapy: Strengthening parent-child relationships through play.* Sarasota, FL: Professional Resource Press.
    I have used this book in explaining basic play therapy to beginning therapists as well as parents. This book is very useful and offers ideas on how to implement filial therapy. I have not written about filial therapy but believe it is effective.

ALL IN A DAY'S WORK—THERAPY WITH ADOLESCENTS

SHARON B. KREIDER

Walking in the front office of the agency, I find Mark is pacing in the reception area, his face creased in worry. Mark looks like many young adolescents except for a pervasive anger that seeps in and fills quickly. His shoulders are tense; he wears his hat so that the visor almost touches his nose and it's difficult to see his eyes. If you did, you might notice a similarity to a dog that has been kicked all its life. Mark is anxious to meet with me. I notice the police car around back and a conference already in session.

For whatever reasons, Mark got in another fight at home this morning. These days he is not the victim, but the perpetrator. Inside the therapy room, I ask Mark to take off his hat. He meekly obliges. With gentleness, I ask what's wrong. Tears begin to well up, spill over, and travel quickly down his cheeks.

I just don't know why I did it, he says, as his foot continually taps and he twirls his hat over and over again in his hand. Eye contact is difficult as he begins to unravel the details of the evening and morning. A knock at the door interrupts the session as Mark is escorted off to juvenile detention and awaits sentencing for his fifth offense. I watch him walk toward the police car, his shoulders and chest locked, his hat drawn further down his forehead. The disrespectful, intimidating attitude creeps quickly in.

In my office, I begin to write up the clinical notes for his file, for his court hearing, for his family, and to oblige the must of every good clinician—documentation. Mark is 15, although he looks considerably older, and has been in several different placements over the years. He has a history of experiencing difficulty with managing his anger, of truancy and behavior problems in public school. His most recent charges include trespass, possession of stolen property, loitering, and harassment. Mark's parents divorced seven years ago due to domestic violence and alcoholism. He now lives with his mother, who has been diagnosed with clinical depression and has chosen to raise Mark with a permissiveness that borders on neglect. Today Mark struggles to follow any structure, which often leads to disrespect, rudeness, arguing, denial, or displacement of responsibility. He tends to choose negative peer interactions and use sarcasm or inappropriate comments to disguise his feelings and encourage negative peer participation.

Family therapy has been minimally successful for Mark because of his pronounced anger and lack of respect for adults, especially his mother. Mark tends to use family therapy as a means to displace and transfer his frustration and anger. Familial problems have become chronic and the symptoms of aggressive behavior, intimidation, bullying, blaming others, swearing offensively, and initiating violent threats are on the increase. Mark has become annoyed with anyone who tries to help and often will exhibit angry and resentful attitudes, actively refusing to comply with even the most basic of societal rules and guidelines. He tends to minimize his responsibility and accountability for his actions, attitudes, and subsequent conse-quences. I suspect he has relapsed, using his drug of choice to cope with his intense thoughts and feelings.

As I formulate the first clinical paragraph in Mark's report, the phone rings. It's Maria's mother. Maria has just been admitted into a psychiatric facility for a suicide attempt. After a long phone call with the mother, I call the attending physician to help with the initial psychiatric assessment. Maria has a long history of emotional difficulty and has made significant strides in individual and family therapy. She has begun to talk openly about her biological father having physically and mentally abused her and her parents' divorce four years ago. Although this 13-year-old girl has physically developed and matured, she can give the overall impression of being much younger than her stated age because of the tendencies towards impulsiveness, immaturity, and acting-out behaviors.

Maria has a history of bipolar disorder and has had previous suicidal thoughts. Chronic familial problems began with her biological father, followed by a conflictual divorce and her mother's psychiatric hospitalization for clinical depression. When Maria's mother remarried two years ago, Maria had difficulty accepting the step-father into the home as a new member of her family. As the months wore on, she increasingly showed difficulty with feelings of anxiety, anger, and frustration, which led to behaviors requiring psychiatric hospitalization and a year at a residen-tial treatment center. After this placement, Maria returned home to live with her biological mother and stepfather with services at this agency. Maria's family social history and assessment include her extreme behaviors such as aggression, self-harming, and negative attention behaviors, which have created chronic stress and anxiety within the family system.

After speaking with the consulting psychiatrist, I learn that Maria will most likely be hospitalized for two weeks and transferred to a long-term residential facility to help in restoring her to a more stable functioning through medication and supportive therapies. I hang up the phone and look at the clock. It's only ten o'clock and several therapy sessions are scheduled. I take a deep breath and look at the card and picture of a young girl who attended therapy several years ago and is now living a successful and happy life. Her words ring in my ears: *Never doubt that you make a difference, for you have made a tremendous difference in my life, thank you.* This is why I do what I do.

My office, Turning Point Center for Youth and Family Development, is located in northern Colorado and provides high-quality outpatient and residential treatment for adolescents who are experiencing family, behavioral, educational, legal, and/or substance abuse problems. Over the last year, Turning Point serviced 190 adolescents and 570 family members. The agency employs 65 full-time staff; some of the treatment staff include doctoral-level consultants, master's-level therapists, bachelor-level counselors, master's-level specialists (art therapist, addictions specialist, recreation therapy specialist), and special education (severe needs) teachers. Some of the offered programs include outdoor-adventure-based recreation, art therapy, equine therapy, music therapy, family services, residential treatment, and day treatment. Adolescents and their families are referred to Turning Point through local or county government services. We are funded, in part, through grants, foundations, corporate donors, and/or government agencies.

I've been working with adolescents, especially those adolescents with emotional and behavioral problems, for fifteen years. People often ask me, *How are adolescents different today than they were fifteen years ago?* My answer is usually *not much.* However, I have noticed that my clients are younger these days, exhibiting more anger. In my last group therapy session I asked how many were from divorced families. Nine out of ten clients raised their hands; the other client had never met her father.

Counseling today is akin to missionary work. Most of us do not get paid very well in comparison to the amount of education and training required for our profession. The hours are long, not many sing our praises, and sometimes we fail. Even success is hard to define due to the sensitivity needed in every case. All clients are individuals with unique histories, individualistic treatment needs, and a unique genetic makeup. Counseling with this population is hard work. Adolescents with emotional and behavioral concerns can be challenging, at best. This population can be the most resistant to therapy, yet when trust with the therapist is actively built through such things as consistent unconditional positive regard and warm acceptance, the rewards are great. To know I've helped with clients' progress toward forgiveness, self-acceptance, honesty, self-confidence, family unity, or emancipation when needed—this is all in a day's work.

On April 20, 1999, I was working with a group of adolescents when news of the Columbine shooting interrupted our day. Most of us were stunned. It was difficult to understand the magnitude of the tragedy. It was even more difficult to sit for the rest of the days, weeks, months, and continue to work with clients who show similar thinking to the perpetrators of these violent acts. We still experience effects of that tragedy; it's taken time for the impact to settle. In the group discussions that followed, the tragedy was on everybody's mind and resulted in core topic issues. Some were upset, fearful of the events and wanting to use the sessions as a means to facilitate discussion of frustrations, feelings of injustice, or resentments. A few glorified the incident and felt vindicated; many of these adolescents were victims of crimes themselves. Columbine is not a singular incident but a witness to the violent, disturbed thinking of many of our troubled adolescents today.

Counseling for youth at risk requires patience, commitment, and a belief that it does make a difference. In fact, maybe it makes *the* difference. Mark and Maria are not exceptional cases; in fact, over the course of this last year, I have worked with seventeen adolescents with similar life stories and similar life difficulties. I imagine many other therapists throughout this country would have similar stories, perhaps many of them much more complicated. In individual therapy, these adolescents may require a great deal of time to nurture trust and to begin to demonstrate honesty and sensitivity to feelings. Learning how to control impulses and express anger through appropriate verbalizations or through healthy physical outlets on a consistent basis seems to be a common theme in most of the treatment plans.

Psychological testing and psychoeducational evaluations are other components of assessment needed to assist in accurate diagnosis and subsequent treatment. Family therapy is another key aspect of treatment. I assist a client's parents in establishing clearly defined rules and consequences and then challenge the parents to follow through on contingency contracts or consult with a family to assess the veracity of issues that can be central to supporting the adolescent through therapeutic intervention. Long-term goals are just that. Treatment with adolescents can take time. It has been my experience that these are the building blocks of adolescent therapy: trust, a sense of self-esteem, responsibility, family unity, appropriate boundaries, a sense of empowerment, social support, a sense of respect for others, awareness and acceptance, and a renewed sense of joy in life. This is often more time consuming than circumstances may allow.

I did not set out to become an adolescent therapist. Fifteen years ago I worked as a bachelor's degree level counselor in a small treatment school and found that working with troubled adolescents gave me a sense of fulfillment. For whatever reasons, I found that I genuinely cared about them, when it seemed that many in their lives did not. A few years later, as I continued to work with youth with emotional and behavioral problems, I went back to school. One or two courses at a time, night school, weekend school, and homework filled my free time. For the most part, as a therapist today, I enjoy coming to work for the ones I do touch in a simple or profound way. As I took a break from writing this, I noticed a fax from a client who had run away from her legal and personal problems. It was a three-page letter from a young troubled girl sitting in jail and asking to begin therapy again. Her mother died of cocaine dependency, her father left her years ago, no siblings, and no grandparents. I pick up the phone to begin the process of having her placed in foster care and consent to treatment.

For the most part, working as a therapist is fulfilling work, and there is not another career I would choose at this time. Why do I do what I do? I am often asked this question. I do not have a definite, methodical answer. Perhaps this career choice can be compared to random acts of kindness—work we do for no reason except that, momentarily, the best of our humanity can shine. When I spontaneously can give, without thinking of myself or of reward, to genuinely help others is the best invitation to move beyond the arena of normal circumstance and into a sense of compassion.

Also, one of the reasons I teach psychology and stress management classes at the local community college is because working as a therapist can be very stressful. To cope effectively with the daily challenges of therapy, I do yoga three times a week to help alleviate the physical symptoms of stress. Daily meditation and affirmations help with staying focused and present. I also converse regularly with my colleagues to help with clinical issues such as transference and countertransference.

Looking back on my career, I find the most valuable lesson has been learning how to pace myself. This means to realize that therapeutic work is not done at 5 P.M. There is only so much that can be done in one day, and then it is time to bring closure and take care of myself. So, I find time every day to walk (especially between therapy sessions) and make a short list of the things I did not get done. My desk usually has several different colored post-its all over, kind reminders of what needs to get done. The colors and size of post-its are an attempt to organize therapeutic intervention and clinical treatment into manageable chunks.

Another important lesson is documentation. I can't say enough about the importance of documenting treatment. My advisor once told me there are three things you need to learn for our profession: document, document, and document. I also find consultations with my colleagues invaluable. A week does not go by that I am not consulting with one of my colleagues on some aspect of my clinical work. Finally, taking the time to attend trainings and workshops is extremely helpful in staying current in the fields of counseling and psychology.

Sharon B. Kreider MA, LPC, NCC works full-time as a salaried therapist at Turning Point Center for Youth and Family Development in Fort Collins, Colorado. Sharon received her BS in psychology from Eastern Oregon University and her MA in counseling psychology from Vermont College at Norwich University. She is currently working on her CCHMC certification. She has been working with youth at risk for fifteen years. She also teaches psychology and stress management classes for Front Range Community College and is a wife and mother of two.

SUGGESTED READINGS

Bly, R. (1996). *The sibling society.* Reading, MA: Addison-Wesley Publishing Co.
   Mr. Bly's book goes beyond sociological statistics to see dilemmas created by familial breakdowns, divorce, abuse of power, and the changes within society. The book can also serve as a good cultural debate or discussion forum.

Finch, A., Nelson, W., & Ott, E. (1993). *Cognitive-behavioral procedures with children and adolescents.* Boston: Allyn and Bacon.
   A clinical guide for mental health professionals for assessment and treatment of adolescent and child issues. This book has theoretical and practical components.

Monahon, C. (1993). *Children and trauma.* New York: Maxwell Maxmillian International.
   This book, on the effects of trauma, offers suggestions and treatment for restoring a child's sense of safety and balance. The book can also be used as a resource for the warning signs as to whether a child may require professional help.

Pollack, W. (1999). *Real boys.* New York: Henry Holt and Company.
  Pollack discusses why so many boys are lonely and in conflict. The book also challenges conventional practices for adolescent males.

Somers-Flanagan, J., & Somers-Flanagan, R. (1997). *Tough kids, cool counseling.* Alexandria VA: American Counseling Association.
  A resource book on user-friendly methods for applying treatment approaches for the adolescent population. Some chapters focus on assessment of suicidal adolescents, basic medication treatment, and when therapy should terminate.

REHABILITATION COUNSELING OF THE BLIND AND VISUALLY IMPAIRED

ANN E. HACKERMAN

At 8:00 A.M., I park the car and go through a security door to enter the back of the building. The neighborhood is less than desirable, yet the building itself has served the blind and visually impaired since the early 1920s. As I enter, I brace myself with my Campbell crutches (forearm crutches) and follow the path between the bright textured yellow lines. I stop by the client break room to visit a man who lost his vision during the Vietnam War; he is studying out of a Braille book while his guide dog naps at his feet. At 8:00 A.M., the dog has my sympathy. That silly dog is always asleep, and he is the butt of many jokes on the laziness of certain guide dogs, the poor thing. They are awaiting the client's scheduled time to go to the computer lab for a lesson. I go ahead and travel to the far warehouse to check on those packaging paper cups and building clamps for utility poles. All report doing well, so I let them know I am heading upstairs, and if they need anything, feel free to call or come by.

I stop by the reception area and put my telephone messages in a cloth bag I have on the grip of the left crutch. The receptionist laughs, as she knows I am rarely alert at this horrific hour, but some messages say *urgent*, and I always prioritize the needs of the clients. I get to my office and retrieve even more messages off the voice mail and right away call back the ones that say it is *important* or an *emergency*. I begin planning for the day when suddenly I hear the *click, click, click* of a mobility cane tapping the wall near the office. I call out to whomever it may be, to let him or her know I am four or so feet to the left.

In walks a strapping young man who was blinded four years earlier. I guide him to the chair nearest my desk, and I ask what I can do for him. He shares that he is fearful of my recommendation that he be evaluated for a prosthesis to fill the void that once held his right eye. We talk again about what could happen to him at his age without a prosthesis. He is reminded that the bone structure of the right side of his facial bones will change shape, causing a *pumpkin head*. He says he does not want to look like a caved-in pumpkin and says he is ready to begin the steps. He laughs at the thought of looking like a rotten pumpkin and agrees to follow my guidance into getting the medical assistance he needs for his fitting.

As he returns to work adjustment training, I realize that I have a two-hour group that will begin fairly soon. I rush to gather material, as today the plan is to focus on adjustment to permanent disability; if we have time, we'll move into the types of questions clients may experience in a job interview. I go to the computer lab and work with the Duxbury software, embossing my typing into Braille for those that are totally blind. For those with low vision I prepare a 24-point Arial font: dark and crisp for clarity. I place the information in the group room and return to the telephone to make more callbacks.

I spend at least 45 minutes easing clients' fears about the waiting lists for work adjustment training, computer training, job development, orientation and mobility training, or any questions relating thereto. To step back a little, I find it necessary at this point to explain this particular clientele, their particular obstacles, and what makes them more unique than others receiving rehabilitation services for blindness.

Obstacles particularly common to the Mississippi Delta region of the United States are the lack of formal education, poor to no transportation, poverty, minimal to no family support, no marketable job skills or work tolerance, behavioral health issues (depression, anxiety, posttraumatic stress disorder, etc.), and lack of motivation to change lifestyle patterns. Many of the clients seeking rehabilitative services have hit their proverbial rock bottom and realize they must change, unless they want to spend the rest of their lives drawing a disability check, federal insurance, and food stamps. They know they cannot change their life pattern alone and need professional intervention.

When it comes to education, the average person calling me for assistance has not earned his or her high school diploma. Many went blind during childhood. Opportunities for education of the blind prior to the 1970s were limited, especially for the African American population in the Delta. The clients share that their families were either too poor to send them to specialized schools for the blind or they were unaware such programs existed. Therefore, most left school before completing elementary school and became laborers on farms and in warehouses. Now that they are in their 50s and 60s, they are compromised further with arthritis, muscle strains, weak backs, or the inability to stand for extended periods of time. They have no other skills to offer the competitive working world.

Transportation is a major issue. For obvious reasons, they are unable to drive and must depend on public transportation or on others for rides. When it comes to employment, they must either be able to utilize the public bus system or have a very dependable person taking them to and from work. For those that are fortunate enough to have someone willing to assist, the drivers typically expect gas money—extra funds the blind person seldom has due to living at the poverty level. For those living in rural areas, public transportation is not an option.

Poverty is a major problem throughout the Delta region of the United States, but especially for those who are blind and visually impaired. Each of my clients either draws a disability check or is in the process of application. In Tennessee, the maximum draw is $512 per month. With such a limited income, clothing for interviews and work is nonexistent. Money for public transportation is allotted. These individuals tend to have poor diets—they must buy the most amount of food for the least amount of money, causing other medical issues (i.e., diabetes and heart disease). They tend to live in high-crime areas and are easy targets for assaults and muggings because they are unable to visually identify the perpetrators.

Family support is another issue altogether. Many do have children or parents (who are now elderly) who are willing to assist, but they either do not know what to do or they enable to such an extent that dependency develops. The inability to do household chores, cooking, or shopping keeps the blind or visually impaired individual dependent upon others for activities of daily living (ADLs). Then there are those who have no family to assist them, either due to lack of a family or having family members who take advantage of them and steal from them.

How are job skills acquired when one is unable to find employment? In speaking with potential employers, fears of safety and higher insurance premiums arise on a continual basis. The higher the degree of vision loss, the more difficult it is to find job placement without assistance. Visually impaired persons tend to become dependent upon the disability check and food stamps. Then they begin to feel an overwhelming sense of hopelessness in relation to finding gainful and meaningful employment.

Multiple disabilities compound employment placement obstacles. For many clients, their vision loss was secondary to a medical condition and/or the medications used to treat medical conditions (i.e., insulin-dependent diabetes mellitus, sarcoidosis, methotrexate, Plaquenil). This is mostly a result of ineffective medical care due to lack of income and insurance. Such conditions and medications require close observation under a specialist, as well as an ophthalmologist. Under proper medical care, vision loss is not always inevitable. Those with diabetic retinopathy, for example, may experience poor circulation, hypo- or hypertension, and limb amputation. For those living with sarcoidosis, complications include severe asthma, arthritis, fibromyalgia, and chronic fatigue syndrome.

Knowing this before I go into group therapy with a small group of clients I've never met gives me insight at the onset. I gather the members together. Today they are all men, which is fine for today's plan. I know many have never spoken of their vision loss, so we start with the standard introductions and then move right into the causes of their vision loss. For these men, it was all due to trauma.

One man shares that he was assaulted by three men while walking out of a corner grocery, causing his retinas to bleed and detach. He is now afraid to leave the near vicinity of his parents' home (where he now resides). He was attacked nearly four years ago. Another man was shot while sitting on a couch. He was misidentified as another man and was shot through curtains. He lost one eye and also lost complete light perception in the other. He has now developed a fear of going to social gatherings. An 18-year-old was celebrating his high school gradu-ation at a dance club when a gunfight broke out near the door entrance. He was hit by a stray bullet while standing near friends in the back of the club. He lost one eye and nearly complete vision in the other. He is now afraid to go into crowds or into dance clubs, even if not alone or in a familiar area. All three men have chronic nightmares, depressed mood, heightened anxiety with panic attacks, general withdrawal, and lack of trust. None are comfortable being outside after dark or riding a bus after dark. For these men and many other clients, behavioral health counseling is mandatory to the recovery and rehabilitation process, as they are all experiencing classic posttraumatic stress symptomatology.

Counseling is at the core of the entire rehabilitative process. Whether it is behavioral health, career counseling, or both, counseling is an ongoing intervention from intake to case closure. So many enter the rehabilitative process without ever beginning to grieve their multiple losses (i.e., sight, independence, mobility, self-worth and dignity, finances, insurance, homes, cars). They have yet to process their fears of disease progression and the general impact and toll their loss of vision has taken on their lives.

In reflecting upon this, I think about the past ten years I have spent providing triage and crisis stabilization to teens on inpatient, residential, and day treatment bases. I remember story after story of sexual victimization and perpetration. Drug addiction. Sitting in my office while I tell a mother her husband has been forcing her daughter to have sex with him for the past ten years. Witnessing a young man remove his shirt in a family session to show his mother the scars across his back and shoulders from being beaten by his father. Working on reuniting a mother and daughter after the mother prostituted the child for years in exchange for drugs. The hundreds of calls placed to child protective services workers and judges. I wonder why I ever left that population behind, when I had such success working with them.

I think about driving through gang-infested neighborhoods taking photographs of graffiti and bullet holes in houses—hundreds upon hundreds of them, all used for the sake of education and perhaps reaching a youngster before his or her life is lost to the streets. Too many funerals.

Then I look over at my forearm crutches leaning against the far wall. I think back when I first started having problems walking, but the severity did not hit until approximately two years ago. Would I now be a target for an angry young man I am confronting for the destructiveness of his cocaine addiction? Would I get caught in the path of psychotic female as she bolts down the hall in full gallop as she strips? Never have I ever been threatened before, because there was always equal respect between the youth and me, but would it all change now? I really do miss those teens.

But then I reflect on the difference between the teens and my present clientele. Both have many issues relating to their childhoods. Both need rehabilitation, whether it is for school or competitive employment. All have suffered some sort of loss and severe family discord. Many have abused polysubstances as a means to cope with the losses. The only significant difference I can come up with is that adults have more rights when it comes to confidentiality.

I document the group session using *BIRP* (behavior, intervention, response, plan) charting and review the clinical data for a woman soon to arrive for an evaluation for the appropriateness to participate in the facility's rehabilitation program. She arrives, and I am greeted by this graceful, immaculately dressed woman. She is just impeccable, not the stereotypical client referred to me. I guide her to my office with my right elbow as she holds her mobility cane in front of her. As she sits, she states that she noticed I walk with a slight limp and inquires if I am feeling okay enough to help her today. Never has anyone asked about me before. That is a new one.

As her story unfolds, I am reminded of my days with the teens. She shared that she and a friend were gunned down in a hail of gunfire by a man who had been stalking her for over a year. He killed her friend by blasting him in the chest, hit her multiple times as she sat in her car, and then he turned the gun on himself and completed suicide. One of the bullets penetrated her skull, causing her to lose one eye and complete vision in the other. She was hospitalized for months. She states that she has forgiven the perpetrator and has turned to her Higher Power, God, to guide her. She is truly at peace, and I am amazed by her strength and courage. I validate her and answer her concerns. She laughs and adds that I am the first person in six years of professional rehabilitation who has ever validated her without showing pity. She closes with saying she has found her counselor and will be back.

I then sit back as I begin writing up her assessment, thinking that I have made no mistakes in changing populations. I am challenged daily, and I know this population chooses to be helped; they are not being forced into treatment by a parent or a judge.

To counsel those who are blind and visually impaired at such a clinical level requires a master's degree from an accredited program, a license for independent practice (LPC or LCSW), and certification as a rehabilitation counselor (CRC). Specialized training and education in ocular diseases is an asset. Communication skills must be enhanced, because such a population is unable to respond to nonverbal communication and cues typically used in the professional counseling setting. The clinician must also be versed in how to approach the client physically, as well as how to speak in a general manner. To be a part of a professional team that enables a blind person living off welfare and government assistance to become an assertive, independent, competitively employed individual is the most reward-ing aspect of this clinical role.

In regard to my educational and professional development, I entered college as a prepharmacy major (both of my parents were pharmacists). It took one day of that schedule to realize it was all wrong. I graduated with a BA in psychology from a small private college; I landed my first job as a psychiatric technician at a freestanding psychiatric hospital with an 80-plus-bed adolescent unit. I was still in college when I was hired, and I stayed on board for five more years until I completed my master's degree in counseling from a large university.

In those five years, I had the opportunity to study under some of the most brilliant and gifted psychologists and psychiatrists in the region, including the medical director, who was known nationally. He became my clinical supervisor for my licensure after I completed my master's degree. During the five-year time frame, that particular psychiatrist moved on to another hospital. Six months after gradu-ation, I had not been placed in a clinical role as promised, so I went to administration and got out of my contract with them (they pay tuition, you work for them for two years). I followed my supervisor to the other freestanding hospital and worked as an individual, family, and group therapist.

After becoming licensed in two states for independent practice by passing oral and written boards, I moved into another environment: private day treatment and outpatient for youth. I learned so much and stayed there until changing to this population after my physical health began to deteriorate rapidly.

All during this time, I worked on research projects and was published in several scholarly journals, including one article of which I am most proud. It was the one I wrote with my mentor and supervisor, Dr. Paul King. I owe him more than he will ever realize, and I am honored that we are still in touch.

Ann E. Hackerman, MS, LPC, NCC, CRC, CCBT graduated from Christian Brothers University and the University of Memphis and is a Licensed Professional Counselor in the Memphis, Tennessee area. She is a member of the American Counseling Association, the American Mental Health Counselors Association, and the Tennessee Counseling Association. She has spent the past ten years working with dually diagnosed persons as well as those adjusting to severe disability.

SUGGESTED READINGS

Crudden, A., & McBroom, L. W. (1999). Barriers to employment: A survey of employed persons who are visually impaired. *Journal of Visual Impairment & Blindness, 93* (6), 341–350.
   A national mail survey of 176 employed persons who are blind or have low vision found that employment barriers included attitudes of employers and the general public; transportation problems; and lack of access to print, adaptive equipment, and accommodations. Strategies to overcome barriers are addressed on an individualized basis.

Harley, D. A., Greer, B. G., & Hackerman, A. E. (1997). Substance abuse and rehabilitation. *Rehabilitation Education, 11* (4), 353–372.
   Substance abuse is problematic for persons with disabilities. There is a gap between the demand for rehabilitation counselors with skills in substance abuse counseling and the existence of rehabilitation programs offering this component as part of the curriculum. Attention is given to terminology, risk factors, assessment, treatment issues, culturally diverse populations, ethical and legal issues, case management, and resource development.

Malakpa, S. W. G. (1994). Job placement of blind and visually impaired people with additional disabilities. *RE:View, 26* (2), 69–77.
   There are multiple problems associated with job placement of persons with severe disabilities, but support, public education, and advocacy can considerably minimize the impediments. Modified training and placement approaches are proving successful with people who are blind or visually impaired and have additional disabilities.

Vash, C. L. (1981). *The psychology of disability.* New York: Springer Publishing.
   The psychology of disability is the study of normative responses from psychologically normal organisms to abnormal stimuli, causing devaluation in the eyes of the nondisabled. Devaluation and acceptance are considered the pivotal variables in adjusting to life when it is complicated by disability.

MEANINGFUL VOLUNTEER WORK AS A COUNSELOR

GERI MILLER

I began to write this chapter in my mind as I was driving to my volunteer work as a psychologist at the local county health department. It was 7 A.M. on a Thursday and I had returned home from the American Counseling Association convention the previous Tuesday night. When I arrived in North Carolina, there was extensive snow in the mountains and I was without electricity (meaning no heat, water, or electricity) for most of the day after my arrival. I was tired that Thursday morning and wondering why I was still doing this half-day volunteer work I began seven years ago. I was chastising myself for making an 8 A.M. appointment with a client that Thursday morning (*Why make such early appointments as a volunteer?*) and driving on snowy/icy roads to get there (*What if she does not show up after all of my effort to get there?*). When I arrived at the health department, my 8 A.M. appointment was early and my next two scheduled clients came also. As I worked with them in session on their issues, I remembered how this volunteer work began.

Its roots are in the poverty in which I was raised. I was the youngest of seven children from the wrong side of the tracks and our family was on welfare. From an early age I watched my mother work with social workers, whom I would now describe as burned out, but when I was a child I simply thought they were mean women. Their disrespectful treatment of our family left me wondering if a person could be a social worker helping people and not be mean. This initial curiosity shaped my first-degree choice: a bachelor's degree in social work. I was also aware as a little girl that when you are poor, you have very limited access to mental health services; for example, if we complained about how our social worker treated us, we would simply get another mean one that we could not choose. Another influence on my future volunteer work stemmed from the role modeling of two of my mentors. My first mentor during my addictions work was a psychiatrist named Dr. Sharon Woods, and my core mentor in my master's program was a psychologist named Dr. Tom Russo. Both of these individuals spoke of the importance of volunteer work as a counselor and then demonstrated this belief by volunteering their clinical expertise in their local communities. These early childhood and mentoring influences resulted in my making a promise to myself that as soon as I was not drowning financially, I would volunteer my services as a counselor.

Seven years ago this promise came into being as I began volunteering at my local health department. I had completed my doctoral program in Counseling Psychology in 1990, taught for two years in North Dakota, and then began teaching at Appalachian State University in 1992. In order to be licensed as a psychologist in North Carolina, I needed more post-doctoral clinical hours than North Dakota required, so I obtained a supervisor for additional clinical work, Dr. Russ Neale. I talked with Russ about my options for obtaining additional therapy hours. I was interested in working at the ASU University Counseling Center in exchange for a class, but I remembered my promise to myself that I would volunteer clinical hours at my first opportunity. I brought up this promise to Russ in our supervision and he suggested that I meet with a doctor he knew who volunteered his time at the local health department.

I met the doctor and nurse practitioner from the local health department during lunch. Our conversation focused on how none of us had ever done this before, but we thought we would like to give it a try. The health department had a social worker who primarily worked with pregnant clients and, while they had professional volunteers in the past, these had not been from the mental health field. I had never worked at a health department and was not sure how to set up such a volunteer arrangement.

In the last seven years, I have donated a minimum of one-half day per week in clinical hours to their clients. There is no typical day in my work. I try to keep my clinical hours to the same one-half day rather than have them spread out through the week, but that is not always possible given client schedules, my schedule, and that of the health department. I do not have my own office, so sometimes I have done counseling in interesting spaces: counseling in a room with a bed with stirrups as a backdrop, counseling in rooms under various stages of construction when the health department was under construction. My forms and scheduling have evolved to suit the agency and client while being ethical professionally. My atypical work has inspired me to write about it for journals: I counseled a woman who spoke only Spanish (and I speak only English) and also a woman who had a premonition of her death.

Each year when I write out my annual malpractice insurance check, at times when my finances are tight, and sometimes during the political struggles of the university tenure process, I debate (debated) quitting this volunteer job. There are no external benefits for me in my volunteer work. As a friend of mine describes my volunteer clinical work: *Geri refers clients who show up with insurance to someone else.* However, the internal benefits of my work are immeasurable.

At the health department, my clientele are predominantly indigent European American women living in a rural Appalachian mountain area. Often they are the head of a single-parent household holding, at best, full-time, minimum wage jobs with few mental health resources available to them outside of the local mental health center. Typically, these women have had few educational or occupational opportunities. Frequently, I work with them on issues related to substance abuse, dual diagnosis, sexual abuse, and domestic violence.

When clients have an issue with their own or a loved one's substance abuse, I often ask them the question, *What can you do to stop feeding the problem of addiction in your life?* I use this question to help women develop a stronger sense of empowerment, self-esteem, and community support that stems from feminist therapy. Generally, this question will help my clients look at the triggers in high-risk situations, their lack of coping skills, and the causes and consequences of their behaviors. In the area of dual diagnosis, I work closely with the physicians and a nurse practitioner regarding these clients' psychotropic medications and therapy needs. In this area I focus on how these two mental health diagnoses overlap (substance abuse, mental health) and fuel each other's existence. When I work with a woman on sexual abuse issues, I attempt to create an atmosphere where she feels safe and can learn ways to nurture herself outside the session. Many of my clients experiencing domestic violence are in these situations. The area of domestic violence has become a focal point in my work as a counselor, educator, and trainer as a result of my volunteer work.

After being at the health department for about a year, I realized that many of the women I saw in counseling were in domestic violence situations. I had not anticipated that simply being at the health department would draw these clients to me. For example, because I do not have an office per se at the health department (I use the office of a clinician who is not needing it for that half of a day), there is nothing identifying me in the clinic. Therefore, my female clients are only known to the receptionist as seeing me (their names have not even been written in the schedule book for the last year and a half because we discovered it was a more efficient system if I simply handled all of my own appointment scheduling). Anyone who sees a female client coming to the building believes that she is there for health problems. This anonymity is very important in a rural area and in domestic violence situations where perpetrators control most of the clients' activities but typically do not have issues with their female partners' having physical health care. I work with women on their safety first in these situations with a sensitivity to the barriers that keep them trapped in the situation. Again, the themes of empowerment, self-esteem, and community resources arise.

While all of the issues women have brought to me in this volunteer work have been important, perhaps the most meaningful and moving experiences for me have been those provided by women in domestic violence situations. Providing a client with a safe place where she can make decisions that fit best for herself and, if she has them, her children, has been powerful clinical work. Even as I write this book chapter, memories of the bravery, decency, and integrity of these women come home to me in their stories. Always the focus has been on the question, *How can I make the world the most safe for me (and my children)?* I believe it is important to state this question because even if a woman's behavior does not look like she is examining this question, in my experience in working with this population, she is. For example, she may decide to stay in the situation and others may tell her that she does not care for her children because she stays. Yet, with me, she has weighed the pros and cons of leaving and cannot find a way to adequately support her children on her income, she cannot find housing, she does not have personal support in her community to leave, or there is some barrier that keeps her trapped. She has in her own way bravely faced the barriers she presently faces and carved out a plan on how to make herself and her children as safe as possible in the situation.

I view myself in counseling these women as providing information and support: not being the one to tell them what to do, yet being a reality check, which means sometimes telling them what they do not want to hear. Their stories have deeply impacted me personally and professionally. They have forced me to learn to live with being afraid for my clients, to learn how to live with the knowledge that I may be sitting with a client for the last time because of the violence in which she lives. They have forced me to examine my stereotypes of battered women because they have come to me in all shapes and sizes: women who have been badly abused historically and women who have no history of abuse, women who have no money and women who *have* a lot of money but who have come to me because they do not have access to that money, women who love their perpetrators and hope they will change and women who stopped loving them long ago but are terrified of the harm that will come to them or their children if they leave.

All of the women with whom I have worked on domestic violence issues have been afraid. It has been hearing their fears and their sense of powerlessness and watching them make the wisest decision possible at that time given who she is and her circumstances that has fueled my urge to do the best clinical work I can for them in this area. The stories have been amazing: the woman who decided to stay so that her children could have the best education possible; the woman who left for another state so her perpetrator could not harm her or her children so easily; the woman who hid repeatedly in the woods with her baby wrapped in a blanket when her partner became violent because she had no phone, no car, no neighbors nearby; the woman who could not go to the local shelter because her perpetrator knew where it was and threatened her there previously; the woman whose partner missed her with his shotgun only because he was drunk.

The stories of survival, bravery, and integrity in the midst of violence that is breathtaking have motivated me to update my knowledge in this area. I received university monies to learn more about this area. I have taken this knowledge and experience and applied it to my professional work when I train at local domestic violence shelters in two counties, train mental health and addiction professionals on this topic, teach it as a part of graduate counseling courses at the university, and present and write on the topic. During the past year I have had the opportunity to present on the topic of domestic violence to two different groups of physician assistants. At each presentation there were approximately 800 physician assistants. I was able to tell the stories of these brave women and encourage them to do what they can to be sensitive to the possibility that their female clients live in these situations not because they want to, but because of societal barriers that keep them trapped. I was able to encourage them to hear each woman's story with compassion for her suffering and yet provide her nonjudgmental information on her options and support for doing what she determines is best in her situation. It was at these presentations that I realized I was a holder of these women's stories and I could help these women the most by telling their stories to other professionals. The women with whom I work are not safe enough to tell their stories, so I tell them via lectures and writings such as this book chapter.

This is the core meaning of why I am a counselor and why I enjoy my work. I believe that I am blessed to have the opportunity to work with women in all types of situations and help them find inner and outer sources of strength and support that empower them to make the best decisions they can make at that time in their lives. I have had women drive a minimum of one hour one way on hazardous mountain roads to see me because they feel safe and encouraged by the work we are doing together. I cannot imagine a more meaningful work. My only regret is that I do not have more time in my life to dedicate to the work.

Geri Miller Ph.D., LPC is an Associate Professor in the Department of Human Development and Psychological Counseling at Appalachian State University in Boone, North Carolina. She received her doctorate in Counseling Psychology at Ball State University in Muncie, Indiana in 1990. She is a Licensed Psychologist (NC), a Licensed Professional Counselor (NC), a Certified Substance Abuse Counselor (NC), and has a Certificate of Proficiency in the Treatment of Alcohol and other Psychoactive Substance Use Disorders from the American Psychological Association College of Professional Psychology. She has worked in the counseling profession since 1976 and in the addictions field since 1979. She has published and presented addictions research and counseling approaches. In 1999 she published a book on addiction counseling, *Learning the Language of Addiction Counseling*, with Allyn and Bacon. She is currently a member of the American Psychological Association and the American Counseling Association.

SUGGESTED READINGS

Gilbert, L. A., & Scher, M. (1999). *Gender and sex in counseling and psychotherapy.* Boston: Allyn and Bacon.

    This book is an excellent overview of the dynamics of gender in counseling. It facilitates sensitivity in the reader regarding gender issues.

Marlatt, G. A., & Gordon, J. R. (1985). *Relapse prevention: A self-control strategy for the maintenance of behavior change.* New York: Guilford.

    This book is considered a core textbook for understanding the issues in relapse prevention work. It provides counselors with a practical framework for both understanding and intervening on relapse issues.

Miller, G. (2000). Sharon's journey. *Counseling and Values, 44,* 124–128.
This article describes the counseling work with a client who had a premonition of her death.

Miller, G. (1999). *Learning the language of addiction counseling.* Boston: Allyn and Bacon.
This book is intended to be an overall addiction counseling textbook for individuals who are new to the addiction counseling field. In addition to basic topics such as assessment, treatment, and relapse prevention, it addresses issues of dual diagnosis, self-help groups, brief therapy, multicultural concerns, personal and professional development, and treatment-related issues regarding sexuality, domestic violence, and eating disorders.

Miller, G. (1998). Triangulated therapy: Cross-cultural counseling. *Women & Therapy, 21,* 41–47.
This article describes the work of an English-speaking counselor with a Spanish-speaking client.

THE DAY-TO-DAY LIFE OF A CLINICAL SEXOLOGIST

ROBERT H. RENCKEN

Establishing an identity in our life's work is obviously foundational. More than work, however, that identity becomes even more valuable when one is in independent practice. My identity, my skills, and my trust are my product in the mental health marketplace. With deliberation, I have chosen the identity of Mental Health Counselor and Clinical Sexologist. I will summarize my road to this choice and positive outcomes.

When I majored in psychology as an undergraduate at Rutgers University, I never thought I would be working in this area. At the time, my career plan was to become a professional Air Force officer. Instead of a twenty-year career, it became a five-year wonderful growth experience. One of those areas of growth was the recognition that my rewards came from dealing with people rather than machines, creating options rather than limiting them. I started my coursework at the University of Arizona even before exiting the Air Force and completed a master's degree in Counseling, followed by a second master's degree in Home Economics (Child Development and Family Relations), hoping for a college-level teaching job.

My career track was to take a different turn into the clinical arena with jobs in residential treatment and in child guidance. During this time frame, I added extra training in testing and became credentialed as a school psychologist. This was to provide me with my day job, which I still value. For these next twenty years, my private practice evolved from child/parent counseling to the full range of counseling and psychotherapy, including the opportunity to engage in clinical sexology. After extra coursework at the Institute for Advanced Study in Human Sexuality in San Francisco, my clinical and educational interest in sexuality blossomed.

Sexology has two credentialing bodies, the American Board of Sexology and the Certified Sex Counselor (or Therapist) of the American Association of Sex Educators, Counselors and Therapists. For several reasons, I chose the former and hold the title of Diplomate of the ABS. My clinical counseling interests led to strong professional organization involvement and also led to the commitment to deal with problems related to sexual abuse. After working with child victims, adult survivors, offenders, and families, I greatly enjoyed training other counselors and, as an extension, the publication of *Intervention Strategies for Sexual Abuse* by the American Counseling Association. I truly felt that I had earned my professional identity.

My current practice is in a small group, with my status as independent contractor rather than a partnership or corporation. My two mental health colleagues are, by background, a rehabilitation counselor and a marriage and family therapist. Approximately 90 percent of our clients at this time are with one managed care organization, requiring the ability to see a wide range of problems and different populations in relatively brief treatment. I use a variety of treatment strategies, from family systems to cognitive approaches, although my training was in Adlerian-oriented counseling and family work. I still focus strongly on power and control issues. My work in the sexological arena is split between fee-for-service referrals and those who have sexual concerns that are a part of their individual or relationship treatment. This day represents a cross-section of those clients.

THE MORNING

The worst thing about living in Tucson is that work generally starts early, between 7 and 8 A.M. for most individuals. Working backwards, my reluctant wakeup is at 5:30 A.M., with a wife-accompanied walk and breakfast, arriving at my practice office at 7:30, about the same time as my colleagues. After making coffee, voicemail revealed only one message—a client who apologized for missing the previous day's appointments because she was ill. She will call to reschedule. Although I sometimes charge a $20 fee for missed appointments, that is used with discretion and with concern about the overall therapeutic relationship. The day's appointments are reviewed. Over coffee, there is a brief consultation with one of my colleagues about a client's decision to divorce.

The first client of the day is seen at 8:00 A.M. for her fifth counseling session. Keeping track of the number of sessions is a crucial survival tool for managed care. Norma is a 65-year-old retired woman, who has multiple somatic complaints including diabetes (type II), fibromyalgia, irritable bowel syndrome, and migraines. She has had several surgical procedures. In the past, she has had difficulty being stabilized on medication (for the somatic complaints), but she is currently doing better in that regard. She also is taking Paxil, 40 mg per day with a psychiatrist prescribing. He was the first to diagnose her with major depression, and he referred her to me. She reports feeling better, physically, and she has had several days that she has been able to do some walking.

Her primary concern today is the continuation of communication problems with her grown daughter, who reportedly avoids Norma or is downright hostile. Most of the session is spent reframing Norma's view of other people's problems so that she can better care for herself, exploring a long history of caring yet controlling behavior in relation to her children. She notes that she seems to have much less control over her life since her retirement and debilitating illnesses. I changed the emphasis to creating some small tasks that she can control and then give herself credit. This included light cooking, writing unsent feelings letters, and walking short distances as often as possible. She agreed to take these steps. It is likely from these contacts that she will need support over a long period of time, and sessions have been spread out to every three weeks, which also reduces the stress of leaving the house.

There is no client scheduled for 9:00. After writing the progress note on the first client, I completed a fax form requesting additional sessions from the managed care system. Our current relationship with managed care is relatively good compared to horror stories we have heard. We have to request extensions every five to six sessions, but the form is very simple, it can be faxed, and it is very promptly returned by fax. Clients typically have an allocation of twenty outpatient visits per year, which is almost always adequate. Dealing with the managed care office requires little extra time beyond normal charting or note writing. The company has not declined any of our requests for routine treatment extensions. We are paid on a capitation basis, where the monthly funds available for mental health are divided up (like a pie) among the providers, based on how much we would bill. Although the reimbursement is somewhat inconsistent, we have been relatively pleased. We are, however, concerned that a major shift will happen in the managed care company soon and we may have more restrictions.

The second client of the day is seen at 10:00 (session 1 for him). This evaluation session drew on my knowledge of sexuality, paraphilias, and sexual abuse. These types of evaluations may also take place under the auspices of the court or Child Protective Services, but this particular case is voluntary and does not bring up the question of mandatory reporting. Mike was referred by a couples counselor who was seeing him and his fiance. He described the problem by saying that his relationship was being affected because he is a *nonoffending pedophile*. He describes a pattern of arousal to pubescent females since he was in high school. He is now 40 years old and has not been in a committed relationship until this one. The arousal pattern would serve as his typical masturbatory fantasy, but now his fiance becomes angry when he looks at a young girl, and she has threatened to end their relationship. Aside from this threat, Mike does not see the pattern as a problem because he has not taken any action on the fantasy, denying either verbal or physical contact with any of the fantasy objects.

Typical dynamics of hebephilia (as opposed to pedophilia) were discussed. *Hebephilia* is the attraction to pubescent females. By the end of the session, he was able to identify how he was being hurt by this arousal pattern and the importance of remaining in control. This is very different from being judgmental about the *wrongness* of the arousal pattern. He was encouraged to write down any time that he noticed this arousal (the setting, whether he was alone or with fiance, etc.). He gave permission to talk with his fiance and/or have a conjoint session with her. Even though this is not a managed care case, it is likely that only brief therapy will be necessary. I plan to see him again in one week to continue expanding his awareness.

Client 3 for the day was seen at 11:00. Nedra, age 38, has been seen sporadically over the last three years for ongoing dysthymia, exacerbated by several losses, including the death of her mother and the breakup of a close relationship. This session is number eighteen cumulative for the year. Her current concern is job stress. She is an elementary school teacher and has been frustrated with the school system's inability to provide special services for some of her students. We discussed ways for her to modify her own approach until she is able to receive assistance. She also role-played appropriate assertiveness in dealing with her principal. Her empowerment should be helped by this technique. I will see her again as needed rather than scheduling, since this strategy has been utilized quite well in the past.

THE AFTERNOON

Lunchtime was spent with a colleague from outside the group regarding our mutually led men's group. We discussed plans for new options and marketing in that specific area, including newspaper coverage.

Client 4 was seen at 1:00 P.M. (session 3 for client). Mark, age 36, and his life partner David, age 28, were referred originally by Pretrial Services, subsequent to a charge of Domestic Violence against Mark for having destroyed some property of David's while in a rage. There is a long history of alcohol abuse on Mark's part, and it became clear that he is also significantly depressed. He has just been started on antidepressant medication by his family physician. After several questions to me regarding my experience in dealing with gay men, both Mark and David have become very open in describing historical and current issues with each of them, individually and as a couple. David describes himself as a rescuer, while Mark has been a consistent victim. Interestingly, both had been involved (at different times) with the same man, who is described as a *major asshole*. Options that could improve the self-confidence of each were discussed for changing the perception of roles and some risk-taking behavior. Even in crisis, the couple was encouraged to focus on mutual support, and they committed to this.

No client was scheduled at 2:00 P.M. I completed notes on clients 2, 3, and 4 and returned one call from a client to reschedule an appointment. I returned another call from a colleague regarding a mutual client family. I also reported progress on Mark (client 4) to his probation officer. Such calls are never billable, essentially becoming a part of the cost of doing business for these clients.

Client 5 (session 10) was seen at 3:00 P.M. Manny is a 40-year-old business entrepreneur who was referred by his stepdaughter's therapist. He was accused by his stepdaughter (age 16) of sexual abuse because she caught him staring at her while she was asleep and he indicated verbally that he wanted to touch her but did not. He left the home voluntarily, and his wife has recently initiated divorce proceedings. The allegation of sexual abuse was not substantiated by Child Protective Services nor by the Sheriff's Department. He has remained in counseling because he sees binge alcohol consumption and, probably, compulsive sexual behavior as the root to these problems. The last two sessions have focused on his depressive adjustment to the divorce process, accompanied by significant guilt. We refocused this session on his sexual history, masturbatory fantasies, and general need for control. He will be seen again in one week.

Clients (couple) 6 were seen at 4:00 P.M. Jean (38) and Harry (47) were referred by her counselor because of significant relationship problems—primarily a lack of any sexual contact for the last year. This is their second session. While both acknowledge that they work very hard and long hours, it is easier to avoid initiation of sexual activity than deal with her feelings of rejection when he says that he is no longer attracted to her because she has gained weight (approximately 100 pounds). They both also acknowledge trust difficulties because of financial problems. Options were presented and discussed that could improve communication regarding the financial concerns, including regularly scheduled appointments for discussion rather than waiting until problems arise. Most of the session was spent presenting and discussing the principles of what I call *Focused Relaxation,* a variant of Masters and Johnson's *Sensate Focus,* and the relaxation, pleasure, and connection that can improve by nongenital touch and nonverbal communication. The couple agreed to pursue some simple touching exercises. I will see them again in two weeks and progress through the exercises as they are ready.

THE EVENING

There were no clients scheduled at 5:00 P.M. I wrote notes for clients 5 and 6. There were no messages. I left the office for the day to go a colleague's office for a men's group—a weekly, ongoing, open-ended group. It has been functioning for ten years, with various participants, some of whom have been actively involved for more than five years. The group theoretically runs from 5:30 to 7:00 P.M., although it typically runs somewhat late. This is a therapy group that focuses on rather typical men's issues such as affective awareness, positive control, empowerment, and relationship concerns. It also utilizes a *mentoring model,* where men with experience assist newcomers both in and out of group time.

There were six group members today. The discussion focused on a crisis of one relative newcomer, who reports that his wife has just announced that she was calling off counseling and wanted him to move out. The possibility of new options and opportunities was explored, as well as validating his feelings of anger, fear, and hurt. The notion of fear was newly recognized by the man, and the group supported the concept of fear, identifying their own experiences.

The day was finished shortly after 7:00 P.M. It was time for a late dinner, catch-up conversation with my wife, and mind-numbing TV. The content of the TV shows are typical—weekly dramas and sitcoms, with somewhat of an emphasis on police shows. I end up being critical when there is a sexual offense or salacious discussion of sexuality, but I usually end up putting the office behind me. After several instances of nodding off, I drag myself to bed at 10:00.

It seems that a day in the life of a mental health counselor and clinical sexologist is not particularly glamorous but is constantly changing. Even at the times when I have worked full time (or more!) in the practice, it has been exhausting but not boring, challenging but rewarding, and occasionally, frustrating but absolutely validating. I am proud of what I do and how I do it.

Robert H. Rencken, NCC, CCMHC, CPC is affiliated with Lundent, Serrano and Rencken, a private practice in Tucson, Arizona. He is also a school psychologist with the Sunnyside Unified School District in Tucson. He received his B.A. in psychology from Rutgers and his M.Ed. and M.S. from the University of Arizona. He is the author of *Intervention Strategies in Sexual Abuse.* He has also contributed journal articles and chapters in other publications on sexual abuse and sexuality. He served as Executive Director of the Arizona Counselors Association for fourteen years, has been on the Governing Council of the American Counseling Association, and is a recipient of ACA's Kitty Cole Human Rights Award.

SUGGESTED READINGS

Allgeier, A. R., & Allgeier, E. R. (1995). *Sexual interactions* (4th ed.). Lexington, MA: D. C. Heath.
   This is an excellent college textbook on sexuality, with an exceptional blend of research and clinical expertise.

Kaplan, H. S. (1987). *The illustrated manual of sex therapy* (2nd ed.). New York: Brunner/Mazel.
   This is the most concise coverage of techniques for sex therapy, including helpful illustrations that demonstrate the techniques available to couples. It is particularly easy to use for general or relationship counselors.

Leiblum, S., & Rosen, R. (Eds.). (1989). *Principles and practice of sex therapy* (2nd ed.). New York: Guilford.
   This is a comprehensive edited book containing the full variety of sexual therapy by the top specialists in the country. It is a very important resource book.

Rencken, R. H. (2000). *Brief and extended interventions in sexual abuse* (2nd ed.). Alexandria, VA: ACA.
   This revision of the 1989 book *Intervention Strategies for Sexual Abuse* is written for all counselors who need information about sexual abuse but who are not specialists in the field. This edition adds brief interventions for victims, offenders, and survivors, multicultural concerns, and prevention research. Case studies have also been expanded.

THE COACH BECOMES A STAGE

CAROLE OLIVER

I was searching for a professional home. I had graduated from William Paterson University with a Master's in Counseling Psychology degree in 1977 and by 1981 still had not found a professional home. I was looking for a professional organization that spoke to me and had a philosophy and perspective I could relate to. I would go to lectures and hear people speak about the etiology of schizophrenia or some such topic, but no one seemed to address the emotional life of their patients. Quite frankly, the speakers seemed emotionless and flat. I was really discouraged after attending a primal scream therapy workshop where I found myself walking around in a dark room, looking into the eyes of total strangers and expressing how I felt about them. I left questioning whether I made the right decision to go into the field of counseling. I wondered if I would ever find a place where I could feel comfortable.

I went back to my isolated private practice in Montclair, New Jersey, and stopped trying to find a specific therapeutic modality. Then one day in my psychotherapy session, my therapist told me that there was a psychodrama conference in New York City beginning the next day. He knew of my interest because I had mentioned that my undergraduate professor had always encouraged me to look into psychodrama. Here was an opportunity to do so, yet spontaneity was not one of my strong parts in those days. I went with trepidation and I went alone, knowing no one. It was at that conference that I found my professional home. It felt safe and the people were authentic; I participated in a drama that was a profound experience for me. Four days later, I enrolled in Bob Siroka's training group and stayed for ten years. I now consider it my life's work and my calling to God's work.

What is psychodrama? Jacob Levy Moreno, contemporary of Sigmund Freud, developed psychodrama in the early 1900s. He felt psychoanalysis was not enough for a client to get better. He believed it was restrictive and that it was not a hopeful model of psychotherapy. So he said, *I want to take the coach and make it a stage.* Psychodrama works with thoughts and feelings and is an action method of psychotherapy designed for individuals and groups. Moreno believed that in order to heal, a person must not just talk about his or her feelings or conflicts but experience them through enactment. Through enactment, which is facilitated by a trained director, participants explore their current issues and concerns in a safe environment with the help of the group.

As the participant, called the protagonist, reexperiences his or her dilemma, numerous results are achieved: The protagonist discovers the depths of emotions; clears up confusing thoughts or feelings, has a catharsis; gains an understanding of the other persons in the drama, called role reversal; and is validated by the other group members. This method helps clients resolve longstanding issues, develop new problem-solving behaviors, increase spontaneity, develop a wider role repertoire, and generate shifts in perceptions that facilitate a realistic view of the world.

My personal goals as a psychotherapist and psychodramatist are to assist clients in discovering their inner truth, express emotions freely, and establish authentic interactions with others. Psychodrama is an active process; the therapist does not remain silent or give advice to the client but rather interacts in a direct and respectful manner. It is a unique, multidimensional ACTION approach to psychotherapy with sound developmental theory behind it.

Because psychodrama explores an individual's world through action, it incorporates modalities such as music, art, and drama therapy to facilitate personal growth. It assists individuals in expressing areas of personal concerns that have been chronically problematic in a new and different way. Another outcome is to develop an authentic self with behavior that matches feelings.

Action methods can be incorporated into an existing therapeutic model, providing a new theoretical framework to increase the effectiveness of clinical skills and facilitate spontaneity and creativity in the therapeutic process. Psychodrama is a group process, but also lends itself to individual psychotherapy session as well.

Colleagues, clients, and corporate training managers have asked me *What is so special about psychodrama?* I answer them by sharing my experiences as a psychodramatist. It is a multidimensional approach to psychotherapy using all of the creative arts. As a psychodrama trainer and psychotherapist, it is my antidote to boredom and even burnout. It serves as a catalyst to expand my creative and intuitive process. A basic tenet of psychodrama is the development of spontaneity and creativity. Moreno believed the more spontaneous a person is, the more creative he or she is in directing his or her life.

This is true for me as a psychotherapist and psychodrama trainer. As a trainer, I allow myself to trust my intuition and let that guide me in the many areas of directing such as doubling, role reversal, and scene development. I use my creativity in developing the enactments. For example, in a drama, the client says, *I feel like crawling into a hole.* I have her create the hole using group members to portray the hole and have her crawl into it. We then explore her feelings as she is in the hole. It is potent and healing for her. What is spontaneous about this process is that I do not have a preconceived scene in mind. I listen carefully to the client, trust my creativity, and direct the drama accordingly.

Each psychodrama session I direct is fresh and unique. As the protagonist's inner life comes alive through action, a sense of wonderment emerges. Both the protagonist and director benefit from the creative juices that flow between them during the drama. It is magical to see a client dramatize a lifelong struggle and recreate endings filled with hope and promise. Because it is a hopeful model of psychotherapy, one of its goals is to empower individuals to reach their fullest potential. The empowerment is contagious. Sigmund Freud, a contemporary of J. L. Moreno, once asked him, *J.L., what is this psychodrama you speak of? Well,* said Moreno, *you analyze their dreams, I give them the courage to dream again.*

Psychodrama works well with children, adolescents, adults, and families. My clientele is diversified. I often do psychodynamic psychotherapy and incorporate psychodrama into it. Since psychodrama primarily is designed for groups, I run several groups per week. I see individual clients during the day and save the evening mostly for groups and couples. I facilitate monthly workshops on different themes such as perfectionism, self-esteem, life's transitions, and so on.

I have two offices, one in Montclair, New Jersey, and one in Manhattan. My Montclair office is 12 by 33 feet with soft peach walls. It has a tranquil and tropical feel to it. I want clients to feel safe there. Besides the therapist's style, I believe colors and themes help create the feeling of safety. I once had a client call it *The Magic Kingdom.* I have an art table in my room for individual and group work. Most of my clients have their own 18 by 24 art pads that they keep in their own slots in a shelf next to the table. This is useful because they get to see their progression through their art. It chronicles their healing journey. It's like kindergarten. They go to their slot, pick up their pad, sit at the art table, and begin to work. The art becomes a warm-up to their drama.

On Thursdays, I start my day at 10 A.M. with private clients. Even though psychodrama is primarily a group experience, I can tell you some ways I use it in individual work with clients. Let's take my client, Ann, who has a history of somatizing her stress. She has headaches often. We may go to the art table and I will ask her to draw her headache, using colors to demonstrate the intensity. I ask her, *What size, shape, and color is your headache?* After she draws it, we place it on a chair, she has a conversation with the art pad, her headache, and she reverses roles with her headache. When she is the headache, I ask her, *What are you trying to tell Ann?* It is in these moments that clients come closer to the truth. What works here is that Ann gets to be her headache, not just talk about her headache. The action allows Anne's unconscious wishes or desires emerge.

She may go from speaking to her headache to remembering an event about her mother during her childhood. I ask her to speak to her mother by placing an empty chair in the room, or she may draw her mother and use the drawing. She speaks to her mother and then reverses roles and answers as her mother. Sometimes, after she expresses her feelings, she is able to develop empathy for her mother through the role reversal. Neither of us is ever quite sure where this exercise will take us. However, it is through the journey that we learn.

Another example is with families. Last week, I saw the family of a boy I am working with who suffers from depression. I have had family sessions before with them so I know them. I had each family member take on the role of another family member. The son was the father, the mother, the daughter, and so on. It was compelling for each member to see how he or she are perceived and understood by other family members. This is a role reversal technique, a powerful tool to use for families and couples. Family members are surprised when they realize their children or parents understand them. It creates an opening for closeness and agreement between family members.

After seeing a few more clients, I leave to teach my class in Action Methods of Counseling at the Montclair State University graduate program. One positive aspect of a private practice is a lot of flexibility. I have almost two days free each week to play, rest, and get organized. I can design my schedule to accommodate my teaching. I love teaching psychodrama to the grad students. They are excited about their careers and eager to learn. I am also lucky to have them intern with me each semester. They experience what it takes to run a successful private practice. As I have mentioned, my work is isolating, so it is wonderful to have young energy around me. The students accompany me and participate in all my presentations, workshops, and conferences.

I do corporate training and include action methods in most of my training classes (i.e., team building, coaching, alleviating stress, etc.). This training is well received and people comment on how much easier it is to participate because they are actively involved in the learning process. I have even applied it when working with police departments, a population usually not open to an experiential process where they might look foolish. I was able to have policemen role reversing with their fellow workers and their significant others. It was quite an eye opener for me. It works mostly everywhere when people are hungry for the truth. Even though I have described psychodrama techniques in this chapter, it is important to know that psychodrama is not just a bag of tricks but a sound, well-developed theory of personality.

The most gratifying aspect of my work is witnessing clients making break-throughs, moving forward, and letting go of some of the emotional burdens that have plagued them. I also love the fun that I have. The process affords much creativity and spontaneity. Because I work from a spontaneous perspective and do not have preconceived hypotheses, there are always surprises in a drama. We may start out with a scene that is painful and end up with the protagonist and the auxiliaries finding humor in it.

Psychodrama has been a tremendous influence in my life and I am forever grateful to have discovered it. Through my own training, I have worked through numerous issues and have come full circle in my own healing. To become a trainer in psychodrama, one learns by doing. I did countless dramas in my training. The only way to learn is by doing. As a wounded healer, I understand how my clients feel because I have been where they are in my own dramas.

Training in psychodrama is an arduous task. To become a certified practitioner (CP), you must have a master's degree in a related field, a year of supervision, take a six-hour exam, and pass an on-site observation. After your CP, you are eligible to become a practitioner in training (PAT). You must then complete 144 hours of psychodrama training under supervision with a trainer, educator, and practitioner (TEP) to sit for the exam and pass an on-site examination to become a TEP. All this, while you are working on probably the most difficult emotional issues of your adult life in your training.

It takes courage to train and to become a psychodramatist. You must be able to go to very dark places and not be afraid. As a proficient psychodramatist, you can't shy away from difficult, undignified emotions. You must be prepared to face them with your clients. I believe you can only do this if you have looked your own demons in the eye. The training, along with individual therapy, helps you do to do that.

Psychodrama is my antidote to burnout. One of the best aspects is that I am constantly discovering and reinventing my creativity. People respond enthusiastically to psychodrama. After they have experienced a workshop or an individual session, they feel affirmed and relieved. I am validated by their response.

The stresses are few, but intense. Because action methods cut through defenses rather quickly, psychodrama enactments can be extremely intense and powerful. We go deep, sometimes to witness intense rage or profound sadness. I strive to be fully present with the protagonist and, as a result, the drama triggers my issues or drains my emotional resources. I learned after directing many psychodramas that I must have a support network of my own. After I direct an all-day workshop, I make sure I am with people who nurture and support me the rest of the evening. I need to have a safe place to unburden my leftover emotional baggage from the day. This is very important for any therapist.

Burnout comes easy if I don't practice self-care. Developing long-term coping skills is always a challenge for me. I easily forget to care for myself. I often agree to see a client when it is not a good time for me. I sometimes let clients' schedules dictate my personal time to a fault. I am learning to say *No.* Not bad after twenty-two years!

One pitfall of my work is that I have to work evenings. I miss out on courses and social and professional events. However, I do have some rules. I do not work past 7:30 at night. I will only work three evenings. I don't work weekends, except for one monthly workshop and some emergencies. I take vacations throughout the year, especially in the winter. They amount to about six weeks per year. I limit my caseload to twenty to twenty-five clients. Most important, I make sure I get a good dose of my two beautiful grandchildren every week. They are a major stress reliever and a gratitude check.

I believe that to really cope over the long term, we as clinicians need to know our limitations—what we can or can't do to avoid burnout. I play tennis often and it is a priority. I make it such. I recently formed a women's support group with my friends and their friends. I go to monthly supervision and often use the time for therapy for me. Still, it is very easy to fall off the self-care wagon. I know. I fall off often, if I am not diligent. My body lets me know when this happens. I get migraine and tension headaches. I feel fatigued. Because I love my work, I often do not realize how stressful it is until my body tells me. Every few years, I need to change something about my practice to keep it stimulating. This year, I plan to turn my attention to teaching and training while reducing the number of my one-on-one clients.

It seems to me that everyone has to find his or her niche—a style that feels comfortable and authentic. Part of the struggle for me was that other modalities were not speaking to me. I did not feel authentic. I felt like I had a script on how to be a counselor. Having discovered my niche, I now feel that I participate in my work as an authentic human being, struggling like everyone else. I am free to be myself. Because I am still a work in process, I learn about myself everyday. In spite of the stresses, I would not give up my work for another career.

Is psychodrama for everyone? *No.* There is not one particular theory that works for everyone. My wish is that more counselors become aware of psychodrama and experience it for themselves. I hope this chapter inspires you to check it out.

Carole Oliver, M.Ed, TEP, LPC is a Trainer, Educator, and Practitioner in Psychodrama and Group Psychotherapy and a licensed professional counselor. She has extensive group and individual therapy experience. Carole has a private practice in Montclair, NJ and Manhattan, and she teaches Action Methods in Counseling at Montclair State University Graduate School. She has been conducting workshops and training in New Jersey and Manhattan for twenty years and is an experienced psychotherapist. Carole has trained the staff at the Caron Foundation, New York University, NJ Task Force for Women and Alcoholism, Montclair Police Dept, NJCA, NASW, NJASW, Mountainside Hospital, Johnson and Johnson, AT&T, and numerous other corporations and agencies.

SUGGESTED READINGS

Blatner, A. (1966). *Acting in.* New York: Springer Publications.
  This easy-to-read book explains psychodrama in simple terms and covers the basic tenets of the theory. I use it for my psychodrama class.

Holmes, P., Karp, M., & Watson, M. (1994). *Psychodrama since Moreno.* New York: Rowledge Press.
  This is an informative, easy reading book on the current theories and themes of psychodrama.

  Note: For information on psychodrama and psychodramatists in your area, you may call the American Society of Group Psychotherapy and Psychodrama at (609) 936-1659.

10

FORENSIC REHABILITATION COUNSELING
WILLIAM J. WEIKEL

While my colleagues in the private sector moan and groan about third-party payers, lack of referrals, and the like, I routinely sit back, booked a month or more in advance and earn from $95 to $450 per hour. Much of that is from those same insurance companies that terrorize my counterparts who do individual and/or group counseling as a major component of their private sector work. Luckily, my specialty of forensic rehabilitation counseling is one that is much in demand in our increasingly litigious society.

My work combines my training in counseling and rehabilitation counseling and allows me to use my skills to the utmost. In my practice, I use the title *Vocational Expert* as I translate medical and/or psychological diagnoses and restrictions into their vocational implications. The counselor working as I do must have a solid base in all three areas—medical, psychological, and vocational, as well as some background and/or training in economic data to translate occupational loss into such things as reduced work life expectancy or lost wages.

Typically, I am retained by an attorney representing either the plaintiff or the defense to interview a client, perform testing, then study the medical, psychological, and/or economic data and render an opinion concerning ability to work, lost wages, and so forth. My training ground, after earning an M.A. in Rehabilitation Counseling and a Ph.D. in Counselor Education with a concentration in rehabilitation counseling, was to work as a Vocational Expert on a contractual basis with the Office of Hearings and Appeals, Social Security Administration, a position that I have continued to hold since late 1976. In this work, I have learned the ropes and at least part of the work required for private practice with the added bonus that it keeps me in contact with attorneys, the major source of referrals.

THE PROCESS

Once a referral has been made by an attorney for either side in the action in question, I make an appointment to interview the client face to face, although on

55

some occasions I simply perform a study of all of the depositions and documents in the case, called a records review. In the face-to-face session, I elicit from clients an educational and vocational history, ask them to list their physical and/or psychological problems, and have them estimate their own functional capacity, such as their ability to sit, stand, walk, lift, and things of that nature. Clients are told up front who I am working for, although I am to be an objective and impartial evaluator. Confidentiality is not applicable since I am retained to share information obtained from the client and use at least part of that *subjective* data along with objective information to render an opinion about his or her employability, loss of access to the labor market, and/or lost wages and future loss.

After interviewing a client and typically giving an achievement test to measure academic levels for reading and math, I study the medical/psychiatric evidence provided to me and render my opinions about work-related issues. My job is not to decide which of the physicians, psychiatrists, or psychologists are most correct in their opinions, but to assume in turn that *each* is correct and relate a series of opinions so that a judge, jury, or administrative law body can then decide. In order to do this, I must first determine the individual's *pre-injury access* to the labor market. That is what percentage of the almost 13,000 different jobs that exist in the U.S. economy could that person, based on factors such as age, education, training, and work experience, have been expected to perform prior to or absent any injury or condition.

Next I plug in any exertional impairments, such as a restriction to not lift more than twenty pounds, and/or nonexertional impairments, such as no exposure to dust or fumes, to develop a *post-injury* profile. If there are psychiatric restrictions, and there usually are, such as problems with attention, concentration, persistence or pace, or problems following work rules or working in close proximity to others, these too must be factored into the profile. It is not unusual to have widely differing opinions from various treating or examining professionals, but, again, the job is not to assume *who* is most correct, but to assume in turn that *each* is correct and determine the client's occupational loss or employability under those assumptions. Excellent databases are a must to back up your opinions.

DIVERSITY OF CLIENTS

I get to work with clients from all walks of life, from a veterinarian who was injured while working on a large animal to a sniper from a S.W.A.T. team (now euphemistically called a marksman) who was injured in an automobile accident. I also am called upon in *wrongful* or *accidental* death cases involving persons from infancy to adulthood to discuss and opine regarding *lifetime lost wages*. In these cases, I may have school or work records; in infant cases I am retained to discuss work-life expectancy and earnings for various educational levels or occupations.

Far and away, my bread and butter work over the years in Eastern Kentucky, where I live and work, has been with coal miners involved in Workers' Compensation claims. The stereotypical miner I see has a low back injury, coupled with at least some level of pneumoconiosis (black lung), and depression or anxiety. These and personal injury cases by way of motor vehicle accidents typically comprise 90 percent of my caseload.

SURVIVING AND PROSPERING

The potential vocational expert in an office practice must have the ability to learn medical terminology and the importance of exertional and nonexertional limitations on a person's ability to work. He or she must become an expert on various sources of labor, wage, and employment information provided by federal and state agencies. I typically use resources published by the U.S. Department of Labor, Bureau of Labor Statistics, as well as the Department of Commerce, along with various state or commercial sources. More and more frequently I go to websites provided by these and other agencies such as the Department of Labors' www.dol.gov to help me render an opinion using the best and most recent data available. Keep in mind that in my practice I am not retained to place a client, but merely to evaluate and render an opinion that may or may not include recommending a referral to a state bureau of vocational rehabilitation, private agency, or pain management center.

BEST ASPECTS

This private forensic rehabilitation work allows me to use the full range of my education and talents to provide a valuable service. When I render my opinions in open court, via deposition or in an administrative hearing, I can represent myself and my profession in an ethical fashion that helps to show the importance of the entire field of counseling and rehabilitation to this nation's health-care system. In every case where I testify, my credentials as a Kentucky Certified Professional Counselor, National Certified Counselor, Certified Clinical Mental Health Counselor, and Diplomate with the American Board of Vocational Experts become a part of the record. Also my fees are in line with other health-care professionals in my area, from $95 per hour while evaluating a client and studying medical records to $450 per hour while giving a video deposition, so I am well paid for my work and efforts.

WORST ASPECTS

In my office practice I am often alone, which can add stress and lead to burnout. While I have my trusted secretary of many years, I also seek out and maintain relationships with the relatively few others who share my same specialty. I try to attend professional meetings, find sources of help when needed, and set time aside for myself. I also teach general counseling courses at a small university and find the graduate student contact an ongoing source of renewal.

LONG-TERM SURVIVAL

The vocational expert in for the long haul must never forget how to learn, because the field has evolved and expanded in my twenty-five plus years in the profession. Also, changes in legislation such as Workers Compensation or tort reform can mean a rapid decrease or increase in business, so you must be flexible and alert to new or changing opportunities. Finally, the practitioner must have a superb sense of ethics and follow the best standards of practice so that he or she is not an expert with an opinion for sale, but an objective evaluator who can help the deciders of fact to make informed decisions.

William J. Weikel, Ph.D earned his bachelor's degree at Temple University, his master's degree at the University of Scranton and his doctorate at the University of Florida. Dr. Weikel is past chair of the Southern Region Branch of the American Counseling Association, past president of the Kentucky Counseling Association, and past president of the American Mental Health Counseling Association. He is a professor in the counseling program at Morehead State University and owner of Eastern Kentucky Counseling and Rehabilitation Services.

SUGGESTED READINGS

Janikowski, T. P., & Riggar, T. F. (1999). Training and competency of vocational experts. *The Journal of Forensic Vocational Assessment, 2,* 2–9.
   This journal is keyed to assessment instruments as they relate to forensic vocational assessment.

Journal of Forensic Vocational Assessment. American Board of Vocational Experts, 783 Rio Del Mar Blvd., Suite 61, Aptos, CA 95003 (abve@abve.org).
   This is the most appropriate journal for counselors in the field of forensic rehabilitation.

Weikel, W. J. (1996). The expanding role of the counselor as a vocational expert witness. *Journal of Counseling and Development, 64,* 523–524.
   An article that elaborates on the counselor's expanding role as a consultant to the court system in vocational matters.

Weikel, W. J., & Hughes, P. R. (1993). The counselor as expert witness. In T. P. Remley, Jr. (Ed.), *The ACA legal series.* Alexandria, VA: American Counseling Association.
   This brief work discusses the role of the counselor in forensic work as he/she testifies in courts, responds to subpoenas, etc.

Weikel, W. J., & Palmo, A. J. (Eds., 1996). *Foundations of mental health counseling.* Springfield, IL: Charles C. Thomas.
   A comprehensive text that discusses mental health counseling in various settings, including forensic work.

A COUNSELOR IN THE
LONG-TERM CARE CENTER

JOYCE M. BREASURE

I work as an independent contractor for a large elder care company in two long-term care centers. First, I do not call them nursing homes because the philosophy of long-term care has changed. With more and more different kinds of people needing care for a host of reasons, nursing care is not all that is done. I serve patients from 90-year-olds with dementia to teenagers with AIDS, from adults with us for rehabilitation after knee replacement to terminal cancer patients, from people with liver failure due to alcohol dependence to a 102-year-old male who is mentally fine but whose body has become weak. Plus, the term *nursing home* conjures up a negative vision. I work in a *community* with fancy dress dances and residents with computers and VCRs. People die, but they also laugh at the pet therapy dog or horse.

I have always had elders in my life, through family, church, and community. I just assumed everyone was comfortable working with people with different needs and people who were dying. Life and death in a farm community is an everyday process. So, I was surprised when a colleague asked if I would mind coming into the long-term care center to work with a quadriplegic who needed counseling for adjustment to his new way of life. He had been an active man until the accident. The insurance company that was managing his care wanted a mental health counselor. I was the only one the facility director knew, so I got the job because the elderly didn't frighten me.

The man was to be short-term rehabilitation—a departure for me. That was ten years ago. One hour a week turned into a contract for ten hours a month for a set fee, in one facility, and last year another facility contracted with me as well. The money is not reimbursed by any insurance provider or agency. My fees for service are paid out of the overall budget. I believe this is a major commitment to my work with the patients and staff at the facilities.

My typical trip to each facility lasts about three hours a week and usually begins with an update from the director of social services (or the director of nursing). One of them tells me who needs to be evaluated, which resident's medicines need to be verified for effectiveness, who needs psychotherapy, and what changes have occurred in the patients I see on a rotating basis. Each nursing station has a *request for services* log where doctors, nurses, staff, residents, and families can request a visit as well.

In one visit I may work with six to eight residents, depending on their communicative ability. I review each record to see if I can detect a pattern or a reason for the behavior's starting. I review the chart each time, before I see the patient. I then interact with the patient, record a note in the medical chart, and assist staff with a plan. This plan may include a referral to a psychiatrist or a medical specialist, medical tests, suggestion of medication, or a diagnosis for the doctor to consider. It may also include counseling from me, family interventions, specifics for the dietary or activities staff to implement, involvement in community programs, or for support and love until the person dies.

The best aspects of the work have been hearing thousands of personal stories. I have met people who outlived all ten of their children, a nurse in the first graduating class from Johns Hopkins Hospital/University, the personal driver of Omar Bradley, the private pilot for General Patton, men and women who picked cotton for one penny a day, every type of doctor and lawyer one can name, and teachers who worked in one room schools and taught for fifty years. I have been taught more about disease symptoms and ways to counteract the symptoms, and sometimes the disease itself, by the people with the disease than I have from any class or book. I have seen people die because they gave up and people live when the cancer had eaten most of their bodies, but they wanted to see a grandchild born or a child come home.

The worst aspect of the work is patients' not being able to give me information orally. My clients often cannot speak or can talk but are living cognitively forty years ago and have no time orientation at all. I have to piece together the information from the charts, the staff, roommates, and family. Sometimes the family member in charge will not give me the information I need to understand a long-term mental health illness. Many clients have been able to exist in a family setting for years with an undiagnosed major mental health disorder, without being treated or even acknowledged. The daughter or son who doesn't visit often or has moved away often provides another picture of the person. We admit what is supposed to be a sweet, docile, loving person. Three days later that person steals food from a roommate, slaps someone in the hall, makes a racist statement, or displays disassociative personality traits. The patient may have been abused or neglected. A number of times, after we feed, hydrate, and resocialize the elderly, the dementia recedes (or completely goes away), and the physical illness diminishes.

I have learned which questions to ask and when to ask them. At times, it appears health providers assume an elderly or even demented elderly person cannot answer a question lucidly. My favorite question is *Are you depressed?* This is a very complicated diagnostic process, but one of the strongest I have. The patient will always answer and the answer almost always is the same as my diagnosis. This is followed by questions on eating and sleeping habits, sadness and crying episodes, lack of motivation in activities and physical therapy, and on and on. My patients often tell me that I'm the first person who has ever asked those questions. I am often told I am the only one who listens, as well.

I teach patients, medical personnel, staff, and families about depression, anxiety, stroke, dementia, and Alzheimer's. Elderly depression is different from the depression of younger people. It affects a different part of the brain, is harder to treat, and comes back quickly without continual medication and counseling. Elderly depression can decrease appetite, increase agitation, decrease motivation in physical therapy or ADLs (activities of daily living), change sleep or day/night patterns, increase pain, cause failure to thrive, and in the end, even cause death.

I have seen death certificates in the last five years with one of the causes for death listed as depression. This is a new phenomenon in the elderly. Depression can onset from a stroke, changes in environment, loss of a spouse of fifty years, loss of physical capability, from a medication, and from any physical illness. Many people say they would be depressed if they were old and sick, but this is NOT a reason for clinical depression. Medication is often required and often must be long term. Currently, there are a number of pharmaceuticals that work well with the elderly. However, they must be monitored for effectiveness and side effects. At times, a particular medication will not effect results, so another is tried.

Anxiety has often existed throughout the client's entire life, but has been passed off as *worrying*. I have met people with elaborate rituals to cope with the panic that they have felt for sixty years. Chronic breathing diseases, trade term COPD, seem to cause the onset of anxiety, maybe because of the fear of not getting their breath, from not getting enough oxygen to the brain, or from the medications for the pulmonary disorder. These patients are often dismissed by others as complainers who want their medications at an exact time. Sleeping and eating patterns are disrupted by the fear. When the patient is placed in a confined setting, the rituals are often taken away, making the panic attacks even worse. I am often seen as their only advocate. One of my former clients knew exactly what day I would visit and was always waiting for me. If she had been given her prn (take as needed) anxiety medication, she was in her room; if not, she was in the front lobby. She also told me on the day she died that I wouldn't have to come back next week.

Dementia is the slow loss of function. Sometimes people are admitted with advanced dementia, but have managed to fool the family until a disaster happens to them, often a fall. I am asked to assess what is happening with the patient when there is a change. At times, a dementia patient will increase behaviors—become negative, combative, or violent; increase demands of staff and family; hallucinate or become delusional or paranoid. The first thing I check for is an infection. Infections can cause severe shifts in behavior. UTIs (urinary tract infections) will cause all of the above symptoms. One wonderful resident with an Alzheimer's diagnosis would experience extreme agitation and aggression three days before the urine sample would show the infection. She would yell *Help me* most of the day. If she knew I was in the building, it was *Help me, Joyce*! The decision to medicate based on symptoms, instead of waiting for the test results, was eventually made, once I could show the chart pattern over a period of time.

Dementia patients will often relive the abuse experienced in their life, especially childhood trauma. Many of these elders were children when a child was considered property. They were sexually and physically abused and nothing was done, because it was not illegal. This basically causes posttraumatic stress disorder, because the brain can no longer block the memories. The patient will repeat phrases like, *I'm a good girl. My daddy will tell you.* Or *Don't let any man get you alone.* The patient may also resist or fight certain activities, like removing their clothes for bathing, bathing, treating skin problems in the genital areas, or changing their incontinence clothing. Finding a way to accomplish the needed procedures without repeatedly traumatizing the patient and staff is a challenge.

I started a technique shortly after I arrived at the center I call *SITR*. This stands for *Stay In Their Reality.* One of the techniques that medical personnel are taught is *reality orientation.* This is often translated into such action as staff members telling the patients with dementia they *can't speak with their father because he is dead* (or offer other similarly harsh messages). I watched patient after patient be retraumatized by the death of their father, mother, spouse, child, or pet. Finally, I began demonstrating to some staff how to redirect, without confronting, a brain that is using another time reference. What I do is simply stay with them and then make statements like *tell me about your father/mother* (etc). *Why do you need them? Can I take care of it for you?*

Another technique is to use their photo books/albums or bulletin boards that have pictures of their family members. Usually, they will easily refocus this way. Another version of this technique is the use of signs. One resident repeatedly tried to exit the building through the front door. A sign was placed on the door that said, *Mrs. Smith, please do not go out the door.* She would read the sign and turn around. Unfortunately, it also stopped several guests with the same name. The elopement behavior ceased in about two weeks and no one had to redirect her. She did it herself without being agitated by someone stopping her and the alarms going off.

The risks with this setting can be quite diverse. I have been bitten, spit on, hit, slapped, punched, vomited and urinated on, and exposed to a variety of contagious illnesses. I have been handed dentures, prosthetic eyes, and artificial limbs. I have been kissed, hugged, given bruises from being held too tightly, given presents (I'm ethically not supposed to take), made an honorary family member, and been listed in estates. The greatest risk, it turns out, is emotional—caring too much and having that person die.

Burnout happens when you don't do the work of mourning, when the person is so negative and depressed (but refuses the medication) that he or she pulls you down, or when you stop listening and looking. I believe that not going through the mourning is one thing professionals omit. We aren't supposed to care. However, my patients know which care providers love them and which ones are simply doing a job. When I am the only caring person the patient has in the world, I do not know how not to care. Nor do I want to do so. I go to lots of funerals, viewings, and memorial services. Many years ago I helped to institute facility memorial services where anyone on staff can talk about the residents' impact on their lives and how they miss them. Each year a remembrance, like a tree or statue, is placed in the courtyard in memory of our lost friends.

Patients have the right to refuse medication, so sometimes the depressed patient is very negative and speaks only of dying. Many times I am the only one left who will still go in and spend time with the patient because staff, and often the family as well, have burned out. It can be very overwhelming. I try to go to one of my happy patients next or walk around the facility. If I am lucky, the pet therapy dog is there and I can pet the animal. It is very easy to get in a mold and see everyone as the same. I cannot afford to get into that mold. I can miss something that is in the chart, in the history, or said by the client. That missed fact or pattern can explain many issues and often will change perceptions of those working with the patient. Seeing every person as a new experience also keeps burnout away.

The biggest honor I have ever been given was to have people share their dying thoughts with me. I feel so awed that I am the last to speak to these precious people before they leave. I am given the responsibility to carry out their last wishes and desires or to hear that they are at peace and not afraid. I cry; they comfort me. I tell them how lucky I am to have met them; they smile. I stay; they leave. I go on to another patient, knowing I have been a part of someone's life and death.

Most of my skills come from experience and training with psychiatrists and other mental health providers who have worked in this field. If the person doing the training about the population has not had experience with the elderly, I usually lose patience. One must be ever vigilant to watch for trainers with severe cases of ageism. It is rampant.

I love working as a counselor in this setting and capacity. The field of gerontology is wide open for counselors. I honestly can say I make a difference in the long-term care centers I work in and in the lives of my clients.

Joyce M. Breasure, LPC, NCC, NCGC, NCC, CCMHC received her master's degree in counseling from the University of Delaware in 1977. She is a Past President of the American Counseling Association and a Past President of the American Mental Health Counselors Association. She is also a past Chairperson of the National Academy of Certified Clinical Mental Health Counselors and the National Board of Certified Counselors. She currently sits on the ACA Insurance Trust and the Commission on Rehabilitation Counselor Certification. She has been in private practice since the late 1970s.

SUGGESTED READINGS

Genevay, B., & Katz, R. S. (1990). *Countertransference and older clients*. Newbury Park, CA: Sage Publications.
    You must have a book about not taking the patients home with you. This is one I liked.

Howard, P. J. (1994). *The owner's manual for the brain.* Austin TX: Leornian Press.
   You must know how the brain works. This is an easy read and a place to begin. I have read hundreds of books on brain function.

Hussain, R. A., & Davis, R. L. (1985). *Responsive care, behavioral interventions with elderly persons.* Champaign, Il: Research Press.
   Older, but lots of specific techniques and charts to help you with diagnosis and behaviors.

Seligman, L. (1996). *Diagnosis and treatment planning in counseling.* New York: Plenum.
   You must also have a diagnosis book and stay current on the diagnostic manual. Seligman is a practitioner, so this is a strong text.

Waters, E. B., & Goodman, J. (1990). *Empowering older adults: Practical strategies for counselors.* San Francisco, CA: Jossey-Bass.
   Another book with lots of specifics and resources you and the families can use.

12

AN ART THERAPIST/COUNSELOR IN PRIVATE PRACTICE
DEBORAH A. GOOD

My work is diverse, combining art therapy and verbal counseling. Currently, I contract my private practice to an outpatient agency. In this chapter, I will give you a feel for what it is like to be both an art therapist and a counselor, what it is like to be in a private practice with many other therapists, what my work environment and clientele are like, and how I cope with the day-to-day stress of this job. I will speak to you from my personal perspective and through what I have learned by working in the field for twenty-seven years.

COMBINING ART THERAPY AND VERBAL COUNSELING

My master's degree is in Art Therapy. I trained at the University of New Mexico and was the first person to graduate from the Art Therapy Program. My program of study included an extensive background in art education, studio arts, and psychology. As the first student in the Art Therapy Program, I worked closely with the administration to form an educational program that met national standards for art therapists.

What Is Art Therapy?

Art therapy is a fascinating profession. Just as many counselors choose a particular way of working with clients, so does an art therapist. I am trained in how to use various forms of art media with clients to help facilitate their self-expression of the therapeutic issues that brought them into therapy. Different forms of art media tend to evoke different reactions and expressions in the clients who use them. This information can be very helpful when assisting clients toward full expression of their feelings, as well as gaining perspective over challenging situations. A very simple example would be to (1) give erasable colored pencils to people who need more control in their life; (2) allow them to choose the subjects to which they bring

65

shape, color, and form; and (3) assist them in transferring some of that perceived control into other aspects of their lives. If a client is able to give graphic form to a particular problem, he or she can work in therapy to change that image, gain power over the image, or dialogue with the image in order to change his or her internal view of the problem.

Art therapy is both a process and product-oriented profession. The process of making art is therapeutic. All of us know that when we engage in the process of doing something that we enjoy, we lose track of time and sometimes enter into an altered space where what we are doing is the only thing that matters at that moment. Many clients work through their reasons for attending therapy by entering into the art-making process. It is the therapeutic art process that heals the client's wounds. The finished product is either of little concern or constantly changes through working and reworking of the image. Sometimes the product is destroyed because the client needs to demolish what is left of the therapeutic issue. One of the most valuable aspects of art therapy is that it allows clients to give shape, color, and form to a particular therapeutic issue. The client no longer has to carry that issue internally. The therapeutic issue is now in a form of its own (the art product) in front of the client and the therapist. Sometimes, there is an incredible relief in the mere fact that the issue has been externalized and that the client no longer internally has to carry the total weight of the problem. Therapy then can take place by working with the art product, which changes the individual. Creating an art therapy product gives distance to the problem. It provides a safe space to deal with many threatening and/or painful life issues.

Art therapists have two credentials, national registration (ATR) and board certification (BC). In order to receive either of these credentials, an art therapist must complete a master's degree program in art therapy or a related field. If the graduate work is in a related field, there must be a certain number of graduate credit hours in art therapy training or post-graduate work in art therapy toward a certificate in art therapy. After the required graduate education is completed, the art therapy candidate then must complete 1,000 to 2,000 hours of supervised client contact hours in order to qualify for registration and/or to take the national certification exam. Please contact the American Art Therapy Association for detailed information on art therapy education requirements, approved graduate programs, and necessary prerequisites in order to enter a graduate art therapy program. Also, you may contact the Art Therapy Credentials Board for information on the art therapy credentialing requirements.

The American Art Therapy Association (AATA) is the national membership organization that sets the standards for the profession. AATA works similarly to the American Counseling Association (ACA). AATA sponsors an annual conference that is held in different areas of the country on a rotating basis. This conference usually takes place in the beginning or middle of November each year. If you want information regarding AATA, you can call 1-888-290-0878, or write to AATA, 1202 Allanson Road, Mundelein, IL 60060-3808. You can also visit its web page at http://www.arttherapy.org.

The Art Therapy Credentials Board (ATCB) creates and administers the national board certification exam for art therapists. It acts very similarly to the

National Board for Counselor Certification (NBCC). Like the NBCC, the ATCB's home is at the Center for Credentialing and Education, Inc. (CCE). You can reach the ATCB by writing to ATCB, 3 Terrace Way, Suite B, Greensboro, NC 27403. You also can call the ATCB at 1-877-213-ATCB (2822), or visit its web page at http://www.ATCB.org.

What About Verbal Counseling?

After many years of working as an art therapist, I wanted to learn more verbal counseling skills. My clinical work led me in a direction where I was using verbal counseling in combination with art therapy. Many of my clients want to talk about their work, verbally process their feelings about the images they create, and sometimes just sit and talk. The more my clientele moved toward a diverse practice, the more I knew that I needed to enhance my verbal skills. Of course, verbal skills are a part of an art therapy program, but I felt the need to focus intently on this area of therapy. I was curious as to what a counseling degree would offer me as a therapist. I knew that, in general, with increased counseling skills, I would feel more confident when engaged in verbal dialogue. It seemed to me that it was an appropriate time in my career to go back to school and add to my clinical knowledge.

I completed a Ph.D. program in Counseling Education at the University of New Mexico. The doctorate gave me many things professionally. First, I feel that I am a well-balanced therapist because of the work that I did during my advanced graduate studies. I have more fully developed skills that positively affect the work I do with clients. Second, I now have dual licensure in New Mexico as a Licensed Professional Art Therapist (LPAT) and as a Licensed Professional Clinical Counselor (LPCC). Given that art therapy is a younger profession (AATA was founded in 1969), many insurance companies and employment agencies still need to be educated regarding the profession. ACA and the counseling profession have been in existence for a longer time and are more widely recognized by the public. I know that to do art therapy and call myself an art therapist, I must be registered, hopefully board certified, and—in New Mexico—licensed as an art therapist. The counseling credentials in addition to my art therapy credentials allow me to work creatively and effectively with many clients and have my work recognized by more accrediting and licensing bodies.

PRIVATE PRACTICE AND OUTPATIENT AGENCY WORK

I have been with Family Therapy of Albuquerque (FTA) for eleven years. The reasons I chose to contract my work to this agency were twofold: (1) There are between fourteen and seventeen therapists of various licensed areas who work at FTA at one time, and (2) the agency is sponsored by and housed within a local church, so we are able to service all people of the community. Referrals come through the agency, as well as personally. I contract to the agency for a set client contact hourly wage and receive that income on a two-week pay schedule. I pay my own taxes and am responsible for the same amount of paperwork as if I were in an individual office. The agency secretarial staff takes care of the FTA office management and insurance billing. When I am at work, I have equipment at my disposal (fax, copy machine, etc.) and sign up for use of shared office space on specific days of the week. I love the freedom of scheduling my own hours, but also enjoy the environment of a working agency.

I enjoy working with other therapists because there is always someone available to bounce ideas around with or to consult with regarding a particular case or intervention. I like the fact that I am not isolated in my work. Several times, I have been very thankful that another therapist was available after or during a particularly difficult session. The director of the agency is also available to me at all times for professional consultation. With a long history working in mental health, I never have been without supervision of my work. I firmly believe that supervision and peer consultation are a mandatory responsibility of a successful therapist. Contracting my private practice to an established outpatient agency ensures that I am around peers and have supervision available.

Many people are able to afford counseling services at FTA because a local church sponsors its counseling programs. Clients are charged a flat fee but can apply for assistance by the church to lower that level. No restrictions or demands are placed on the clients regarding their personal belief systems. People of all walks of life are welcome. Having my private practice at FTA has allowed me to work with people I otherwise might not have been able to see and still be able to support myself financially. My paycheck is not affected by whether the insurance payment came in for a particular client. I often assist the agency in insurance reimbursement recovery, but I only bill the agency according to the amount of client contact hours that I have accrued during a pay period. For me, it is a win-win situation.

The down side of private practice is that there is no income if I am unable to work. I provide my own benefits. For several years, I paid for health insurance through my local membership to the Chamber of Commerce. Small businesses that are members of the Chamber of Commerce have the right to sign up for various kinds of group insurance as a membership benefit. Membership in the national organizations such as AATA and ACA offers benefits for professional liability and disability insurance. These are just a few ways that a small private practice business can provide the benefits necessary for today's professional. Unlike an employment situation, the therapist in private practice pays out of pocket for all taxes and working benefits. Vacations and time off have to be carefully planned. I had to learn to save enough money out of my paycheck to take care of my taxes, insurance, accounting, and vacations. It takes a lot more planning and financial responsibility to work for myself instead of being employed by an agency or institution.

WORKING WITH CLIENTS

Through the years, my clientele has changed, sometimes dramatically. Working for an extended period of time in hospitals and mental health agencies with patients experiencing different kinds of abuse fine-tuned my diagnostic skills and clinical intervention techniques, which are vitally necessary for a successful and productive private practice. I have been fortunate to work with many very talented clinicians and doctors throughout my clinical experience. Hours of in-service and continuing educational opportunities trained me to work with various forms of abuse: substance, physical, emotional, and sexual. For years, my practice focused predominantly on treating people with severe abuse issues, life-threatening diseases, and chronic mental illness. I strongly believe that a therapist is not prepared for private practice right out of graduate school. It takes years of experience properly to prepare a therapist to work privately with individuals. The responsibility is immense and the liability risk is intense.

Currently, I see mostly adults, some children and families. I have worked with couples who are seeking psychological evaluation to adopt a child, families who have a parent with newly diagnosed schizophrenia, many dissociative individuals, posttraumatic stress disorder survivors, families with teenagers who are acting out in ways that are dangerous to their health, clinicians who are dealing with secondary stress issues from working with severely traumatized clients, and children and adults with chronic pain or illnesses. These are just a few of the client populations that I have worked with within the past year. Because of the diversity of my practice, it is vital for me to continue to educate myself about new ways of working with many different diagnoses. Having a wide variety of clients keeps private practice interesting and makes me more aware of ways that I can continue to improve my skills as a therapist.

A Typical Day

I contract for the use of my office on Mondays, Tuesdays, and Fridays. My Mondays start off slowly, and I often schedule supervision of professional therapists who are working toward state licensure and national certification. Periodically, I will supervise graduate students who need an off-site supervisor for their internship placements. I taught graduate school for eleven years and enjoy staying involved in the education process. I see approximately three clients in the afternoon at my office.

On Tuesdays, I will see two to three clients in the morning and then go to a two-hour staff meeting where we eat lunch together, socialize, and either have an in-service or group client consultation. I then will work with clients from 2:00 in the afternoon until 6:00 or 7:00 in the evening.

My hypothetical day begins with a client who is a dental hygienist who recently injected an HIV-positive client and then accidentally stuck her hand with the needle. Fortunately, she has tested negative on all the follow-up tests for HIV but considers this experience a wake-up call regarding the need to focus on what is important in her life. This client has kept a personal journal during the course of her therapy. She has been able to work through many life issues by using a workbook between sessions. The workbook is *The Creative Journal,* by Lucia Capacchione, ATR. The author is an art therapist and provides a step-by-step activity-oriented journal process for introspective adults. Many of my clients have found this book to be supportive between therapy sessions. Sometimes, this client will bring her journal and sketchpad with her to session and we will review her progress and insights. My goals for this client are to build her self-skills to a level that she can move past this traumatic event and make changes in her life that will sustain the growth she has achieved because of this experience. I see this as a short-term case.

I usually ask my clients to keep a journal and to buy a book that has blank pages so that they can also sketch and draw out some of their issues. Most of my clients have found that this process has allowed them to immediately work on problems as they arise in their daily lives.

My second client is a male nurse with chronic depression. This person has been one of my longer-term clients. He came into therapy as an avid journal writer and discovered a love for drawing and sketching as a way to track his thoughts. His therapy focuses on relationship issues and maintaining an emotional balance with his depression. Recently, his therapy has been based more on verbal than art therapy. This is due to the fact that we are working in a more cognitive manner through an intimate relationship that has had its share of ups and downs. Role-playing interactions have proven to be a helpful tool to the cognitive work that he is doing verbally.

The third client in the morning is a woman in her sixties who is working through an abusive marriage that has ended in divorce. She keeps a journal and likes me to read it in session. We will often discuss the things that have presented themselves in her writings. I often give her assignments to work on during the week between therapy sessions. These mostly have to do with self-care, monitoring her inner thoughts, and maintaining a balance in her life. She is a caregiver by nature and is working on turning that skill into self-nurturing. If she is able to stay in therapy for an extended period of time, it would be useful for her to work on the abuse issues that were part of her marriage, trace the pattern of picking abusive partners, and find ways to interrupt the behavior that leads to poor choices in personal relationships.

After our staff meeting lunch, I will work four to five more client contact hours. Often, there is a cancellation and I will use that hour to catch up on paperwork, clean my office, or take a walk outside. I work in an office that is very pleasant, but has no windows. I find that I need to stick my head out the back door between clients and debrief a bit by sitting in the sunlight—even if it's just for a few moments. I try to keep therapy sessions to 45 to 50 minutes so that I have time to myself between clients.

The first client in the afternoon is a woman in her forties who was hit by a drunk driver while she sat parked in her car alongside a highway. The driver who hit her was going 75 mph and had fallen asleep. My client suffered pain upon impact and has been recovering for the past nine months. She is a musician and tends to relate to her environment through her feeling and hearing senses. It seemed important for her recovery to more fully develop her self-awareness through her sense of sight. I use metaphors that have to do with her vision in directing her art therapy and assign projects for the week for her to be more aware of using her sight as a sense of awareness. She documents her weekly experiences in a journal/sketchbook.

Recently, I asked her to draw an image that showed where she was in her recovery process. She drew an image of a large dark hole in the middle of a spiral. I asked her to go into the large dark center and draw it as large as the paper to see what was in there. She did and found that there was a small stick figure caught inside a deep, concrete-lined hole. The walls were smooth and she identified the figure as herself. I tried to stick with the image she drew and not read any of my personal interpretations into her work. I noticed that the figure had no hands or feet and remarked that it would be difficult to climb out without them. She immediately stated that she was not strong enough to climb out at this time, but that she could see a ladder that she will use to climb out when she becomes stronger. As someone who works with image and metaphor, I see her description of the picture as a mirror of her recovery process. I pointed out to her that, although things seem bleak and dark right now, she is quite aware that there is an end to her pain, as well as a way out of how she is currently feeling. We both saw what initially appeared to be a hopeless situation as a sign of hope for a full recovery in the future. The assignment that I gave her was to surrender to the recovery process by resting and taking it very easy for the next week. By directing her to do this, I was supporting the image she drew and encouraging her recovery process.

Later in the afternoon, I see an 11-year-old boy who was referred to therapy by his psychiatrist. He is diagnosed with an intermittent explosive disorder, severe anger expressed mostly at his father, and selective episodes of mutism. He was referred into outpatient art therapy after completing thirty days at an inpatient psychiatric hospital. He is very isolated, has no friends outside of the family, and experienced the death of a close relative last year. His parents report that he has opportunities to make friends, but chooses not to socialize verbally with his peers. Fortunately, he is able to attend art therapy once a week and his parents are supportive. I have been able to coordinate therapy with his psychiatrist, as well as his parents' therapist. Release of information forms were signed so that all the professionals involved had permission to work together in support of the family.

We began therapy by working on three-dimensional projects. I wanted him to be physically involved in the art media, especially because it was going to take time to build trust before he verbally spoke to me. I believe that making art is a form of language and our first months of working together were mostly done in silence. After several sessions, he started to respond to me with a head nod, or shrugged shoulders. I was encouraged to receive this response. I learned that his relative who died almost a year before had made a model of a home he wanted to build some day. My client always admired the model and began to draw architectural drawings of homes. I suggested that we build a model of his drawing and purchased the materials to do so. He liked this idea. We worked together building a model of a large home, yard, and stables out of foam core. I wanted to work with him to develop trust and a positive working environment within therapy.

Over the course of three months, we built the model in layers because the house had a second floor and roof. When he first began to talk, he would mock me when I made a mistake. He would throw things short of my body to get my attention. It seemed that all of these gestures where a deficient attempt to make social contact with me. By the end of the project, he was speaking in more appropriate language to me. He would listen when I told him that I did not like something that he did or that a gesture was inappropriate. Ironically, the project was completed at the same time as the one-year anniversary date of his relative's death. We have a long way to go, but we are making progress.

My workday ends by working with a family. I have found that it is necessary to extend the length of time that I work with families to $1\frac{1}{2}$ hours in order to complete all the issues that arise. That means that I end the session at $1\frac{1}{4}$ hours, which leaves time for rescheduling and paperwork. The family consists of two parents and two teenaged girls. The parents are in their late forties and the teenagers are 13 and 15 years old. The presenting problem has to do with the 15-year-old daughter's testing the family boundaries and limits on her outside activities. Both daughters are very bright, do well in school, and are very loved by their parents. This is the first time the family has been in therapy. In the past, they have considered themselves well adept at dealing with problems as they developed. Recently, the 15-year-old daughter has been staying out past her curfew, spending time with people her parents do not know, and hanging out with men who are 20 and 30 years old. The family is very astute verbally and, obviously, has discussed this problem numerous times before. In order to assess the dynamics of the power struggle, I ask the family to draw a picture together. The family is instructed as a group to decide the theme of the drawing; each member picks one color to use in the drawing and must stick to that color. It is easier for me to track what each person drew with each one using only one color throughout the drawing. The art therapy directive allows me to watch and observe the family as they choose what to draw and how to draw it. This directive can also be done in silence, meaning that the family is not allowed to talk during the art making—all decisions are made nonverbally (Langarten, 1987).

When the drawing is completed, I ask the family to title the picture and pick a spokesperson to explain the drawing process to me. It is important whom the family picks to verbalize the drawing. I wonder if the chosen spokesperson is the one who usually has the final say and attention in the family. Each member of the family is asked for his or her input into the drawing process. The final product (the drawing) is used to review each person's contribution. In reviewing the final product, I consider several questions: (1) Did the family members stay in isolated areas of the paper, or did they cross over into each other's space? (2) Did any family member intrude upon another person's drawing, or were they welcomed? (3) Is this the way the family usually interacts with each other? (4) How are these patterns of behavior like the current crisis within the family? With these new insights in mind, I work with the family to create new behavioral contracts with boundaries that are decided upon by the whole family. Curfews, consequences, and rewards are built into the contract before it is signed by all members of the family and me. We review this contract on a weekly basis and have found that the strong foundation for the contract serves as a base for all newly introduced situations. This family has grown in mutual respect and trust. I have been privileged to notice the parents regain control of the household, the 15-year-old test and then respect new boundaries, and the 13-year-old offer more information about her role in the family dynamics.

HANDLING DAY-TO-DAY STRESS

I start my day with exercise. I have learned the hard way that regular physical exercise is necessary for my own mental health. I live near a nature path along the Rio Grande River and have surrounded my private life with quiet and tranquility. I can walk out my door and be in nature. I like to walk, bicycle, but most of all, swim. I swim from one-half to three-fourths of a mile three to four times a week at a community pool. I get up at 6:30 A.M. and am in the pool by 7 A.M. The people I swim with are now my friends and the pool has taken on a social atmosphere. On other days, I walk or do Pilates floor exercise. I like to start my day with exercise to clear my head and begin each day fresh. It has become somewhat of a positive ritual in my life.

I try to get to the office at least fifteen minutes before my first appointment. I do not like to greet my clients with a feeling of being rushed. Sometimes that is unavoidable, but I work toward not having that happen on a regular basis. I schedule clients each hour and try to stick to a forty-five- or fifty-minute session. If I am doing art therapy with a client, I leave extra time at the end of the session for cleanup. I start to warn the client about time when ten minutes remain before cleanup. This attention to scheduling helps me not to run over the fifty-minute hour and into the next client's session. Also, as I mentioned before, I try to walk outside for a few minutes between clients. This helps to break up the routine of seeing one client after another by refreshing me and helping clear my thoughts.

My doctoral dissertation focused on secondary traumatic stress experienced by counselors and therapists. Self-care led me to this topic. I had worked for ten years with severely abused adults with complicated dissociative disorders and posttraumatic stress disorder. I still enjoy working with this client population, but now I am more aware of the personal toll that this work entails for the therapist. I knew that my stress level had been stretched to the maximum, and I wanted to research an area of interest that would help me to manage the day-to-day stress that being a therapist encompasses. Research shows that therapists who work with severely traumatized clients often take on the symptoms of their clients. Recovery from secondary stress is quick once it is recognized and given attention. This factor alone makes it dramatically different from burnout. Also, the stress that the therapist feels and describes pertains to the abuse suffered by the client, not the therapist. I have listed some readings at the end of this chapter for further research into this area.

I feel that it is very important for therapists to be grounded in their own spiritual belief system. Not that this is ever imposed upon the client, but, rather, it serves as a foundation for the therapist's support system. We constantly hear the horrors and pain of others and must have some frame of reference to deal with these human atrocities and realities. Often, the therapist questions how these stories fit into a larger picture of the world or benefits his or her own growth as a human being. In some way, we have to figure out how all these experiences fit together to make us who we are, or we can never help others who are on the same quest.

CONCLUSION

The combination of art therapy and verbal counseling sets the stage for many opportunities in a therapy session. It is important to realize that there is a big difference between using art in a therapy session and doing art therapy. Therapists trained in art therapy develop an educated way of seeing the use and value of art as therapeutic within itself, as well as a therapeutic intervention. Art therapy is more than a tool. Combining art therapy and verbal counseling skills has offered my clients many ways to express themselves and develop new life skills for the future. Those planning to use art in a counseling session should improve their therapeutic skills by studying art therapy and becoming an art therapist.

Deborah Good, Ph.D., ATR-BC, LPAT, LPCC is a past president of the American Art Therapy Association (1997–99). She has worked in mental health systems since 1973. She holds a master's degree in Art Therapy and a doctorate in Counseling Education. Nationally, she is a registered and board certified art therapist (ATR-BC). She is licensed in the state of New Mexico as a Licensed Professional Art Therapist (LPAT) and a Licensed Professional Clinical Counselor (LPCC). Deborah is the past Director of the Art Therapy Graduate Program at Southwestern College in Santa Fe where she taught for eleven years. Currently, she contracts her private practice to Family Therapy of Albuquerque in Albuquerque, New Mexico, where she resides.

SUGGESTED READINGS

Capacchione, L. (1981). *The creative journal: The art of finding yourself.* Athens, OH: Swallow Press Books.
    This is a self-help book by an art therapist. It is an art-making and writing directed journal process focused on self-growth and discovery. Many of my clients work on this journal between therapy sessions and have found it helpful.

Kramer, E. (1993). *Art therapy with children.* Chicago, IL: Magnolia Street Publishers.
    Edith Kramer is one of the founders of the art therapy profession. This book will give the reader a good understanding of art therapy from a psychoanalytic perspective. Kramer firmly believes that the process of making art is therapeutic.

Landgarten, H. B. (1987). *Family art psychotherapy: A clinical guide and casebook.* New York: Brunner Mazel.
    Helen Landgarten is one of the original art therapists who focused on working with the entire family system. This book covers a variety of issues faced by families, a review of

the developmental stages of relationships, and the Landgarten Family Assessment. If you are using art in family therapy sessions you should read this book.

Landgarten, H. B., & Lubbers, D. (1991). *Adult art psychotherapy: Issues and applications*. New York: Brunner Mazel.

This book contains a thorough collection of chapters written by various authors on pertinent information regarding art psychotherapy with adults. Some of the topics included are a philosophy of art psychotherapy, suicide and developmental issues, borderline and personality disorders, mothers of incest survivors, AIDS and terminal illness, and termination. Presented in the readings is a thorough review of clinical work, and great care is devoted to the topic of art therapy and termination.

Stamm, B. H. (1995). *Secondary traumatic stress: Self-care issues for clinicians, researchers, and educators*. Lutherville, MD: Sidran Press.

Beth Hudnall Stamm has gathered some of the leading authors on traumatic stress and PTSD to write chapters on the experience of secondary stress. This book focuses on the need for the therapists to be aware of secondary stress symptoms and to build self-care techniques into their work, especially when they work with clients who have been traumatized.

13

A FAMILY COUNSELOR'S TYPICAL DAY

PETER EMERSON

T his opportunity to examine a "typical day" in my life as a family counselor provides a unique opportunity to utilize a technique by the same name— "typical day"—that I frequently employ with my clients. I will use the same basic questions from the typical day interview, with minor modifications, to outline the text of this chapter. As I began to further examine my typical day, I quickly came to the realization that my entire day is approached from the same Adlerian systemic perspective employed with my clients, co-workers, and family. This chapter will reflect both of these concepts as the foundation for how I approach the day in the life of a family counselor.

How does the morning go? Daily variety is an important element for my personality style and was a critical factor in my decision to enter into this profession. I am the type of person who would dread knowing my entire agenda in great detail for the day, week, and month. Following such a prescribed routine would be difficult, if not impossible, based on my family counseling experience, so this aspect of family counseling should be carefully considered by any prospective family counselor.

Immediately after awaking, I try to have some kind of contact with each of my family members. Since I will be dealing with family-related problems all day long, I want to begin my day with no regrets concerning my own family. Prior to my family's dispersing for the day, I make contact with each family member. Conversely, if there is an unresolved issue carried into my work for the day, I find it much harder to attend to the clients, colleagues, or students with whom I will work. Specifically, listening to a client while my attention is focused on my own family is, at best, distracting.

Next, I need to check the times of activities that I have scheduled for the day, so that I can see how the day can be balanced. Since attending the National American Counseling Association Convention in Reno, I have attempted to apply William Hettler's admonition for counselors to balance their own lives. If the activities in the day are sedentary in nature, such as sessions with families or the mountains of paperwork that is attracted to everyone in a private practice, my day begins with physical activity. If my day starts with a high degree of activity, then I do my physical activity in the afternoon or evening as a way to unwind from the day.

I have noticed two critical benefits for investing my time in these physical activities. First, I believe working effectively on plans with clients depends on my belief in the plan. If I don't believe that physical activity is a key to a balanced life, my credibility suffers. In my work with children in families, I've concluded that children have a keen sense of whether I practice what I teach, as opposed to being merely another adult exposing them to "do what I say not what I do."

Another benefit is that my overall stress at work and home diminishes. When my stress level is lower, my productive energy levels are higher. Under these conditions, I attend better in sessions, handle mundane paperwork more easily, and actually enjoy work. I look forward to the end of the day, not to just rest, but to enjoy some family time.

Included in my daily activities are conjoint family sessions, supervision of counselor interns, crisis intervention, family education on a wide variety of issues, visits to homes of elderly, teaching graduate marriage and family courses, documenting case material, and serving on a variety of community service committees. I attempt to balance activities each day. For example, I schedule supervision of counselor interns on different days. If there is a family session scheduled, I'll try to follow with a teaching activity. Alternating the activities has assisted my staying more refreshed for each activity of the day.

A big component of my attitude is the agency and set of co-workers I am preparing to encounter. Examining my workplace from a family systems approach helps me to understand what might be expected or needed from me at each setting in which I work. If it is a healthy setting, my attitude is naturally positive. So, if I notice that I do not enjoy going to a particular work setting, my first reaction is to ask, *What purpose does my not enjoying this setting have, for me and the system as a whole?*

After analyzing the purpose of the system, co-workers, and myself, I adjust my behaviors, so that the work setting is both enjoyable and productive. I frequently find work settings need ongoing evaluation and adjustments prior to the helpers' being ready to help. Sometimes I feel as if my most important clinical work occurs prior to the arrival of any clients. If I don't spend this up-front time on my attitude and the worksite atmosphere, my energy is spent dealing with situations that were potentially avoidable.

What are my behaviors at work? Since I am writing the chapter on the family counselor's typical day, the reader might expect that a majority of my time is spent in session. The reality is that a majority of my typical day is spent in a variety of activities other than providing direct services in the form of family counseling sessions. The variety and volume of noncounseling activities required to function in the profession of family counseling was initially a bit of a surprise for me.

My workday generally begins with indirect services of various types. I start with electronic paperless work at the screen of my computer, listen to phone messages, and check with various administrative support workers prior to any counseling activities. The next paperwork activity is to go over the billing for services. Billing for counseling sessions, presentations, consultation and supervision must be reviewed on a daily basis. Other nonclient daily activity includes reviewing case notes prior to the session, writing case notes after each session, consultation relating to the session, and preparation of a disclosure statement prior to every initial session.

My work behaviors in each session are oriented to a family systems approach. I begin the counseling relationship by giving each client a declaration of practices, as required by Louisiana law. In the discussion of the declaration statement, a variety of aspects of the counseling relationship are illuminated. First, I let my clients know that I do not work with individual clients if the presenting problem is a family issue. For example, if a child is having difficulty at school, the parents must be active in family counseling with the child. I do not see the child as a client without at least one parent participating in the process. In my work with couples, I let them know that to render appropriate marital or relationship counseling, I must work with both of them to be effective. To do relationship counseling with just one person risks facilitating more problems for the couple. If the issue involves several family members, I require the appropriate members' involvement. The bottom line is that no one gets dropped off for counseling without the dropper participating.

Another area is confidentiality within the family counseling relationship. The family counselor deals with confidentiality on a daily basis. In the state of Louisiana, the client owns privilege. Clients' owning privilege dictates that I need to develop ongoing methods to monitor and maintain the confidentiality of each client in the family counseling session. An example of the complexity involving confidentiality in family counseling is addressed in the following case.

SUSAN

Susan initially presented herself as having several concerns involving her parenting skills with her son Josh. She informed me that she was in the process of divorcing her husband Dan and that the divorce had been extremely difficult for Josh. Josh's grades were much lower since Dan had moved out, and his ability to concentrate on his schoolwork had suffered enormously. Susan, Josh, and I entered into an agreement to work on Susan's parenting skills and school-related issues with Josh. Three weeks into the counseling relationship Dan, the husband, told Susan that he wanted to join her and son Josh in counseling. Susan was immediately concerned that Dan wanted to join in the counseling process to monitor what was being said about him. She indicated that Dan had a history of controlling behavior in their relationship and feared his entering counseling would destroy the work already started. Josh indicated the same concern apart from his mother.

When Susan brought up this issue in the fourth session, I assured her I would not disclose that she and Josh were in a counseling relationship with me unless she directed me to release that information to Dan. A signed release indicating the nature of the information would also be required. As in the case of Susan, I conduct sessions using a modified Conjoint Family Therapy Model. The initial joining with the family is accomplished with all members who will be a part of the counseling relationship present. Once the counseling process has started, another family member seeking to join in would need the consent of those with whom I have already initiated the relationship to join. The agenda of the person or persons seeking to join would also need to coincide with the established relationship for joining to occur.

CONFIDENTIALITY

The limits of confidentiality in terms of issues that must be reported are also established during the disclosure. Each person reaches an agreement with me and all other participating family members that all material except issues requiring mandatory reporting are kept confidential. I do not release such confidential material to anyone, including another family member not present for the discussion, without the permission of the family member/s making the disclosure. Additionally, I do not encourage family secrets or family members not sharing information with one another concerning issues they might have with one another. To this end, I meet separately with children and parents for a portion of each session. Individual goals and issues with other family members are discussed at this time. Family members are encouraged to bring these issues before the entire family in the joint family time or to address other family members directly in one-to-one sessions with me present. Each family member is allowed to discuss issues at his or her level of comfort and at his or her own pace. Strict adherence to this confidentiality process creates a strong mutual bond of trust that facilitates my ability to join with the entire family.

There are other procedures that I employ for the purpose of establishing confidentiality limits with children and teens in addition to those already stated. During the first session, when I am working with minor clients, I always discuss the limits of confidentiality with parents present. Once I carefully outline mandatory reporting requirements, I tell the parent/s that all other discussion between the minor client and myself must remain confidential. If the parents do not agree, I do not continue counseling. If the parents agree, I assure them that I encourage minors to disclose when ready because I do not believe in family secrets. I will also allow the minors to read, or I read to them, a draft of my notes on individual sessions prior to writing them into the case notes. If there is something they don't want in the notes, assuming it is not a mandatory reporting issue, I respect the minor clients' wishes and delete it.

JOINING

I spend much of the time in initial sessions joining with the family and employing techniques that are family systems oriented. Joining is the process of developing a mutual bond with all members of the family. It is extremely important that, during the joining process, no one in the family perceives or feels that I have sided with another family member against him or her. Besides joining, a variety of other techniques indicative of a family systems approach to counseling are used. On occasions marriage and family techniques are different from the basic skills counselors learn in community, school, or student affairs settings. One such example is a common blocking technique that operates seemingly contrary to the standard listening and attending skills utilized in most basic techniques courses. In blocking, the goal is to disrupt dysfunctional communication so that healthy communication can be facilitated. My work with a couple, Dawn and Gary, concerning their communication skills, illustrates one of the several blocking techniques I've employed. It also reveals how members of the family system attempt to triangulate the counselor into the counseling process, which frustrates the joining process.

DAWN AND GARY

Dawn and Gary sought counseling to save their marriage. Their communication was intermittently nonexistent and volatile. When they entered the room for the first session, they moved their chairs, which were initially placed four feet apart, to different sides of the room. Both Dawn and Gary sat with arms and legs crossed and would only have eye contact with me. They attempted to triangulate me into the presenting problem by seeking to talk through me to the other. My initial attempts to get the couple to establish eye contact while speaking to one another failed. Each would exhibit a different nonverbal cue that would shut down the communication. Gary would roll his eyes upward, which would completely shut down Dawn's communication, causing her to look away from him and turn to me for help with her husband's bad attitude. Dawn would get a grimace that would immediately elicit Gary's finger pointing at her and saying to me, *See what I have to put up with?* At the point that each attempt at direct communication failed, they both escalated trying to triangulate me into the system.

When I attempted the usual individual techniques of having them face one another squarely with open posture, using eye contact and leaning toward the other, the communication between them became more dysfunctional. Instead, I needed to completely disrupt their dysfunctional communication process. Since Dawn and Gary could not look at each other's nonverbal cues, I blocked that dysfunctional communication process by turning their chairs back to back. Once they were no longer looking at one another, the nonverbal communication was successfully blocked and open dialogue began. The triangulation attempts were negated when I refused to let the couple talk through me. As they sat back to back, each would be directed to talk to the partner instead of me. I employed a second blocking technique by refusing to participate in the triangulation. Both blocks facilitated my ability to join with both Dawn and Gary without either thinking or feeling I was taking the other's side.

COMMUNITY SERVICE

What are my behaviors outside family counseling work? A substantial part of my days is spent in some form of community service. When I was first establishing a private practice, the community service was focused on getting me known in the community. Providing free workshops and presentations was the most effective recruitment tool for my marriage and family practice. Subsequent to my initial community service focus, I find myself redirecting my time and energy. Now I desire to participate in the community in a way that is beneficial to individuals with less access to paid services. I find I am also freer, at this point of my career, to do the volunteer service that I have a desire to do.

Currently, I have had the ability to work with older members of the community in my area on issues of abuse prevention and intervention. My work in this area was initially voluntary. In many respects this particular volunteer experience became as rewarding as any paid employment I have ever performed. I have also done pro bono counseling at the local university's counseling center, for members of the local community, and sheriff's office personnel. Although the focus lately has been on my ability to assist the community, and not on recruitment, I continue to have the experience of receiving paid consultation opportunities as a direct result of my community service work.

CONSULTATION

Consultation is another regular aspect of my work. I have consulted with numerous private profit and nonprofit agencies. I enjoy the specific, time-limited parameters involved with this type of work. It provides me with an enjoyable contrast to the more ambiguous, open-ended counseling process. One of the most frequent venues for my consultation work is within the local schools. My family systems training has prepared me to facilitate healthy parent-teacher relationships, initiate appropriate counseling services that contain a family systems focus at several school sites, and provide a variety of in-service training sessions to community schools. The case of Millie and Shawn provide a good illustration of the type of family counseling/consultation conducted in the school setting.

MILLIE AND SHAWN

Millie sought family counseling because she was fearful that her son Paul was about to be diagnosed with Attention Deficit Hyperactivity Disorder. Such a diagnosis at the school Paul was attending almost certainly meant he would be referred for evaluation for medication. His mother Millie wanted to use medication only as a last resort. Paul presented as a brighter than average 10-year-old full of the usual energy present at that age. Paul and Millie both reported that he was able to concentrate at home much better than at school. Paul's teacher and principal were both willing to try alternatives to medication prior to referral for medication.

Using a common family counseling technique, my first step was to expand the symptom to all system members (family and school). Expanding the symptom is a technique that examines the role each person in the system has in maintaining the symptom. In this case there were two primary roles to expand. The first was that of the teacher. Paul was, in fact, easily distracted. His ability to focus on the task at hand was made more difficult by the teacher's style of teaching. She utilized learning centers that consisted of groups of four students working in cooperation at different tasks at each station in the class. The problem was that Paul was distracted by what each of the other students in his group was doing, making it impossible for him to focus. The teacher was vested in her way of teaching. Since it had worked for most of the children, she had been taught to use learning stations, and her performance would be evaluated on using this style of teaching. So she kept trying to use the style she knew, which maintained the symptom of Paul's not paying attention in class. Once her part of Paul's symptom was brought to her attention, she was willing to try something new. Paul was allowed to sit at an individual study station for part of each day.

The second expanding of the symptom involved the other children at Paul's station. They enjoyed talking to Paul and he helped them in their part of the activity whenever he was off task. The other children maintained the symptom to elicit Paul's help and attention. This too was stopped when Paul went to his individual station. Paul never needed medication once the intervention of expanding the symptom was completed.

OTHER ACTIVITIES

What are my nonwork-related activities like? I am active in my state counseling association, currently serving as editor of the state journal. This experience has allowed me the opportunity to be exposed to the cutting edge in research and practice within the state. I am also involved at varying levels of activity with several other professional organizations that are essential to my being the most productive and knowledgeable family counselor I can be. These organizations are the American Counseling Association, the International Association of Marriage and Family Counselors, and the American Association for Marriage and Family Therapy. This involvement has offered both social and recreational opportunities for me throughout my life.

What are social relationships like? To help assure a healthy balance, I also have found the need to have other social relationships related to my work. Perhaps the most crucial of this type is the ongoing consultation relationship I like to maintain. I find I need to identify at least one other family specialist with whom I can process my caseload, supervision, and crisis intervention work on a regular basis. A benefit of this is that I can process work in such a way that it can now stay at work and not follow me home. I've found the separation of family and work essential if I don't want a separation of my family from me. I can also use consultation to check the appropriateness of my procedures in difficult situations.

A final area of social and play life that I need to spend some time engaged in each day is nonwork related. I need to spend regular time, in addition to the physical activity, concentrating on an activity that has nothing to do with counseling. Two activities that I currently am engaged in are reading fiction (any fiction will do) and watching the nightly news with family members. Taking this daily mental break is helpful in refreshing and renewing myself for the next day's work.

Peter Emerson, Ed.D., NCC, LPC is an Associate Professor at Southeastern Louisiana University. He is a Certified Family Therapist and a Clinical Member of the American Association for Marriage and Family Therapy. He has worked in the area of marriage and family counseling for over twenty years, in a variety of settings. He is a detective in the Tangipahoa Parish Sheriff's Office, working with elder abuse. His areas of specialty include parent education, working with issues concerning older family members, and family development using a systemic approach. He is married and has five children, one grandchild, and a second grandchild on the way.

SUGGESTED READINGS

Dinkmeyer, D., & Caldwell, E. (1970). *Developmental counseling and guidance: A comprehensive school approach.* New York: McGraw-Hill.
     This book contains the format for using the typical day interview. The typical day interview is a tool I modify and apply to all of my family counseling work and implement with my own family.

Fenell, D. L., & Weinhold, B. K. (1997). *Counseling families: An introduction to marriage and family therapy* (2nd ed.). Denver, CO: Love.
     This text provides the reader with an excellent introduction to the spectrum of family counseling theory, including the Conjoint approach I utilize extensively. The text is intended for readers with no background in the family approach to counseling. Theories are presented in a clear precise way, outlining the essential elements needed to understand each theory.

Sherman, R., & Dinkmeyer, D. (1987). *Systems of family therapy: An Adlerian approach.* New York: Brunner/Mazel.
     This is the only thorough source for implementing the major family counseling theories from an Adlerian approach, the theory used to construct this chapter.

DEALING WITH DIMENSIONS OF DIVERSE POPULATIONS

THOMAS ARBAUGH, JR.

Was it the second ring or the third that woke me on a cold February Sunday morning? Through blurry eyes I saw it was 5:30 A.M. Knowing no friends would call me at this hour, I didn't bother looking at the caller ID. Trying to focus on the reality of the early morning, I smiled in the dark as I remembered the secretary in the school counselor's office who once told me it didn't actually matter what time I made it to school since I wasn't really of much use to anyone until 9:00 A.M. How accurate she was. With fleeting hope I did intensely wish this to be a wrong number and nothing of importance. How inaccurate I was.

As the plaintive voice on the phone spoke my name, I recognized Dave even before he began to tell of the return of depression and desperation. Dave had not mentioned these old enemies when last I saw him the previous Tuesday night. For that matter, during our last three sessions he had said nothing of slipping back into depression nor even hinted of suicide.

Dave had attempted suicide during the Thanksgiving holidays last year shortly after we had begun counseling. Feeling depressed, he decided to limit an evening meal to a combination of diet pills, pain relief medication, and sleeping pills. Fortunately, Dave had had second thoughts and called a friend who drove him to the emergency room.

Wide awake now, I focused on what I was hearing and, at the same time, remembered other important details I had gleaned in our prior counseling sessions. From his voice tone I knew he was deeply troubled and realized he was conveying inner thoughts he had never shared in sessions. Something was terribly wrong.

Without conscious thought I became a professional counselor and began functioning in that role. My partner heard the shift to my counselor's voice. The precision, clarity, and intensity of one side of the conversation told him this was not to be a regular Sunday morning for the two of us. He got out of bed and headed for the bathroom, realizing in these early moments that this was not to be a brief call. We both had inklings of the extraordinary Sunday morning about to ensue.

Dave, a client of only four months, said he had loaded his pistol and was ready to kill himself when he remembered our agreement to call me if thoughts of suicide returned. In the first moments of our conversation that morning, I was quite frustrated with Dave and myself. Even now, I don't know if it was the early morning hour or my own dashed thoughts of making some progress with this client. Regardless, I worked at staying focused on Dave and the immediate situation and away from what I could have done differently to prevent him from coming once more to the point of suicide. My major concern was to keep Dave alive through this crisis.

Dave was referred to me by both a local physician and by a hospice worker. Both of them knew I was at ease working with diverse populations. My clients include gay, lesbian, bisexual, and transgendered people, in addition to HIV positive and AIDS patients. Fortunately, with the onset of new drugs for those who are seropositive, the latter population of AIDS clients declined.

Dave will eventually develop full-blown AIDS if he does not soon decide he wants to find a way to get AIDS medications, which may cost as much as $2,000 monthly. At the time Dave started counseling in early November, he had no desire to live. His lover had died from an AIDS-related disease.

In our early sessions, Dave, 28, hardly looked up and had very little to say. Together this client and I struggled to find even a remote reason for him to live after the death of Jerry, with whom he had had a relationship of nearly seven years. When Dave first came to me, Jerry had been dead for almost a year. The final stages of the disease had lasted only a few months.

Dave had learned he was HIV positive even before Jerry got sick. Neither Dave nor Jerry knew who gave whom the disease. They both honestly did not know when the disease was contacted. Now Dave resented the fact that he lived when his lover died. Dave's grief was compounded by the uncertainty of not knowing if he was the cause of Jerry's death.

I believe a counselor must be willing to take the risk to ask those questions that may uncover issues for which answers are not known. Some such answers may be so ambiguous as to be meaningless; others may be quite frightening. Still others may be heavy veils and masks that cover even greater pain. Dave and I worked at exploring issues in his life that did not have clear answers. There would never be answers for Dave on some questions around Jerry's death. I was hoping comfort with ambiguity would help Dave to deal more readily with issues for him that had no direct answers.

In the beginning of our sessions I worked on loss and bereavement issues, believing this to be the way to help Dave make progress in therapy. Recognizing the grief in his life, I wanted to work toward Dave's acceptance of Jerry's death and, at the same time, establish a firm reason for Dave to continue to live. I was ready to work intensely on this and other issues to try to bring Dave peace of mind. I soon learned Dave wanted to sleep all day. He did not want to be with his friends. In response to that attitude, some of his friends responded in like manner and told him they did not wish to be with him. More often than not, I sensed Dave was nowhere near as ready to work on these crucial issues with the same intensity as I. That realization made me try all the more. The Sunday morning call reaffirmed to me indications that I was more committed to Dave's mental wellness than he was.

Dave was a licensed realtor and worked in real estate just enough to keep his bills paid. He emphasized to me these bills were not going to include the huge cost of anti-AIDS cocktails. His wish to sleep all day made me believe him when he stated he had no desire to undertake the regimen required to take dozens of pills all day long. Coupled with these reasons was Dave's acknowledgment of a pending death he could hasten by not taking medications.

It was clear to me that progress was made with Dave during the month of November. He started looking at me by the third session and a relationship formed that provided some basic elements of trust. He paid his bill for counseling every other week, a practical sign of progress. His payments acknowledged he was investing more than 50 minutes per week in counseling sessions. Another indicator of early progress was Dave's inviting a close friend to his house. That friend eventually proved to be a vital link at Thanksgiving when he drove Dave to the hospital.

After Dave's suicide attempt at Thanksgiving, counseling took on a more serious and desperate tone for me, but not for Dave. The suicide attempt was a significant fly in the healing ointment. Dave rejected the essential chord of harmony I was trying to establish. He continually bounced his right leg up and down nearly the entire session each Tuesday night. He reverted to not looking at me during the counseling sessions.

I sensed Christmas was going to be difficult for Dave, perhaps more difficult than Thanksgiving had been. With signed consent for release of information, I contacted the physician who referred Dave. The physician told me that Dave was never actually his patient. Jerry was his patient and he only knew Dave through treatment of Jerry. We collaborated on possible medications to treat Dave's depression. Dave agreed to see the physician and take the medications. Christmas went smoothly for me, with regard to my concern for Dave. There were no suicide phone calls. We'll come back to Dave in a bit, but I also want to give you some other case examples from my practice.

Sam was a mature married man who had fallen in love with a man less than half his age. He was an ideal client. In every session we would see some growth. He would explore deep and sensitive issues. Sam showed up on time for appointments and would always call if he could not keep the schedule. Eventually, he decided that life would be much easier and safer if he continued to live with his wife. I had some concerns about this decision, although there had been much growth in counseling. I did, however, feel good about his increased self-awareness, his acceptance level in having some attraction toward men, and the new levels of communication he had with his wife. The couple decided to move to another state, some distance from his boyfriend. Sam continued to keep his same-sex attraction a secret. Before termination, I expressed to Sam my personal reservations about his plan to deal with his same-sex attraction by moving away. He cited other reasons that made moving the best option. At this point I realized that I could only make myself available if Sam ever wanted to talk again.

Jean came to individual counseling from a local lesbian support group. One of the co-therapists of the support group had been a graduate student in my classes.

This former student asked if I would see Jean pro bono. This request made me realize Jean needed help and, additionally, my former student had complimented me by asking for my assistance.

Jean was a veteran and a physiological male. Even though her sexual organs were male, she identified as a woman and was waiting for the day when she could have an operation so that she could be a female physically. Jean was referred to individual counseling because she did not fit well in the lesbian support group. Jean had problems dating because she was attracted to women. Jean told me women would not want to date her when they found out she was actually a man. Jean was unsuccessful in dating nonlesbian women because they did not want to date a person who was physically a man and living as a woman.

One day Jean did not keep her appointment. I never heard from her again. A few months after Jean had stopped coming to counseling, a friend who is a lawyer mentioned a transgendered woman who came into his office looking for a job. From the woman he described I was sure it was Jean, though I never revealed that to my friend. I still have no idea why she stopped coming to free counseling sessions.

Bill helped fill my evening schedule and was a client who made great progress in counseling. Being a minister and a schoolteacher is no easy task for any gay person. When a local policeman accused Bill of coming on to him and filed charges of sexual assault, Bill began to seek support in counseling. Since Bill lost both his jobs because of the accusation, we decided on a sliding payment scale so he could continue in counseling. Bill insisted on paying as much as he could for the counseling service. Together in counseling, Bill and I found various issues connected to his initial acceptance of all the abuse perpetrated on him by law officials, the local school system, and the church.

Bill terminated counseling when everything settled down and he moved to another town. He sold his house and all the contents and lived with friends for a while. He obtained a lawyer who got all charges dismissed. Bill was reinstated in his teaching job without a blemish on his record. Given the separation of church and state, however, the church was free to punish him with anti-gay pronouncements and vocal destruction of his local ministry. Bill's personal growth was augmented by support from his friends. This growth and support were amazing, even though there was a sadness that this specific event had to be the impetus for such growth.

Now back to Dave. Even though he lived in the deep South, he never talked about being bothered by other people's opinions of his being gay or even HIV positive. Dave stated that he was indifferent about his family and their reaction to his visible life with Jerry. Dave and Jerry had many connections with other gay friends in the area and Dave would state proudly that they lived openly without concern of the opinions of family and community. Not until Jerry became very sick did they begin to isolate themselves from other people. Then the isolation became important more for the danger to Jerry than the danger of Jerry to other people. There was nothing about being a gay man that presented as an issue for Dave, and, since it was not important for him, it was never addressed in our counseling sessions.

Both as a counselor and as a person who felt strongly about not hiding any part of myself, being openly gay was an important issue for me. I began my counseling experience as a school counselor where I had to be circumspect in order to keep my job. Research demonstrates that lesbians and gay men are not the group most likely to molest children. However, it is not uncommon for the general public to use child molestation as a scare tactic to rid the schools of openly gay people. I was a teacher before I became a school counselor. I witnessed reactions of students and other teachers to gay and lesbian issues. These reactions were far from the open-minded and accepting attitudes that I thought were important to any educational systems.

For years I silently loved another man and only listened as colleagues talked freely of their spouses, children, vacations, and sometimes their love lives. Since I enjoyed my work with children and adolescents, I kept my voice and my life quiet. Upon entering graduate school to work full time on a doctorate in counseling, I resolved to find the strength to bring more integrity into my life. I knew that getting better in touch with my own issues of being a gay man would allow me to be a better counselor. I firmly believe that being an effective counselor is grounded in continuous and ongoing personal and professional growth. Such growth leads to an empathetic understanding of clients, among them students, teachers, and sometimes school administrators.

As a graduate school intern, I counseled with perpetrators of violence, substance abusers, and clients who were in the local institution for the criminally insane. The internship assured me of the kind of counseling that I knew I did not want to do upon graduation. I became more and more confident that I wanted to teach counselors and I wanted to live in a climate that was warmer than the Midwest. By moving south and teaching at a university I accomplished both goals.

Working in counselor education is a good fit for my personality, though I sometimes miss the structure of regular hours as a school counselor. It did not take me long before I started seeing clients in the evenings after class or during the day before classes. Doing private practice counseling allowed me to keep current in counseling issues and to keep my skills of counseling fresh. I very much enjoy teaching and watching students grow into persons who are self- and multiculturally aware. I also have a passion for working with clients and being a part of their personal growth as they discover themselves and recover the positive life elements needed to live and love. Being a counselor educator allows me the income to pay necessary bills without relying on my counseling practice as my sole source of income.

I began to see some renewal in Dave when he returned to counseling after Christmas. He started shopping with a friend of Jerry's who, with Dave, had watched the progression of HIV that ultimately killed Jerry. However, Dave continued to struggle with personal issues and was still resistant to talk about family issues. I believed progress was being made before the phone call early that Sunday morning in February changed my thinking. Dave had almost become part of my weekly ritual and not someone who needed special attention or special focus.

Having a loaded handgun beside his phone helped me give him all the special attention he needed. I sat on the edge of my bed and talked to him until he returned the safety lock to the pistol. Only after I assured him I would call the police if he removed the safety lock did Dave decide that he would be willing to call his shopping buddy and have him come stay with him for the day. Dave used his cell phone so that I could hear the other conversation in the background. I knew I must not terminate our conversation for him to make another telephone call.

Once I knew Dave's friend was driving over, Dave and I talked some more about what led him again to this point of desperation. He had used recreational drugs late the previous night. He also said he had not slept in a few days. Finally, his friend arrived and together they unloaded and disarmed the handgun. When his friend was with him, Dave became settled and sounded like he was out of danger of self-harm. His friend also had to relax a little and the two of us discussed how to keep watch over Dave. I believed both men were safe and Dave would actually be back in my office Tuesday night. I concluded this now lengthy conversation with confidence that Dave did not need more attention or police interference. Only then did the gravity of the situation cause me to tremble a little and be unsettled for a few minutes until I could relax enough to start the day.

Dave came to counseling the following Tuesday and agreed to start taking the antidepressant medication again. Although he had not mentioned it to me, he had stopped taking medication sometime after Christmas because he was feeling better. It was not unusual for Dave to miss an occasional appointment. Even so, I did not see a severe decline in his mood.

It wasn't long before Dave was spending more time working and more time shopping. He still refused to take any medication other than antidepressants. He was not going to take medicine to effectuate his HIV status. One Tuesday evening Dave did not have his checkbook with him and said that he would pay for three visits after his next session. He said that he wasn't sure he could make it next week and he would call to let me know about the week after next. Dave never called and never returned my calls. I saw him once in a store, in the men's clothing department. I talk to my clients when I see them in public if they initiate the conversation. He said Hello, but only that. He never paid for his last two sessions. Perhaps he needed the money to pay for all his new clothes.

Thomas Arbaugh, Jr., Ph.D., LPC, NCC earned his master's degree from Bowling Green State University in 1989. He was a school counselor before working for a mental health and substance abuse clinic in Athens, Ohio. In 1994 he was awarded his Ph.D. from Ohio University and began teaching school and community counseling at Augusta State University. It was there that he began private practice counseling in addition to teaching and research. He has researched and presented on the sexual abuse experiences of men and has given various presentations on the national, state, and local level. Presently, he is training school counselors at the University of Southern Mississippi–Gulf Coast campus and is the President of the Mississippi Association for Counselor Education and Supervision.

SUGGESTED READINGS

Dworkin, S. H., & Gutierrez, F. J. (1992). *Counseling gay men and lesbians: Journey to the end of the rainbow.* Alexandria, VA: American Counseling Association.
There will soon be a revised and updated edition of this book. This has helped me in my practice and assisted many counselors in a better understanding of issues for gay, lesbian, bisexual, and transgendered clients.

Kain, C. D. (1996). *Positive: HIV affirmative counseling.* Alexandria, VA: American Counseling Association.
Information, terms, and medications around HIV disease are changing all the time. This book was quite helpful to me in working with HIV clients.

Marcus, E. (1992). *The male couple's guide to living together.* New York: Harper & Row.
Eric Marcus is a clear thinker and a great guide for someone to better understand the nuances of same-sex relationships.

Unks, G. (Ed.). (1995). *The gay teen: Educational practice and theory for lesbian, gay, and bisexual adolescents.* New York: Routledge.
This is a good collection of articles by a variety of authors on this specific topic. A great addition to a library for the counselor.

White, M. (1994). *Stranger at the gate: To be gay and Christian in America.* New York: Penguin Books.
The counselor should not underestimate the spiritual and religious role that is a part of any client. This is certainly true for clients who grew up with specific Christian ideals that do not fit well with sexuality.

FIVE MINUTES
NANCY PITTARD JONES

It is not quite daylight as my tires crunch the gravel in the parking lot behind my school. My parking place (I am a creature of habit) is open; a good sign, I think. I swing in, kill the motor, and sit for a moment, as I do every morning, and mentally lift myself for the day ahead. I used to try to prepare myself by reviewing my day's schedule in my mind, but now, in my sixth year at this school, I know that flexibility and openness are more important, as the planned schedule for my day is likely to change several times, all before I eat lunch. I need this five minutes to get myself focused.

I get out of my car and walk in to the building. This is Clara Nesbit Elementary, a Gwinnett County school in a suburb east of Atlanta. Only eight years old, Nesbit is a very attractive building. We have beautiful grounds, spectacular murals done by a local artist, and many modern school conveniences afforded to newer schools in our county. Gwinnett County is one of the fastest growing counties in the country, and nowhere is that more evident than at Nesbit.

Our school has close to 1,200 students in kindergarten through fifth grade. My students, at last count, came from over forty different countries, and the kids and their families speak as many languages. Many of our students are the only ones in their homes to speak any English. The socioeconomic level of the students is mixed; most of our kids live in apartments, some in town homes and houses. There are many single-parent homes and many kids living with relatives or foster families. We also have a high level of free and reduced lunch families (over 60%).

We are a very transient area. Our school mobility rate soars above 50 percent. That means that if you were a teacher in my school and you had 20 kids in your class on the first day of school, you would still have 20 kids at the end of the year, but you'd only have about 8 of the ones you started with in August. We routinely have kids in second or third grade who are in their fifth or sixth school since beginning kindergarten. This is extremely difficult on our teachers and staff, especially when the newspapers, the county office, and the government are looking over our shoulders at test scores. It's hard to hold a teacher accountable for a student he or she has to test even though that student has only been in his or her room for three weeks.

Our principal is a Gwinnett country veteran who has been a principal for some twenty years. We have three assistant principals: busy, talented ladies. We have nearly sixty regular education classes plus one self-contained physically disabled class. Our support staff is large: art, music, PE, computer labs, media specialists, ESOL (English to Speakers of Other Languages), special education classes, reading teachers for several specialties, paraprofessionals (teaching assistants), and gifted education teachers. And then, there's us.

We are the school-counseling department. There are four of us all together, although two of us work part time and actually share one position. Our principal, Connie, is and always has been a champion of school counselors, and she has always had more counselors on staff than the state says that she needs. We earn, according to funding points, one and a half counseling positions; Connie has doubled that, and truthfully, she could have tripled that and we would still be busy all the time.

Sherry and I are the two half-time counselors. Sherry is a veteran, a counselor in this county for fifteen years. I can stand next to her and learn something. Like me, Sherry has young children, so working part time is ideal for both of us: We get to be mommy as well as counselor. Our two full-time partners are brand new this year. Heidi and Ginny are troupers; they have jumped in with both feet, and sometimes I forget that they are new. They are both learners, who ask good questions and bring good ideas to the table. Sherry and I have worked hard this year to help get them acclimated. Together, the four of us make quite a team. Where I am weak, I know one of my partners is strong, and vice versa.

The four of us meet quite often in the summer and in the early part of the school year to map out our plan for the year. Our goal is to provide a developmentally appropriate program for every student at Nesbit. We offer services to all children and their families. We cover many academic and affective skills that are necessary and beneficial to everyone. Crisis response is also a part of my job, and some days, it is more prevalent than others.

This morning, I have a meeting of the discipline committee at 7:50, and I have a million e-mails to read before that. After my meeting, I have several classroom guidance and group lessons planned, as well as a very important phone call to make. That is how I spend a great deal of my time; I go in to classes and teach lessons on everything from personal safety/sexual abuse prevention to study skills, from conflict resolution to career awareness. I also lead small group sessions for kids on similar topics but also for more specialized needs, such as changing families (my CF group today has three kids who are each on their fourth dad, none of whom have ever met their real dads), anger management, and a neat group who call themselves the Second Chances group—kids who are all repeating the fifth grade this year. I am also expected to see individual children, teachers, and parents by request, as well as to plan and instruct a great deal of staff development and parenting classes. I serve on and chair several committees as well. I have so many of these things mapped out, but again, I never quite know where my day will take me.

By the time I reach my office, I have already run in to several teachers in the hall. One has stopped me to ask if I can help her with a personal situation; she wants to know if I will counsel her. I listen, a bit dumbfounded that she could talk about this so easily in the middle of hallway, and a bit understanding of why she has been in such a bad mood lately. I tell her that it isn't appropriate for me to counsel her because we are colleagues, and that I would be glad to give her the names of some people in our area who specialize in those types of problems. She is grateful and wants to know how soon she can have the list of names. With a sigh, I tell her she can have it by the end of the day. It's a list I use often and I know right where it is. We spend five minutes together in the hallway, and I know her deepest secret.

The other teacher who stops me in the hall is the one who called me at home last night, hysterical. She had called home to the mom of one of her students to let her know that the child, Joe, was not following the rules and wasn't getting his work done. The mother's reaction stunned this sweet, young teacher: Joe's mom simply said, *You know, he doesn't follow the rules around here either, and I am just plain tired of it, and tired of him. I am tired of calls about him not behaving and doing the same old _____ . The bottom line is, I just don't want him any more. I am going to pack his bag and send him to school tomorrow with his stuff. You can call the police to come get him, or send him to a foster home, or whatever you want. Just don't send him home.* The mom went on about this for a few minutes while the teacher sat frozen in shock and fear.

When the mom hung up, the teacher called me at home, crying that she never should have called home, that this was all her fault, what were we going to do, and so on. Five minutes, Nancy, she tells me, I totally changed his life with a five-minute phone call. I did a lot of listening, and calming her down was a big task over the phone. I explained to the teacher that I would be contacting the Department of Family and Children Services (DFACS) first thing in the morning—my very important phone call—and let them direct our actions from there. We talked about how she should treat Joe when he came in to her room the next day, and how we would proceed. She is still nervous about it this morning. How do I help a teacher prepare for that?

And now, I've reached my office. As I unlock the door, kick it open, and go in to drop my belongings, I see the answering machine light blinking, signaling four messages. Two teachers come in on my heels with quick questions about students in their rooms. By the time I have sufficiently answered their questions, I am 5 minutes late for my discipline committee meeting. So much for unread e-mails . . .

Back in my office after the discipline meeting, I make the call to DFACS about Joe. The cheery voice on the other end of the phone asks me questions and takes notes of all of the details. She asks what time we get out of school that day, and I tell her 3:15. She tells me she will try to have someone come by then. As I hang up with her, I see a face hovering at my door—it's Joe. I signal him in as I set down the phone. He pushes open my door, and there it is at his feet: his suitcase. He looks shattered. I call the front office and ask the secretary to cancel my first two classes for me. Joe and I talk for a long time.

When Joe leaves, I cast a weary glance at my clock. Hmmm . . . I have definitely missed my first two classes, but I don't have another one for five more minutes. I am grateful for this gift of 300 seconds, because I know I can get a lot done. I hit play on my answering machine and jot some notes:

Call one—Ms. Smith, mom of two students with whom I work. Her electricity is being cut off today if she doesn't pay her three-month-overdue bill. Can the school help?

Call two—Mr. Horn, with whom I met last week to discuss his son's lack of progress in fourth grade. When we met last week, we gently approached the possibility of an attention disorder. Mr. Horn cut us off and said he didn't want to hear it. However, according to this message, Mr. Horn was contacted again yesterday by his son's assistant principal to tell him that his son was being suspended again as a result of his impulsive and inappropriate behavior. All of a sudden, Mr. Horn wants to talk to me again and hear more about possible interventions for his son.

Call three—my husband, wishing me a happy day and telling me that he loves me. I am a lucky woman to have his support and encouragement. I wonder if he knows how much those calls mean to me?

Call four—a private therapist who is working with one of my fifth graders. We have a signed consent form to release information from the school to this agency. He and I have been playing phone tag, but I need to talk to him. I am seriously concerned about this boy.

I am now trying to decide who to call back first. I am reluctant to tackle the financial issue of Ms. Smith. Part of my job as a counselor is to help dispense funds in our Care Team account. This group raises money to assist our families in time of need and crisis, as well as providing benefits for all Nesbit students, such as agenda books and character education programs. The administration basically leaves it up to the counselors as to who gets that money. I lean back in my chair and close my eyes, thinking of Ms. Smith. She calls two or three times a year, wanting money for some bill or rent. She comes to get food from our food pantry about every other month. Every year, I have signed her up for a holiday assistance program so that her kids receive gifts and clothes for Christmas, as well as meals for Thanksgiving and Christmas.

At the beginning of my second year at Nesbit, Ms. Smith called me, yelling at me for embarrassing her children by not getting them school supplies; after all, I had done it LAST year, and didn't I have enough sense to do it again THIS year? I have arranged for free eyeglasses for all of her kids, as well as shoes. My basic dilemma with Ms. Smith is twofold: One, I feel that she abuses the system by expecting Nesbit to bail her out and to supply many of what should be her responsibilities. Two, the last time she came to pick up food, she was driving a relatively new car, with cigarettes falling out of a designer handbag on her arm, and a case of beer on her back seat. If she has money for these things, why doesn't she have money for milk, bread, crayons, and so on? But this is a downfall of working here; not everybody thinks like I do, or has the same priorities as me. And the worst part is, I don't want to deprive the kids because their mother makes poor choices!

Maybe I should call back the therapist working with my fifth grader, Michael. Michael has been diagnosed as having Attention Deficit Hyperactivity Disorder (ADHD), Oppositional Defiant Disorder (ODD), Obsessive-Compulsive Disorder

(OCD), and depression. He is on a host of medications and has been in and out of in-patient treatment facilities. He is very intelligent and has blown through several psychologists and therapists. This new therapist, Mr. Griffin, has been very condescending in his messages to me. He told me on one message that there is a new type of behavioral therapy that will fix Michael's behavior at school. I am anxious to talk to him to hear about this new wonder therapy; I'll believe it when I see it! I have noticed that many private therapists feel that they are way above school counselors. I have had several who have tried to pull rank on me. I have had to bite my tongue on many occasions to keep from pointing out that in many cases, my qualifications are equal to theirs, if not advanced. Many of them are Licensed Clinical Social Workers (LCSW), or, like me, Licensed Professional Counselors (LPC). The best therapists I have worked with are the ones who ask good questions, make practical suggestions, and waste no time trying to impress me with who they are. We don't have time for that at Nesbit.

Before I can decide who to call, my phone rings and I answer it on autopilot. It's the school secretary, and she politely intones that she needs me right away in the front office. Upon arriving, I am greeted by a couple and three children, all standing in front of the secretary. The couple wants to register the three children for school, but there are complications that were not covered when the secretary was trained on registration procedures. In a confusing twenty-minute conference, the story emerges.

This couple is Terrance and Dianna. Dianna has a daughter already enrolled at Nesbit. Terrance is her boyfriend, and these three children are his. They had been living with their biological mother, who recently decided that she wanted their father to take care of them, so she dropped them on Terrance and Dianna's doorstep. Of course, Terrance has no papers on any of the children: no birth certificates, no immunization records, no previous school files, nothing. Furthermore, he explains that he needs a paternity test to be sure that he is actually the father of one of the children. Dianna is insistent and belligerent, saying that they need to go, and can't we just take the children?

The secretaries often call on the counselors when a confusing custody situation arises, because we are in-serviced every year by our school board attorney on these types of circumstances. I get the pertinent information, make a plan with the secretary and the parents, and take a glance at my watch. Well, now I've missed my third class of the day. No surprise there; this happens regularly.

Heading back to my office, I run in to one of the assistant principals. Walking with me, she asks, *Can I have just five minutes? I need to update you on a situation from yesterday.* We had a student yesterday who got in trouble with his teacher by mouthing a pretty serious curse word at her. He denied it, and when the assistant principal called his mom to tell her that her son would be put in administrative detention for this offense, as well as for other classroom disruptions that occurred at the same time, the mother hit the ceiling.

She tells the assistant principal that her son will NOT be put in any kind of detention, that the assistant principal does not have her permission to do that, and that if she DARES to do that, the mother will seek legal action against us. We hear things like this from parents constantly. I wish I had a nickel for every lawsuit threatened against me or the school. This is another difficult aspect of this job: The parents seem to think that they can make the rules for the school to fit their own wishes. We have pages and pages of policy on student offenses; the assistant principal and I consult these documents and conclude that she is well within her rights to impose this consequence and that the boy is actually getting off easy!

When the assistant principal leaves, my phone rings. It's Mr. Griffin, the therapist working with Michael. In listening to him, I inwardly groan: His *miracle* therapy that is *so new* is play therapy! He speaks to me about it as if he had personally discovered it and as if it had come in to existence only yesterday. I calmly wait until he takes a breath and explain to him that I am a Registered Play Therapist (RPT) and that at Nesbit we actually have a fully supplied playroom complete with a video monitor. Michael has been receiving play counseling for many years now; that is how the doctors got much of the information they used to diagnose him! Because so many of Michael's problems are chemical, he needs medical monitoring, and his family needs counseling. Mr. Griffin is much less smug with me by the time we end our discussion. A waste of five minutes, if you ask me.

It's been fairly busy so far. And it's only 10:40 A.M. I head out to go pick up my *student buddy.* I serve as a mentor to a first-grade girl named Ciara whose home life makes me cringe every time I think of it. Her mother is only 22, and this 6-year old is the oldest of four children. Her mother is a single parent with virtually no parenting skills. We had to have her mother arrested last year because she came up to the school and beat Ciara with a board in the middle of the hallway because she had gotten in trouble for talking in line. Ciara's mom received probation; Ciara received the worst berating of her life, and this special little girl now believes that she is worthless. Ciara and I talk, laugh, and play games together for thirty minutes once a week. She tells me her dreams of being an actress; she says it would be neat to get to be somebody else for a while. Ciara is the best part of my day so far.

And this is one of the best parts of my job: being with these precious children. They are the reason I get up in the morning to come here. I have so much that I want for them. I want them to know that I care; that they can learn if they make good choices; that there are role models who don't curse, commit crimes, lie, cheat, steal, blame others, or otherwise behave irresponsibly; and that I have high expectations for all of them, no matter how old, what color, or where they go to sleep at night. But I don't have even one minute on most days to convey that directly. I have to rely on the little things: hugs, winks, a note left on a desk, arranging my guidance schedule to be there to clap for them at Honors Assembly when no one else is there.

I drop Ciara off in time to finally get to do at least one thing that was on my schedule: I have a parent conference with a third-grade parent and the teacher. Ms. Park, the teacher, meets me in the front office. We greet Mr. and Mrs. Carrington, parents of Jimmy and head to Ms. Park's room. Ms. Park, a first-year teacher, asked me to attend this conference because she needs to tell the Carringtons that Jimmy will probably not pass third grade this year, and she is nervous about their reaction. I spent quite a bit of time with Ms. Park prior to this conference, role-playing how she could tell the parents, and helping her prepare what she needs to have ready as her explanation. This time pays off; although the parents are initially critical and defensive, Ms. Park uses the techniques we discussed to diffuse them, and she eventually gets them to hear her concerns.

The Carringtons want me to tell them how this will affect Jimmy's self-esteem. I talk bluntly with them about not coming down hard on Jimmy, about using language with him that helps him understand that he has done nothing wrong but just needs more time to develop third-grade skills. I am thankful that the Carringtons are receptive; at a conference when Jimmy was a first grader, the parents screamed at him for not knowing all of his letters and colors.

We are not talking about a lazy or unmotivated kid; we are talking about a kid who desperately wants to please his teachers and parents, but because of his innate intellectual ability, he is behind. We had Jimmy tested that year for special education classes, thinking that he had a learning disability, but he was two points above the qualifying score. We have no formal programs to offer him. Nonetheless, the parents ask me if I could help them find a tutor for math, Jimmy's weakest subject. They sign the papers for him to attend summer school. They agree to read with him for thirty minutes every night and to buy him a musical tape that will help him learn his multiplication tables. They are good parents; they listen and they want to help their son. This was a conference with a happy ending.

As I leave the conference feeling good about Jimmy, I suddenly hear an all-too-familiar noise coming from the kindergarten hallway. I am run-walking that way in an instant. Two of my partners are already on the scene: Kimberly, our first-grade *queen of the tantrum*. We have spent way too much time chasing Kimberly as she bolts from class and sometimes from the building. We actually attended a class to learn physical restraint techniques in order to keep her from hurting herself, others, or us.

Sitting on Kimberly is a LONG five minutes. Was that in my job description? She has spit on me, punched my partner in the stomach, and called many of us curse words that I have never heard from a 6-year-old. Kimberly lives with her aunt; her mother is in detox in Indiana, and her father has been in jail since she was a year old. Her aunt is a respectful, tired woman; she comes to get Kimberly every time we call her following such an outburst. She apologizes to us, tells Kimberly quietly and firmly that this behavior is unacceptable and must stop, and slowly leads her out of the building. Over her shoulder, she tells me, *I got her an appointment with that therapist, one from the recommendation list you sent me, Mrs. Jones. My insurance don't cover it, since Kimmy ain't mine; but I done asked for an extra shift twice a week so I could pay for it.* I encourage her efforts. As she reaches the door with Kimberly, she says, *Please don't give up on us, Mrs. Jones. We tryin'.*

Now it's lunchtime. I usually eat with Sherry, Ginny, and Heidi. Some days we actually get to sit down and eat; sometimes we eat while conferencing with a teacher or consulting with another staff member. Sometimes, we don't eat at all. It just depends on the day. I value this time; it is precious to me for mental-health reasons. One way to stay sane here, where the surprising no longer surprises and the outrageous becomes ordinary, is my network of colleagues. We shut the door, and we laugh, we cry, we complain, we act silly, we vent. It is in the strictest of confidences, my three partners and myself. It's what helps bring me back down. It's what refocuses me on reality.

Today, Sherry tells a funny story about her fifth-grade classroom guidance lesson. Heidi tells us about a new student in kindergarten who is going to be a handful. Ginny tells us about her boyfriend. We talk about movies, about our children, about politics, about sports. Five minutes ago, we were sitting on Kimberly, wiping her saliva off our faces. Five minutes after that, we are cracking up about something we saw on TV.

When lunch ends, I have what I call *errands*. I generally accumulate a dozen little things that need to get done, so I try to do them after lunch each day. Today, I drop by a fifth-grade class to give a check to the teacher. One of my favorite kids is in her class, and the student told me yesterday that her mom couldn't afford to send her on the fifth-grade field trip. She said she was praying that her mom would get the money. Her mom has seven kids; I can spare $11. I ask the teacher not to tell Rose—I like to do *good deeds* anonymously. I drop by a second-grade class to check on a teacher who is pregnant, after much infertility treatment. She is going to tell her class next week, once she is a little further along. She has been feeling really sick—a good sign! I go next door to another second grade class where the teacher is already out on maternity leave.

I met with the long-term substitute last week to give her some suggestions on the Nesbit discipline philosophy and want to see how she's doing with it. On the next hall, I confirm a time with a kindergarten teacher who wants me to come observe her teaching. The teacher had an observation by an administrator as part of her official evaluation; it didn't go well, and she needs some help to fix some basic mistakes. I am going in for half a day tomorrow. While I am there, the kindergarten teacher tells me that one of her students has been absent twenty-seven days; when the teacher asked the mom about it, the mom replied, *It's only kindergarten. He can't be missing that much.* Unfortunately, there is no official penalty for elementary students who miss a lot of school. I ask the teacher to send me an e-mail and tell her I will call the mom.

Errands are over. I am actually due to teach a classroom guidance lesson in five minutes. I swing by my office to gather a puppet and a book. These are my basic and favorite teaching tools. I personally own over 1,000 children's books, and they are the basis of my guidance program. There are fabulous literature selections, appropriate for children of all ages, that illustrate nearly every topic I teach. Although I have been fortunate professionally to publish book chapters, articles in professional journals, and a resource book for counselors, my dream is to publish one of the several children's books that I've written. Some day . . .

The class is enthusiastic. I am confident in my teaching; I am generally upbeat and entertaining, and I have a firm foundation in my disciplinary style. I believe in mutual respect, giving choices to children, and in letting them experience natural and logical consequences rather than punishment. I have read so much on these subjects and taught them as part of our schoolwide discipline philosophy, and so I am comfortable with them. I wear them like a second skin.

I am reluctant to leave the class, but there is more to do, and the day is running short. I finally check my e-mail; I have 58 unread notes. I scan through a few of them and realize that the rest will have to wait until after school is over. I take a few minutes to make myself a *to do* list for tomorrow:

1. Send flyer about our upcoming parenting class to the county printing office.
2. See Amy, a third grader who reported to a staff member that she has to share a bed with her 14-year-old brother, and he *bothers her* during the night.
3. Call DFACS again; they never came to see Joe, and his suitcase is still in my office.
4. E-mail three teachers to see if they were able to secure parent conferences they had asked me to attend.
5. Plan my classroom guidance lessons for next week.

In five more minutes, I have added eight more things to my list. Rolling my eyes, I realize that I better get up thirty minutes early tomorrow morning so that I can get here earlier. Some of these things I can do before the students arrive.

Finally . . . school ended two hours ago. The building is mostly quiet, although a couple of teachers who are late ones like me stopped by for a consult, to vent, or just to chat. I get many things done before the custodian appears at my door with the keys to the building in her hands. It's time to go.

As I trudge to my car, trying to balance my purse, my lunch bag, my water bottle, and the three bags of school stuff I am hauling home, I notice that it has cooled off. Spring is here. School is out in seven more weeks. Many of our students will cry on the last day; they don't want to go home. Nesbit is a safe place for them, and for some, it's the only consistent thing they know.

As much as I love my job, I am tired now. I am also excited: I get to go get my 1-year-old daughter from her little *school* near our house. I can't wait to hold her. But first, I have to stop at the gas station; I am riding on a fume. The attendant inside the gas station notices my name badge, which says *Nesbit Elementary* at the bottom. *What grade do you teach?* he asks. *Oh, I'm a guidance counselor, actually,* I tell him. He looks surprised. *A guidance counselor? In elementary school? What do you need that for?*

I smile. I've heard this a million times before. I tell him, *I'd love to explain it to you, but I gotta go. I have to pick my daughter up in the next five minutes.*

Nancy Pittard Jones, LPC, NCC, NCSC is an elementary guidance counselor in Gwinnett County in Atlanta, Georgia. She received her master's and specialist's degrees at Georgia State University and she is Registered Play Therapist (RPT). She is the President of Kid Choice, LLC, an educational consulting and publishing company. Nancy has published several articles, book chapters, and a book for elementary counselors. She has presented over 100 workshops nationally at professional meetings. Nancy was named National Elementary Counselor of the Year in 2000 by the American School Counseling Association (ASCA).

SUGGESTED READINGS

Dinkmeyer, D., McKay, G.D., & Dinkmeyer, D. (1980). *Systematic training for effective teaching.* Circle Pines, MN: American Guidance Services.
Dinkmeyer et al. describe methods for understanding student behavior and suggest appropriate ways for educators to respond.

Fay, J. (1996). *Teaching with love and logic.* Golden, CO: The Love and Logic Press.
Jim Fay, one of the founders of the Love and Logic Institute, provides insights for educators on diffusing tense situations in a systematic manner that puts the work on the child, not the teacher.

Flynt, M., & Jones, N. P. (1999). Changing the philosophy of school discipline: a comprehensive Adlerian approach. *The Journal of Individual Psychology, 55* (3), 383–388.
Flynt and Jones describe the methods employed at one elementary school to research, design, and teach a schoolwide discipline philosophy based in Adlerian psychology.

16

LIVING/DIRECTING/GUIDING— ONE PROFESSIONAL SCHOOL COUNSELOR'S VIEW

CHRISTINE LARSON VANSLYKE

I am a Director of Guidance in a public school setting, and it's Sunday, late in the afternoon. It has been a great weekend. I've been able to enjoy needed activities, to get centered again and ready for the week ahead. I just got back from skiing with my family partner and two kids and did a hot tub soak to warm the core temp back up. Laundry's going; dishwasher is just loaded. Now to get to the typed-out, taped-up daily schedule of the upcoming week for us, the family. My kids are 13 and 15 and each has a full life.

My son has just finished his first week of his first job. After school and on Saturdays he is a bagger and carryout person at our local grocery store. He's also finishing the last pieces of achieving the Eagle Rank in Boy Scouts and dreaming about the track season beginning in the spring. Another part of life that flavors all he does and all we do is the fact that he's got a learning disability. It is amazing how much his everyday life is challenged by this and the lack of understanding that is still found even in the professional and educational communities. But this kid is great. His college and career goals are ever changing, but they are out there.

My daughter was elected as Student Council president this year after having run for a position every year since third grade. Always facing the challenge of defeat, she did not give up, and here she is president. She, too, had a difficult start. She was also in the Resource Room and did not read until late in elementary school. But now, this kid is in regular ed classes and she just announced this past Friday that she is getting all As—her goal. She's busy too, with equestrian, voice, piano, and gymnastic lessons. She's also a Girl Scout and she participates in Math Study Table two days a week. I guess I'm telling you all this because everything they do, I do too.

My kids' lives impact me personally and professionally. One would think that, in my line of work—dealing with special needs kids' and special needs for all kids—I would have been prepared for what was ahead in dealing with my own children as their learning differences became evident. Not so. The teachers in this case were my kids. By being faced with front-line disabilities in my own children, I had to deal with serious issues of my own. These children were not the kids or the parents I'd counseled so effectively, but they were MY kids. Having been more-than-educated, I felt I should be able to handle the educational and emotional adjustments ahead of me. I'm handling it, but only because my kids forced me to learn, to dig, to accept, to examine my own self, to accept them, to learn as they learn, and to view life through the eyes of special needs children. We are managing and each day I continue to learn and celebrate. My day-to-day experience with my kids has helped to help others in much broader and yet specific ways. My sense of compassion and empathy was already great, but I now can speak the language, communicating in both spoken and unspoken ways, as I seek to help others with special needs become happier, more fulfilled people. I clearly have become a better counselor through these experiences.

Well, Monday morning is here, and I try to hit the ground running. Well, maybe it's just a bit slower than running. Anyway, the alarm goes off at 4:45 A.M., and facing a Monday is not all that inviting. As I get my mind and body ready for the day and the week, I do enjoy the quiet early morning to myself. I have that peace for about an hour while checking e-mail, picking up dirty clothes, folding clean laundry, and so on. Then my daughter hits it, and my son. Then, I'm out the door for a luxurious and peaceful, 30-minute drive north. I listen to the news and then I sing along with the radio, switching stations as soon as someone starts to talk.

I usually beat my secretary to work (she's got kids, too). I unlock the office and the records room, turn on the lights, and start the copier. I did something great for myself this Christmas—I bought an office fountain. I start that up, as well, and it is wonderful. The students love it, too, and the other staff members are jealous. I keep low lighting in my office and do not use the overhead lights. I've got a floor lamp and a couple of desk lamps. My secretary arrives and hollers a wonderful good morning. We support each other—trying to stay positive, limiting the negatives, and accepting Mondays. She is efficient and organized. I try to be too.

I also have a work partner and he is great. We both have different gifts and we complement each other's work style. My cohort has that genuine, infectious love of kids and laughter. It is wonderful to be surrounded by that feeling of inclusion and belonging he gives us. There are times, however, that while he's smiling his smiles and sharing happiness, I'm left to pick up a few of the pieces. That's OK! I'm great at reminding and sharing ideas about trying another way to stay organized, getting back to parents, teachers, kids, principals, and maximizing the minute. My partner and I have learned to stay out of each other's space while, at the same time, lending a hand when we sense one is needed. We have developed specialties within the big framework of counseling in a public high school and each cover our own areas, although we cross over. Whenever necessary, we can become the other's consultant, expert, or counselor. Lucky me to have these two wonderful people working with me.

As my day progresses, my secretary gives me my schedule. Not that one day is anything like the next, but I usually see about ten kids individually, plus several staff members who have questions/concerns. I also make several classroom visits, given whatever might be the special needs of the month, per our counseling curriculum. As Director of Guidance, I handle the scheduling of students and staff for a building of 800 students. I do personal counseling as well as academic and career counseling. Sometimes I'm very efficient with this and I am able to work with larger groups of students. Other times I'm not as efficient (or the needs cannot be met via group intervention). I still enjoy being an in-the-trenches counselor, utilizing *Response Services* from our Michigan Comprehensive Guidance and Counseling Program to handle crises and meet individual needs.

On Mondays the building's administrative team—counselors and principals—meets to format our week. We review who is doing what and when, all the while sharing concerns regarding students, staff, and parents. The week takes off. We have just completed the beginning of our second semester. One of my gifts is that little mini-computer (nonmicrochip variety) that I carry in my brain. The needs of kids, parents, and staff ebb and flow throughout the school year and much happens *by instinct* as we begin a new semester or a new year. What teaching style of staff complements and is healthy for the learning style of a particular student? What teacher is always willing to go the extra mile to individualize instruction? What student is willing to hang in there with a particular staff member for the rest of the semester? These are all questions being processed in my brain at any given time.

As high school counseling has grown into its own and beyond over the past several decades, gone are the even infrequent moments of down time. With the growth and maturation of the Information Age and technology, so has our access and responsibility grown. The information is out there, always, and easily accessible through a myriad of software, hardware, and distance-learning opportunities. For our high school students, this increases the size of our local school communities, taking them to distant and unfamiliar places, but these new ideas now have become familiar. Back in the *old days,* and despite the lack of technology, some of us were able to find out about *life out there.* I, for one, was able to do some exploring before I settled down. For example, during my summers between college years, I worked on a dude ranch in North Dakota, meeting people of varied backgrounds and life experiences. After I got my bachelor's degree, I was a flight attendant for TWA for several years and flew domestically and internationally.

I was one of the lucky ones who was able to begin personal exploration and the whole process without the Internet. However, our students today are guaranteed new ways to access life via technology. They have more advantages and opportunities and, at the same time, more challenges. In our Media Center we have immediate connection to life in any neighborhood in the world. Virtual travel and study equate to possible careers, college dorm roommates, apprenticeships, and actual travel opportunities. This brings home the world to our students, making anything possible in their post–high school years.

We, as counselors, need to be aggressive in our leaps to facilitate guidance and decision/choice-making skills in our students on a day-to-day basis. The College Information and Financial Aid Meetings that we offer twice a year for students, parents, and community members, as well as SAT/ACT preparation workshops and career fairs, are all enhanced with the use of technology and our Internet access. The yearly February experience of choosing life-altering coursework for the high school years, while building the next school year's master schedule, is a worthy commodity and an investment toward the future of each of our students. Today, students, as well as we, the counselors, must stay ahead of the game and remain competitive with the world around us. By offering the programs we do and providing the technological support, they can be.

It always amazes me how our adolescents make it through the day-to-day grind of a teacher's lesson plans. Somehow they do it, and even many with academic challenges succeed. I love teenagers. Wow. My work partner and I talk about how lucky we are to come to work every day and spend time with people on the edge of the world—people ready to take their first worldly steps—and most are unafraid. They teach us. They keep us young and less fearful and more confident. Yet we, as helping adults, are there to help them with some of the scary thoughts of post–high school life, coddling them in some instances until their own inner strengths really take hold. They can do it, and we help them know that about themselves.

What college shall I go to? How can I pay for it? What classes shall I take to best prepare me? How much money can I make working in this field? What about letters of reference? Can I do anything about my teacher that disregards me? My ADD, and my learning style. How can I cope? My friends say . . .—what do you think about that? We constantly face these questions and even tougher ones. *Where will I sleep tonight? How do I deal with my parent or parent's boyfriend that comes home drunk, with the hitting, the swearing, the fighting, etc.? They are always telling me that I am the cause of all their problems.* On and on it goes, as we tend to face both the pleasures and the pain of life with our students, all of us managing to survive and, in many cases, thrive.

As the day is coming to a close, I check my voice-mail. The District Office needs this and that. I'll get at it tomorrow. And, one more thing—report cards were due out yesterday, but the computer still is not working right! We can't access the info we need, and my secretary still cannot process the work through her printer. Oh well, tomorrow is a new day. We'll meet the challenges again, head on, but not until we've shifted gears, and had time with our families, helped with home-work, provided transportation, called our own kids' counselors about their is-sues, tucked the kids in, and found some time for professional association work and communication.

It's a great life and part of what has made it great has been my ability to blend my personal and professional lives. How do I do it? Here are a few suggestions about things that work for me. Have a best friend you trust implicitly and regularly communicate with that person. Exercise regularly in any way that can fit into your schedule. Eat and drink moderately. Save time for some celebration and relaxation on the weekends. I truly believe that there are only two ways to look at things, positively or negatively. Strive for the positive and make that happen in your life.

Develop a personal mission statement and test your life choices (big and small) against it. Mine is to *surround myself with life-giving people and activities.* When I find that my interactions are not measuring up to my mission, I deal with it, move around it, and/or remove it from my life ASAP.

An important part of my life, both professionally and personally, is my professional association work. As I began my career in education, and as I continued on as a professional school counselor, my principal liked most everything I did except, he said, that I did very little outside of my workplace to enrich myself professionally. But how could I? *They* couldn't possibly get by without me there at school! *What about the crises? What about getting all that paperwork shuffled?* Well, thanks to that administrative thrust, I became involved with association work, and as I progressed and processed, I found a space in time and in the lives of others where I could have an impact. It worked for me personally—I found a way to contribute to personkind and promote the counseling profession.

I started out at my local chapter of the Michigan Counseling Association, where I ran for president. I continued on at the state level and became president. I still serve as an annual statewide conference chair and ours is a great meeting (800 counselors attend our conferences). I also became involved at the regional level—I served on the governing body of the national American Counseling Association (ACA), chairing the ACA Strategic Planning Committee, and I am serving as chair of the thirteen states for our region. Busy, yes? But why not? It's fun and fulfilling. That's why I do it.

Best wishes to you personally and professionally as we continue to hit the ground running on those Monday mornings!

Christine Larson VanSlyke, PhD, LPC, NCC, is the Director of Guidance for Cedar Springs Public Schools in Michigan. She received her BS in Education from Central Michigan University, her MA in Guidance and Counseling from Central Michigan University, and her PhD from Michigan State University. She currently serves as the American Counseling Association's Midwest Region Chair.

SUGGESTED READINGS

Covey, S. R., Merrill, A. R., & Merrill, R. R. (1994). *First things first.* New York: Simon & Schuster.
    This is a book that has all kinds of tips and information on managing time and space that allow us to sort ourselves and our activities towards optimum performance and happiness.

Michigan School Counselor Association. (1997). *The Michigan Comprehensive Guidance and Counseling Program, A K–12 guide for program development, implementation, and evaluation.* Grand Rapids, MI: Michigan School Counselor Association.
    This is a published notebook of materials that lay an excellent foundation with clear guidelines and specific information for a complete school guidance and counseling program.

17

SCHOOL-BASED PLAY THERAPY

JOANNA WHITE

The play therapy setting in which I work is wonderfully unique. I am fortunate to be a counselor educator at Georgia State University in Atlanta. My counselor education career spans nineteen years. My primary areas of interest and my teaching assignments have been in the areas of school counselor training and play therapy.

I have always valued a career that involves a variety of counseling activities along with continued connection with children. I believe that the practical application of my skills enhances my teaching and provides my students with current information regarding counseling children.

In my role as program coordinator for the school counseling program at Georgia State, I have always had close connections with school counselors in the local school systems. One counselor, in particular, was a professional colleague, teaching assistant for my classes, a seasoned veteran of over twenty years in the schools, and a friend. I began to spend time consulting at her new school.

This school, which had just opened, was a large elementary school with a highly diverse population. The school community was housed in a beautiful new building with two elementary counselors for over 1,000 students. The needs of the students and the teachers were intense due to the nature of the student body. These needs were especially related to the large number of children who spoke English as a second language and who were recent immigrants to the United States. The low socioeconomic status of the majority of the students' families was another difficulty. The school counselors were aware of and sensitive to the needs of these students. The school principal was totally committed to school counseling and its importance in the elementary school setting.

Each time I visited this school as a consultant-colleague of the two school counselors, I left feeling good about the environment and the effort that the counselors were making in training teachers and solidifying their developmental guidance program. To make things even more appealing to me, both counselors believed in the importance of using play as a conduit to connecting with children. They had play counseling corners in their offices where they worked with individuals and groups of children. With so many children just learning English, play was the *great leveler* that helped children feel safe at school. All children (unless they are extremely traumatized) eventually respond to the toys as a way to share metaphorically who they are and what they are feeling and as a means to work through traumatic life experiences.

My school visits were at the same time that I was phasing out my private practice. I wondered how I could fit in, if at all, in the elementary school as a volunteer counselor. When I expressed this desire to be a regular volunteer at the school, the counselors were excited to have me, and their principal was extremely supportive. She was so supportive that she dedicated space for a play counseling room in the school. I was also fortunate to have the support of my department chair. He agreed that this work would be categorized as part of my service commitment. Eventually, it became a large part of my research agenda. I have been a volunteer play therapist/counselor one day per week at the school for the past seven years. I am pleased to have the opportunity to share with you one of the most rewarding experiences of my life.

TYPICAL DAY

I arrive at school each Tuesday ready for a rewarding day of counseling children in the school's playroom. After so many years, the teachers and the children know me, and it feels good to be a professional in a public school again. I see at least six, sometimes seven, children each Tuesday. The school counselors refer to me the children who have severe emotional difficulties. Because of a lack of finances, cultural mores, and/or family stress, these children would probably not receive counseling services outside of the school setting. I obtain written parental permission to work with these children. I see each child for play therapy for approximately forty minutes in the playroom.

Other play therapy related activities that I engage in during a typical day would be consultation with the teachers of the children that I see in play therapy. This connection with teachers has proven to be an invaluable resource. Teacher consultation not only helps me to understand how the child functions in the classroom, but it also helps me to develop positive relationships with the teachers so that they are open to my suggestions.

At the request of other school professionals (psychologists, assistant principals), I sometimes take a child into the playroom for observation. Because the playroom is the most natural setting for the child at school, it provides an opportunity to observe aspects of the child's personality that may not surface in the restricted classroom setting. These observational sessions also point out strengths that the child has that have not been noted by the teacher or other professionals who work with that child.

A final activity during a typical day at the school is peer supervision with the school counselors. It is imperative that all counseling professionals engage in some type of supervision on a regular basis. We provide support, insight, information and feedback to each other on a weekly basis.

CHILDREN REFERRED FOR PLAY THERAPY

After seven years of play therapy experiences with over sixty children at the school, it is impossible to describe a typical case. Rather, I will attempt to categorize some of the presenting issues.

1. Loss or illness of a parent
2. Abuse (physical, sexual, emotional, neglect)
3. Abandonment by a parent that results in anger turned inward or outward
4. Parent incarcerated
5. Poverty (families living in cars, no money to feed the children)
6. Academic difficulties that lead to emotional difficulties
7. Family violence (spouse abuse), crime
8. Illness of a sibling
9. Acculturation issues
10. Drug use in the family

CHILDREN'S ISSUES THAT I KEEP IN MIND AS I ENTER THE PLAYROOM

It is essential that I view children from a developmental perspective. Play is the natural language of children and is a metaphor for the child's life. Through play, children make sense of their world, engage in mastery activities, learn to cooperate, and develop critical cognitive skills. Children do not have the cognitive skills to engage in the abstract process of talk therapy. For children who are struggling with emotional issues beyond normal developmental stressors, play is even more important because it helps them work through traumatic events and strong emotions. For example, when Ashley rearranges the people in the family house over and over again, I must keep in mind that this is meaningful to her. Ashley has recently lost her mother in a car accident. Everyone in her family is in crisis, and even though Ashley does not cry and get upset at the adults in her family, it is clear that she is processing the loss from her 5-year-old perspective.

I must always keep in mind that as the child plays, I am a privileged witness to the child's private world. The toys provide children the opportunity to work through emotions related to difficult life events. Therefore, there must be a variety of toys representing the continuum of emotions so that each child can access those toys that will help him or her relive these events in order to gain mastery over them and resolution. There is nothing random about this play and everything has meaning to the child. Paul, a kindergarten student who was kidnapped and abused by his father, is obsessed with the handcuffs. He uses them to get control over adults by handcuffing me and putting me in jail. I know that when Paul changes his play theme and the choice of toys that he is moving to another level of healing.

Because play is the language of the child, the school's playroom is the one place that I can know who the *real* child is. For many children, the classroom is a difficult setting. Traumatized children are often easily distracted, dissociative, and have great difficulty sustaining behavior that is expected of them in a group. In the playroom, they come to a comfort level that allows them to express (through play) their fears, pain, and life themes in a safe and accepting environment. Play never occurs in frightening or stressful situations. The playroom becomes a safe haven for children to engage in fantasy and relive issues that they choose to work through in order to learn to control their emotions and their behavior, release tension, and practice new ways to respond to familiar situations.

An example of one child who was able to let us know her true personality through her experiences in the playroom was Debbie. Debbie's teacher was suspecting that she was autistic. She would not talk in class and appeared to be unresponsive to any type of communication or stimuli. Debbie came to the playroom for observation, and it was apparent that she felt safer there than in her classroom. After a few weeks, it was clear that Debbie could communicate when she felt safe. She began to make eye contact with her teacher, and she eventually began to talk (softly and infrequently) in her classroom. It would have been a tragedy for Debbie to have been misdiagnosed. She would not have responded to traditional testing, and it would have been an inaccurate diagnosis.

I must remember that it is fine for children to choose not to talk. Play therapy may be the only occasion when an adult is not pressuring a child to verbalize. Adults bombard children with questions and directions day after day. I can be different with the child, and I must keep in mind that the child's play is his or her talk. Robert was a Korean-born 5-year-old who could not speak English. Robert delighted in being able to use drama, facial expressions, and tone of voice to let me know what he was playing and how he felt. Even though Robert and I could not speak each other's language, it did not affect the play therapy relationship.

I also keep in mind at all times that I must respect the child's ability to do things without adult direction. In order to avoid interrupting the child's attempts to learn and feel competent, I am aware of not doing things for the child that he or she can do. It is very important for me to follow the child's lead rather than to attempt to direct the child's play. If I interrupt the flow of the play, it is like interrupting an adult client in mid sentence. Children have the incredible ability to choose play themes and toys that meet their emotional needs. When Victor asked me over and over again to draw for him, I responded each time with, *I know that is something you can do.* Eventually, he began to create his own artwork.

I must remember that reaction to trauma is unique to each child and that he or she has a unique style of life or predictable way of dealing with life. This process of lifestyle development is grounded in the child's phemomenological field. Culture plays a major role in the child's lifestyle development. I must be open to understanding the unique culture of the child's family, religious group, race, and nationality.

PLAY THERAPY SKILLS

It is important that professionals wishing to work in the field of play therapy have proper training and credentialing. Play therapy skills are advanced skills that are not taught in the core counseling courses in most master's-level programs. This is a specialized area of study that requires play therapists to suspend many of the attitudes and approaches that they usually have regarding children.

The core of the play therapy process is the relationship between the child and the therapist. This relationship must be different from any other that the child has experienced with adults. The relationship is built on accepting the child exactly where he or she is, mutual respect, tracking, encouragement, reasonable limit-setting, acceptance for the child if he or she chooses not to talk, a minimum of adult questioning, and a developmentally appropriate setting with the toys.

Tracking is a play therapy technique that allows the play therapist to verbally follow the child without demanding a response. Examples of tracking would be *Now you've decided to go over there* or *You are painting several colors on your picture.*

Encouragement is another technique that serves as a foundation of the play therapy relationship. Encouragement involves recognition of the child's efforts and courage to try. Examples of encouragement would be *You know a lot about that* or *You thought you couldn't do that, but you figured it out.* Encouragement requires a nonevaluative stance that is difficult for many adults. Directly related to encouragement is the play therapist's belief that children are capable.

The last technique that is basic to play therapy is limit setting. This is a unique approach used in the playroom that provides the child the opportunity to make choices and take responsibility for his or her behaviors and decisions. Play therapists set only those limits that are necessary to ensure safety, manage the time, and protect property. In setting limits, the play therapist recognizes the child's feelings and wishes, gives choices, and allows the child to decide which choice he or she wants. Children are always able to *save face.*

BEST AND WORST ASPECTS OF THE WORK

The privilege of knowing the children is the best aspect of play therapy. I find children to be courageous, creative, inviting, and wonderful. Even the most troubled and resistant child can relate to the process and the playroom in order to make change and find happiness with others. This growth process is fascinating. I am fortunate to be a part of it.

I also like and am well suited to following the child's lead in therapy. I have few needs for children to be other than who they are. I have faith that they will naturally grow and change if I provide the right environment for them.

Another positive aspect for me is the peer supervision that I have discussed in this chapter. As a counselor educator, there are few opportunities to receive supervision on campus. I have learned so much from my school counselor peers.

I like the school environment. As a former school counselor, I have never strayed far from my roots. I feel comfortable in an elementary school. I also like the relationship with the teachers that I have developed over the years. It is a tremendous help to have them available for consultation.

The most difficult aspect to this work is being privy to the traumatic situations that children deal with on a day-to-day basis. This can become overwhelming, so I must take care of myself. I do this by keeping my life in balance and not letting work override the importance of my family and friends. I find that sharing with the other counselors is a great help. Finally, I have begun to balance my direct work with the children with my Kinder Training research. This new approach provides me an opportunity to focus on something new, while helping the children through teacher consultation.

KINDER TRAINING

Kinder Training is a teacher and school counselor consultation model based on play techniques and the theory of Individual Psychology. I developed this model with three professional colleagues (one counselor educator and two school counselors at the school where I volunteer). This approach trains teachers in basic play therapy techniques along with Adlerian techniques and principles that will help them in the playroom and in the classroom. Teachers practice their skills with children in the school's playroom under the supervision of one of the counselors or myself. The intent is to use play to develop a positive relationship between child and teacher and to help the teacher view the child from a different, more encouraging, perspective. After all, teachers are the most important people to the children at school. The research results indicate that after six weeks of child-teacher play sessions, the children showed improvement in social skills, behavior, academics, and encouragement. The teachers increased their facilitative and encouraging statements along with appropriate limit-setting responses in their classrooms.

PLAY THERAPY PRACTICE

Most play therapy services are provided in a private practice, agency, or hospital setting. In setting up a play therapy private practice, it would behoove the therapist to acquire credentialing from the Association for Play Therapy as a Registered Play Therapist (RPT). It is important to have a state license to practice. In addition, RPT status sets one apart from those who claim to have expertise in counseling children, but who approach children in the counseling relationship just as they would adults.

I encourage private practitioners to monitor the time and energy that it takes to attend to children in therapy. Seeing one child after another in a play therapy setting is taxing. Each child deserves your total attention.

Another important issue in private practice is the question of when to terminate. A strong background in play therapy training will make it easier for the therapist to determine the proper time for termination. The pressures from managed care surely compromise this process for children in play therapy.

My situation is unique. The opportunity for a counselor educator to provide play therapy in a school setting is not the norm. However, I encourage counselor educators who train school counselors to become involved in the schools in some way. It will add so much to your teaching, your supervision, and your professional life.

JoAnna White, Ed.D. is Professor and Chair of the Department of Counseling and Psychological Services at Georgia State University in Atlanta. She has served as program coordinator for the school counseling program at Georgia State University. She developed and currently coordinates the Play Therapy Training Program in her department. JoAnna has experience in a play therapy private practice setting, and she has been a volunteer play therapist at an elementary school for seven years. She has presented over 100 workshops at professional meetings, and she has published over fifty articles in refereed journals. JoAnna has also published five book chapters on the topic of play therapy. Her current research focus is Kinder Training, a school counselor-teacher consultation model that combines play therapy skills with Individual Psychology.

SUGGESTED READINGS

Kottman, T. (1995). *Partners in play: An Adlerian approach to play therapy.* Alexandria, VA: ACA.
Kottman provides the reader with an excellent play therapy primer using the theoretical approach of Individual Psychology.

Landreth, G. L. (1991). *Play therapy: The art of the relationship.* Muncie, IN: Accelerated Development.
This book is the definitive textbook on play therapy. In this book, Landreth introduces the reader to the philosophical basis for the approach, informative chapters on how to conduct play therapy, and chapters that deal with special issues such as Filial Therapy.

Landreth, G. L. (Ed.). (2001). *Innovations in play therapy: Issues, process, and special populations.* Philadelphia: Brunner-Routledge.
This book provides current information on special considerations in play therapy (cultural issues, medications, ethics), clinical innovations (abuse, diagnostic assessment), innovative procedures (group play therapy, short-term play therapy), and play therapy with special populations.

White, J., Flynt, M., & Draper, K. (1997). Kinder Therapy: Teachers as therapeutic agents. *International Journal of Play Therapy, 6,* 33–49.
This article is an introduction to Kinder Therapy, a school counselor and teacher consultation model combining play techniques, the model of Filial Therapy, and Individual Psychology to enhance the teacher and child relationship. A case study is included.

18

JUST ANOTHER MANIC MONDAY

JANE S. TURNER

I am a high school counselor in a suburban school near the West Virginia state capital city. We are on block scheduling and have recently adopted an innovative, highly academic curriculum. We have approximately 865 students this year, served by three counselors. Most years, approximately 65 to 75 percent of our graduates go on to college. This is a pretty high percentage for West Virginia in 1999. We draw students from two working class communities. When you read about this day—Monday, September 13—I think it might sound a little dull. It was anything but dull. It was, however, very real.

I arrived at school this morning at 6:45 A.M. and, as usual, Dee, a junior who has been identified through our district's process for identifying exceptional students (students with behavior disorders), came in right behind me. After she hugged me (as she does each morning), she said, *This reminds me of "Another Manic Monday," you know the song?* Little did I know the truth of her words. It was not long until manic became a good thing, as I was called upon to shift from one task to another with the rapidity that I have faced almost every day of my professional life.

Each year we do presentations in senior classes to remind all students of the courses needed for graduation and to inform them of how to apply to post-secondary institutions and request financial aid. We also make sure they understand the services that the counseling department provides them as seniors preparing to take that final step out of high school. Thus, Monday, September 13, was the day we were set to begin the presentations this year.

I was eager to check out the materials that we had readied on Friday to make sure that we would have everything just right. That, however, had to wait as Mrs. W., a very upset parent, came to my office to tell me about the problem she and her family had faced with her son's impulsivity and anger at home on the previous Friday. His behavior had caused them to hospitalize him at a local adolescent psychiatric unit. She was in tears, yet she was trying to take care of business by informing us and making sure we would provide the schoolwork needed at the hospital, while maintaining confidentiality at school. After comforting her, we discussed how to handle his return to the family and to school. She left reassured, yet she was worried and saddened by her son's problems.

Now I could leave to go to the class where we were to be doing our presentation. The other counselors were there but this was our first presentation— our dress rehearsal—which we always do together. As it turned out, I was delayed just a little more. Leah, a student with health and attendance problems, came by to see if I had been successful in adjusting her schedule. She needed a schedule that offered her more flexibility to leave class during the morning hours, as she often becomes ill in class. I was able to work this out and I sent her out happy (I guess) with a new schedule. Then I headed to class myself. All three of us were in and out of the room during that class period as teachers, students, and parents came to the door asking for just a moment of our time. When we do these presentations, we try to be interchangeable and truly we were such, as we took over for each other mid-sentence when necessary.

When I returned from class, one of the other counselors met me at the door to let me know that a new enrollee and his mother had arrived. When I greeted them, I recognized the situation and the boy. He still had a term of alternative school to complete before he could reenter day school. His mother was not pleased to hear this and went off vowing to return after she *took care of things* at the County Board of Education Office. There was no time to wonder what would come of this, however, as it was break time and in came Carrie, a regular visitor to the counseling offices.

Carrie came to report that her friend, Hanna, had scratches and bruises all over her face and neck from a Saturday night fracas with Hanna's mother. Monday mornings frequently bring these situations to counseling offices across the nation. As my readers can guess, I did not make it to class during the second block as I had planned. Instead, I called in Hanna, who confirmed the violent situation. I felt lucky that day as the school nurse was in the building. She examined the girl and agreed to talk to the girl's father and to the Child Protective Service agency, doing the mandatory reporting of the event. I am not a coward, but these reporting situations are always difficult for the student, the counselor, and the parent(s) to face. The student usually is fearful of further abuse after a report is made. Child Protective Service workers are extremely overworked and underpaid individuals. It usually takes several days of very tense waiting for a response to come to the student. All in all, it's a bad scene.

As Hanna and I headed toward the nurse's office, I found Jimmy sitting in our waiting area. He is a senior student who dropped out last year but reentered school to try to get his two required credits for graduation. He came by to see if I could do something to exempt him from the school's summer reading that he had not known about (Gee, I'm sure I told him!). He did not take the test and was not ready to do the report either. Hanna, a student with a learning disability, had sound advice for him. *Get the tapes*, she said, as a way of taking her mind off her own troubles, *they don't take too long at all.* He left miffed and we went on to the nurse.

I returned to my office after leaving Hanna with the nurse and there I found a stranger waiting for me—Mickey Moore. He was from a local agency and was serving as a case manager for one of my students who'd been identified with a behavior disorder and who was also on probation. Mr. Moore was new on the job.

I took him to meet the teacher assigned to work with the behavior-disordered students. She had worked with the boy most of last year.

Now, surely I would have time to take my turn in the class presentations for block three. As I prepared to head down the hall, Mrs. T. came by with her son, Matthew. She is a single parent and just wants to do the right thing toward getting her son's college papers filled out properly. She needed to hear about what they should do on college planning and when they should complete and file necessary forms. Since she took the trouble to come by, I felt I needed to take the trouble to help the two of them. We discussed college entrance exams, his free-lunch application, the college fair, the financial aid workshop, and scholarship searches.

I had stepped out a moment to get papers for Mrs. T. when the special education specialist who covers our school entered our waiting area. We stepped into another office as she tried to ascertain why I had called the school psychologist the past week. She happened to be at the school and had volunteered to relay my message to the school psychologist, who had found trying to contact me by telephone a frustrating experience since our school's phone lines are perpetually busy. She also took the opportunity to fill me in on some problems one of my students (her neighbor) was having. She initially felt the problems stemmed from his reaction to his parents' recent divorce. Now, however, he had begun letting his temper fly at one of the school's athletic contests, and she was looking for other possible causes of the behavior.

Never go out of the room (if you can help it) while working with someone in a school—it is hard to get back. Then the phone rang. It was Mr. Moore again, inquiring as to the time and nature of a school meeting that would be held for his student the next day. I did not know and agreed to find out. I never did find out; but he did, fortunately. Finally, I got back to Mrs. T. and Matthew with the required information and sent them on their way.

Matthew got to class and that, as it turned out, is better than I did that block. That's because I now had a phone call from Mrs. S. Her son, Stevie, has a 504 plan for which I serve as case manager. A 504 plan is put in place for students who have disabilities not specifically addressed through special education, but that require adaptations of regular classroom instruction. These disabilities often are related to Attention Deficit Disorder or, occasionally, to physical disabilities. She had missed last week's meeting to revise his plan, so we discussed it over the telephone and she seemed satisfied that her son was making good progress in his subjects, thanks to our plan.

As I hung up the phone, Mr. Nicely, our school's computer teacher, came in to discuss one of his students, Jeffrey. This boy also has a 504 plan, for which I also serve as case manager. At our school, the principal generally expects that the counselors will handle the 504 plans. Thus, we become the case managers, handling coordination of services and communication with parents for these students. Mr. Nicely wanted me to know about a special privilege he had granted this boy and told me how he is handling him in class right now. We discussed that, along with ideas that I had on how Mr. Nicely, whom Jeffrey really likes and respects, could further impact Jeff's life, both in his class and in other areas, by modeling behavior that will directly assisting him with learning better social skills.

By the time Mr. Nicely left it was noon, and several students who must take the state-mandated *Students for Success* basic skills remediation course came to the counseling center. Some needed to find out to which class they needed to attend, since this was the first day. Others came to grumble about their required participation.

The vice principal dropped by the Counseling Center as he made his usual rounds of the school. I took the opportunity to inform him about the hospitalization of Charlie (Mrs. W.'s son). The vice principal and I had been watching Charlie carefully since he had been in trouble three times in the first six days of school. We had previously held a Student Assistance Team meeting with him to determine what our school can do to help him be more successful. A Student Assistance Team meeting is a meeting of teachers, administration, the school psychologist, the counselor, the parent(s), and the student, called to brainstorm solutions to problems that the student is having in school. While the vice principal was in the Counseling Center, Kit, a very troubled young man, came to tell us about the impending divorce of his aunt and uncle, with whom he lives. He didn't ask for help. He just wanted us to know that he was hurting because of the family breakup.

I followed this with a quick restroom break and a bite of lunch on the run. Then I checked with the nurse on the status of Hanna's case. Hanna and a friend came by to see what was happening regarding the reporting of her case. She also tried to convince me to call her boyfriend, at another school, so she could talk over with him whether she should go home that evening or go to his house. I refused. Hanna replied, *But Mrs. Turner, they won't call him to the phone if I call.* It is difficult sometimes to be the positive, caring helper, yet draw the line and not be used by troubled students.

Before the lunch period was over, Dee and Kit came by once again, laughing and picking at each other. Each of them loves the attention they can get from any of us counselors, and they are smart. When we are busy, they wave and disappear, knowing we just do not have time for hugs and jokes right then.

The bell rang and I scribbled a few notes for teachers, thrust them into the hands of our student aide, and rushed off to finally take my turn at doing the class presentation. With questions, it took one hour and ten minutes. This happened to feel like one hour and ten minutes of heaven since no one was calling me on the phone and no one was presenting me with problems that are too tough for me to solve. The class was just filled with students who needed the information I was delivering, as they looked to planning their post-secondary experiences. It was fun. When class was over, I came back to my office and finished my lunch—*tuna, tuna, tuna*—as the screen saver our office helpers made for me says.

This year we have set as one of our goals to do a better job in documenting what we do for students. This is for our own benefit, but also because the state accreditation standards call for it. To begin on this goal, I established the common documentation folder and placed in it the agenda we followed today in our classrooms, along with a list of students we saw. Having done that, I spent a few minutes discussing the West Virginia Counseling Association election and bylaws with the other counselors. All of us are active in that group. We believe professional activism is very important. Our administrators have always accepted this involvement, as long as the work we do with our students does not suffer.

Several times today I tried to get the computer to print out a transcript. I must prepare it for the clerk to send to the NCAA clearinghouse for a young man. The computer makes our work easier (and harder). It has clearly changed our work. Earlier in my career I might have complained about preparing such a transcript. It is a clerical duty. Now with the wherewithal, usually, to make a transcript in seconds, it is hard to complain.

Our relationship with our clerk is a rocky one. By Board of Education policy, she is to work for us one half day. However, she is often assigned duties by administration and athletics, so it is hard to get her attention sometimes. It is a battle we have to fight nearly every day. Bearing all that in mind, near the end of the school day I began preparing tasks for her to do. She loves to do permanent record cards and we still use them, in spite of (and in addition to) the computerized records. Since double duty must be done, it's good that she likes that part of the duty. At this time she does not have access to the transcripts on the computer as we counselors do. That is a matter still left for discussion with the county computer people (who really like to limit who can access what data) and our administration (some of whom think she should have access and others who believe the fewer people who can call up student grades the more confidential these records will remain).

Also near the end of the school day, I informed the other counselors about the arrangements I had made for our presentation schedule for the rest of the week. Following that, the school psychologist came to follow up on the messages we had exchanged by phone mail and through the special education specialist. We talked at length about my work with a student who has some serious home problems and who is creating some serious school problems for herself with lack of attendance. I have been working with her for about six months, off and on. Although she is polite to me, I feel she is defensive and has not worked with me in good faith and has not been trusting enough to let me help her. That is hard to admit because I would like to think I can do some good for all the students assigned to my caseload (super-counselor that I am!). This young lady, Lorrie, has expressed the desire to try to work things out with the school psychologist and thus I have arranged it. We talked about consent forms to meet with the psychologist, as well as my perspective on her situation.

Although school is out for students at 2:25 P.M., we counselors are still there at 3:30, working on paperwork. Sometimes I stay much later than this, but the paperwork I have today can wait. I have another important task to do this evening. I have to drive across town for an appointment with one of the State Senators. He is the Chairperson of the Joint House of Delegates–Senate Committee on Safe Schools. I want to meet with him to see if there is a chance that legislation will be introduced to increase the numbers of school counselors or to set a reasonable ratio for counselors in the middle/junior high and elementary levels. Right now, school safety is a hot button issue and there is much talk about metal detectors and surveillance cameras (which we have at our school, by the way). There is also much talk by principals, superintendents, and the public about more counseling—more *real* counseling in the schools, as well. If there is even a hope that such legislation will be introduced, the West Virginia Counseling Association must not let this opportunity go by.

My talk with him is very cordial. I really expected nothing less, since I have known him for years, yet I was very nervous as I knocked on his office door at the Capitol. I asked a few questions and he asked more, really picking my brain, I think, about the realities we face as public educators. I left our meeting encouraged, yet I know he will approach the situation with the realism of a politician, knowing that he cannot accomplish everything he hopes to accomplish to make the schools of West Virginia safer, better places for our students. But, he must try in his way. He is an idealist, in spite of being a politician. And I must try in mine. Since my way is being a school counselor, I will go home, get to bed early, so I can be fresh and alert, and arrive at school again on Tuesday, to meet and serve my students.

I have been a counselor in West Virginia public schools for twenty-six years. I chose to become a counselor because, after completing student teaching, I knew I would not make a good teacher. With that in mind, I made a very calculated short-term decision to go on to graduate school in counseling, little knowing that I would still be a counselor more than a quarter of a century later. Since then, I have become very committed to the profession. I have held several offices in the West Virginia Counseling Association and currently serve as newsletter editor for this group. I have spent a lot of time working for improvement of the profession.

When I first became a counselor, I loved it so much that I would have done it for free. Thinking back over all those years, I can certainly see why they pay me. It is very stressful work. Some of the stress comes from helping students deal with the very intense problems that they face every day. Stress also comes from trying to convince my co-workers (teachers, administrators, and clerical staff) that we counselors are not administrators or clerical people. And some additional stress comes from additional duties being added to the unofficial counselor job description each year.

I am a very good group facilitator. That has been apparent to me since I led my first group during practicum. Despite all of the stress and added duties, each year I make time for one group. This is my love and it keeps me fresh, so that I can deal with student problems, advising, assisting with scheduling, field trips to colleges, and organization and administration of tests. For the past several years, my group has been a support group for teen mothers. I set the time and place and arrange for them to be excused from class, so that they can encourage each other. It is so rewarding when I see those young women graduate.

I am proud of the work I do. I may change someone's life, but I probably will never know it. The rewards in this job do not come from thanks or recognition. The rewards come from doing my best for young people every day. That is what makes the job worthwhile.

Jane S. Turner, LPC, NCC received her AB degree in Secondary Education from Marshall University and her MA degree in Counseling from West Virginia University. She is a Counselor for South Charleston High School in South Charleston, WV. She has written an article on Legislative Activism and Licensure for a monograph for the American Mental Health Counseling Association and served on the Editorial Board for *The School Counselor,* publication of the American School Counselor Association. She has held various offices and committee chairs in the West Virginia Counseling Association, and she currently serves as Newsletter Editor and Legislative Chairperson.

SUGGESTED READINGS

Arman, J. F. (2000). In the wake of tragedy at Columbine High School. *Professional School Counseling, 3,* 218–220.
This article was important to me as I wrote about my day since at the time I was meeting with legislators who had interest in working on school safety issues, including the funding of more elementary and middle school counselors. I think the article clearly states reasons to have mental health professionals in the schools.

Burhans, L. L. (1999). A fable: Seven counselors and the plan. *Professional School Counseling, 3,* 3–4.
This article helps to present the whole picture of the role of school counselors in a humorous way, which brings home to the counseling student or practitioner what we are about as a profession.

Dahir, C. A., Sheldon, C. B., & Valiga, M. J. (1998). *Sharing the vision: The national standards for school counseling programs.* Alexandria, VA: American School Counselor Association.
These standards really can help counselors and a school system know what counselors should do and how to implement needed services. They give us guidelines and goals for which to strive.

Harris-Bowlsbey, J., Dihel, M. R., & Sampson, J. P. (1998). *The Internet: A tool for career planning.* Columbus, OH: National Career Development Association.
I am always looking for resources on how to better use the Internet with students since they really like to use it. There is just so much information available at one's fingertips and not enough time to investigate it all.

19

THE COP AND THE COUNSELOR
RANDAL TOWN

My background and training is mental health and drug treatment. I worked in that field for ten years. My undergraduate degree is in psychology and my master's degree is in counseling psychology. I always knew that I wanted to work in community mental health and that was my goal from the very beginning of my post-secondary educational process.

I have worked for the past dozen years in the K–12 school system, coordinating intervention programs for kids who experience mental health and substance abuse problems. I work directly with school counselors and substance abuse counselors in schools. I provide clinical skill development, program development, technical assistance, and consultation. This involves working with school administrators to review and write student policy and procedures for substance abuse, weapons, and student code of conduct. In addition, I am very active in providing training and leadership for schools in the area of crisis intervention and management.

Twelve years ago, when I assumed the position with the schools, I was ready to leave direct service and take on a new task. Teaching the school system that good mental health and clean and sober youth are important parts of their charge has been very rewarding and challenging. For me, I have taken counseling to a new and different level. When I finished graduate school in 1979, I never envisioned that I would be doing what I am doing now.

Five years ago I joined the Yakima County Sheriff reserve program. I am now a fully commissioned reserve law enforcement officer. I patrol on my own, on the average of fifty hours a month, in addition to working for the school system full time. I became involved in law enforcement because I was observing that many of the youth involved in our school's intervention program were also involved with the law. This concept is nothing new. However, something about it intrigued me. I needed to know and to experience more. I wanted to feel *the other side*.

I thought this experience would give me a better sense of what our *high-risk* kids face. I talked with friends, who encouraged me to get involved. I had doubts—I felt that I was much too liberal (politically) and that I would not fit in with other law enforcement officers. I did not know if I had what it would take to arrest people and be part of a system that could ultimately and literally take their freedom away from them. I have always been one who has criticized court systems and law enforcement for being too punitive. Nevertheless, I took the plunge and I have not regretted it for one minute.

Other deputies and police are surprised when they find out about my background. During my interview for the academy, I was asked if I could potentially take someone else's life. I hesitated for a moment before I answered, because, at the time, the concept was totally foreign to me. The interview team picked up on my delay and said *that type of hesitation will get you killed.* I then answered *Yes, I could take someone else's life, if my life or the life of an innocent person were in jeopardy.* Underneath, I still had doubts, but my interest was piqued. After the interview, I was told that my background could be an asset to their effort and I was accepted into the fold.

The reserve training academy was six months long. Classes were Tuesday evenings and all day Saturdays. We covered the same curriculum as a full-time law enforcement officer training academy, just doing so over a longer period of time. In my mind, I was making an adjustment from being a counselor, with a liberal point of view, to a career in law enforcement, with a conservative perspective. The academy class was comprised primarily of students who were, on the average, twenty years younger than me.

The academic curriculum covered constitutional law, Fourth Amendment and state laws, and a variety of other topics. Included was a section on child abuse recognition. Much to my surprise, I noticed no instruction about intervening with people who suffer from mental illness or substance abuse/addiction, both of which are commonly seen in the field. If I were in charge, I would certainly add these components to the curriculum. There was training in the more practical elements as well, such as patrol procedure and firearms training. Much to everyone's surprise (including mine), I graduated from the academy as the top shooter—99.6 percent of 100 shots were in the bull's eye of the target. Academically, I graduated second.

I was beginning to notice the psychological transformation from a thinker with lots of gray areas to a *black-and-white* thinker. I now can see the practicality based upon the need to make split-second decisions and not spend too much time looking at alternatives. However. I also see that veteran cops adopt the *either ___ or ___* mindset as a way of life. From time to time, my wife notices the same change in me. I relate to life differently, and I am becoming less tolerant of differences. This concerns me and is something I have to continue to monitor and work with. I don't want to portray that line cops are not sympathetic or empathic or don't want to listen because, very often, they do; however, time often does not permit such luxuries.

Fast-forward five years. It is December 23, 1999 at 11:00 A.M. Most schools are closed and office life at my school agency is very slow. I decided to take five hours of annual leave and log some patrol time. I went to the sheriff's office and picked up an available cruiser. Then I went home, donned my uniform, complete with all of the extra gear, and I was on the road by noon.

Whenever dispatch assigns two deputies to a call, we know it is a potential *hot* call. Typically, someone's life is in potential peril. Whenever we are given a call, the dispatchers will always give their call sign before any other transmission. If dispatchers want to give or get general information, they will hail our badge number only. Radio silence was broken about 12:30 P.M. "973, 195 and 83" (973 is dispatch, I am 195, and deputy 83 is my backup). There is always a different tenor to the dispatcher's voice when a *hot* call is given. I can sense the tension in her voice. My heart jumps and I can feel the adrenaline begin to invade my being. The dispatcher relays that an 11-year-old girl in foster care is assaulting her foster mother and the foster siblings, and a knife is involved. Domestic violence is always unpredictable. Emotions run high for the parties involved, as well as for the responding emergency personnel.

I reach for the panel of buttons below the dashboard of the patrol car—the ones that control the entire emergency signaling system—and I activate the siren and overhead lights. My vision narrows as I punch the gas and begin to negotiate through traffic. I am heading from downtown to a rural area east of Yakima. I have to do a little *self-talk* to remind myself that I need to continue to breathe normally, relax my grip on the steering wheel, and look from side to side for traffic. The tendency for cops in these situations is to *tense up,* altering their breathing and literally restricting vision. The chance of accidents increases greatly. Graduate school behavioral psychology class comes back to me in a hurry when I am in this situation. My thoughts turn to a phrase my field-training officer once told me: *Being a cop is hours of boredom spiked by seconds of shear terror.*

When I reach the interstate, I immediately proceed to the passing lane of the freeway and watch the speedometer move past 100 mph to 110. I hold steady for about five miles. At that speed cars move by quickly and many drivers become confused when trying to decide how to yield to my emergency vehicle. I exit the freeway and turn eastbound onto a state highway. Once again the speedometer moves up to 100 mph. The highway is more narrow and I am aware of side streets that intersect the roadway. I am nearing the road I need to enter. I quickly turn north onto Riverview and then turn again, heading east to Hedgeway Road. Next, I turn off the lights and siren. I don't want to alert the parties that I am getting near. In domestic violence, coming up on a residence with lights and siren will often make unpredictable people act impulsively and exacerbate their violent acts. I proceed three blocks to the driveway.

As I pull into the driveway, everything on the outside is calm—too calm. I radio dispatch to let them know I have arrived. My backup indicates he is at least five minutes away. Proper procedure indicates that I not do anything else until my backup arrives. I get out of the car and I am careful not to shut the car door too loudly. Right now, I don't want anyone to know I am there. I stand against the house near a window so I can listen to what is going on inside. I also want to delay entering until my backup is closer.

Inside the house it is silent. I peek into the window and see it is a bedroom. No one is in the room. The door is open and I have a partial view into the living room. I see no one and it is still quiet. Then I hear voices and the talk is calm.

I decide to proceed to the back door of the house. I knock. An older woman looks through the glass in the door and then opens it. I enter the kitchen and I ask her if everyone is all right—physically, at least. She confirms that no one is seriously injured.

I asked if she was Ms. Stanton, the foster mother (her name has been changed to protect her identity). She says yes, and I am somewhat surprised, because she seems to be close to 80 years old. She says she's 78 after I ask her age. I thought to myself, *this woman is too old to be a foster mother.* Ms. Stanton says she has been taking foster children for the last twenty-five years. She said that she has cared for more than seventy-five children during that time. This is the first time any of her children had become that violent.

Two young girls come into the kitchen. Ms. Stanton indicates both girls are foster children, but not the ones in question. She says Linda has locked herself in her room. I thought to myself that as long as no one else is in the room with her, I would continue to let her cool off. For now, I will see if I can get a picture of what happened from the other parties.

Ms. Stanton indicates that Linda has been with her for two weeks and was placed in her home because of an unexplained emergency. Linda has been a handful from the very beginning. Stanton said Linda became angry over a conversation that occurred during lunch. Linda was slopping her soup and when Stanton attempted to correct her behavior. In response, Linda exploded and began yelling at the others around the table. She got up, came around the table, and hit Stanton in the face with a closed fist, four to five times. The other two foster daughters came to Stanton's rescue and were assaulted by Linda in the process. Linda then sought refuge in her room and Stanton followed her into the room. Linda reached for her purse and pulled out a small box-cutter knife with a retractable blade. Linda pointed the knife, with the blade retracted inside the body of the knife, and said, *If you come any closer, I will slit your throat.*

My backup arrives, and, when I see Mike, I share with him that the situation is under control for the moment and he can clear the call, after we check in with Linda to be sure she is all right. I approached the room, knocked on the door, and asked Linda if I could enter. I was wary as I introduced myself through the closed door, not knowing what she would try to do while being so angry. I assured her that I was there to help her and try to resolve the situation. Linda said I could come into the room.

As I opened the door, I noticed a small little girl in blue jeans, a sweater, dark blond hair, with tears running from her sky blue eyes. She was lying on the bed. I asked her to go outside with me, away from the others, so I could get her side of what happened. Her story matched what the others had told me. The only difference was she blamed the others for what happened. She did not see herself as the problem or the instigator. This is a fairly predictable response in family violence situations, even with adults. Once contact was made with Linda, Mike informs dispatch that he is returning to his patrol duty.

As we approached the kitchen door to go outside, Linda became combative with me. She began to struggle and, when I took hold of her arm to keep her moving, she struggled even more. I decided to put her in handcuffs until she could become calmer. Her attitude went from cooperation to defiance. I placed her in the back of my patrol car to let her cool off. I would get her statement later, and, for now, I went back into the house to start my mountain of paperwork.

I used to be a therapist at the local mental health agency—the same one that is managing Linda's foster placement. I called there for her case manager. Of course, being just before Christmas, no one was around the agency. I finally got Steve, the program supervisor, at his home. Being a former therapist and case manager, I know the mental health and social service system. This is knowledge that other law enforcement personnel may not have and for which other deputies often rely upon me. This is one of the strengths I bring to the force.

I get Steve on the phone and he said he needs to contact Linda's caseworker at mental health before he can go any further. In the meantime, I start calling other agencies. I called the Crisis Residential Center, Child Protective Services, Juvenile Detention, Department of Family Services, and Children's Crisis Response System. I am looking for temporary placement until her disposition can be determined. Because of her violent act, I am told, another emergency foster placement is not possible. In the state of Washington, an 11-year-old cannot be arrested for a crime, unless it is so egregious that a superior court judge signs an order placing her in the juvenile jail.

The bottom line is that I now have an 11-year-old girl that I cannot place, and I cannot just let her go on her own. Steve calls me back and says that he is looking at a variety of alternative placements, one of which is a placement in a secure psychiatric hospital. I told Steve that if he could place her in the psychiatric hospital, I would not approach the judge for a charge of second-degree assault (and placement into the juvenile jail). He agreed to vigorously pursue the psychiatric placement.

I definitely stumbled upon a crack in the system. Linda was beginning to calm down and become very cooperative. In fact, I was seeing sadness in her eyes. I took her out of the handcuffs with the understanding that I not see any more violent behavior. I radioed dispatch and let them know I was transporting her to the central precinct.

On the way, Linda began to share that she has been in foster placement since she was 2 years old and she had not seen her biological mother in over three years. Linda didn't even know if her mom was currently alive. The caseworker shared with me that her mom's parental rights were terminated because of physical abuse and drug addiction. Yet Linda defended her mother as being a wonderful person. From a counseling perspective, Linda's attitude is understandable—she wants desperately to be connected to her mother.

We arrive at the precinct. I accompany and place Linda into a small holding room while she and I await her fate. Steve calls me back and said that he is placing her into the hospital. Because the only adolescent facility is over 100 miles away, Steve also arranged for transportation. I feel a sense of relief. I told Linda, and, while it is not her first choice to go to a hospital, she realizes that it is probably in her best interest. I run into another deputy in the hallway and he asks me what is happening with the young girl. I told him the story. He then shakes his head and says, *I can see we've lost another one; there is just no hope for her.* I walked away from him feeling discouraged. *Is he right?* I certainly hope not. My counselor persona is coming to the surface, sensing there is still hope for Linda.

I began to talk to Linda once again. I can see a young girl who is confused, very sad, and detached. I wanted to know some of the reasons she has had such short foster placements. She says she does not get close to her foster families because she wants to get back together with her mom. In fact, she said she even creates chaos so she does not have to get close, so others will hate her. I thought to myself that her response is just too textbook and a little manipulative. She seems very therapy wise. I could tell she has been involved in a lot of counseling. Soon Linda's transportation arrives and she is on her way to the psychiatric hospital.

I am hopeful that her life will get back on track, and I feel a sense of sadness that here is an innocent girl who has had a rough time from the very beginning. She has had no consistent person in her life to teach her right from wrong and no one to bond with. I feel a need to debrief the case. Not many situations get to me any more; however, this one did. Critical Incidence Stress Debriefing is mandatory for all personnel who are involved with violent scenes and situations. With emotional tragedies like this one, I am left alone to fend for myself.

My thoughts return to finishing the report. I don't have the energy, but it has to be done. After I finish the report, I return to the road and dispatch sends me to a barking dog call. Law enforcement is just that ironic, going from trauma to the somewhat mundane.

I sometimes wonder if other line cops experience countertransference or are even able to realize that it is happening. I make a point to debrief the call with one of the other deputies that I trust. Russ tells me that he knows it is time to take a vacation when the psychological stress reaches the point where he is beginning to project his angst onto others. He also confides in his best friend, his wife, when things reach a breaking point. In so doing, he confirms for me that my thoughts and feelings are indeed within the realm of normalcy. It's a good conversation. I think to myself that, if I had the time, I would begin a support system for cops. A kind of debriefing process to deal with the psychological and emotional stresses that build over time.

I've noticed that many cops build a tough exterior to deal with the high emotions that are built into the job. They often attempt to portray that tough situations don't bother them. However, it is easy to see that certain stressful situations have a great impact. I also see that many cops have developed streetwise counseling skills. I have been amazed and impressed with the skill level of many cops who can walk into emotionally charged situations and develop calmness through empathy. Many do so with the precision of a surgeon.

Counseling and law enforcement are often intangible professions. We often do not get to see our work completed. We are usually establishing contact with others for short periods of time and then leaving in midstream. For me, it creates an existential angst. From time to time, I feel a sense of incompleteness. My counseling contacts are always a work in progress and I rarely see the finished product.

I build furniture for an avocation. I do so with the purpose of filling the existential void. Because it is tangible, I can put it in my hands, shape it, mold it, and ground with it. I can see something through from beginning to end and put the finishing touches to the work, literally and figuratively. I enjoy being a deputy sheriff. I also like being a counselor. As a program coordinator in a school system, I am removed from the direct clinical contact the counseling profession offers. I am beginning to get the urge to return to direct counseling practice.

There are many parallels between the cop and the counselor. We both intervene in the lives of often-troubled people. We do so with some hope that life will become better for them, yet we realize people will make their own choices and our intervention may mean nothing to them. We hang in there and continue to work for the satisfaction of knowing we are indeed making a difference in the overall scheme of life, our life.

Randal Town, LPC received his BA degree in psychology from Central Washington University and his M.Ed. in counseling psychology from Lewis and Clark College. He is the Coordinator of Intervention Services for Educational Service District 105 in Yakima, Washington, and he is also a member of the Yakima County Deputy Sheriff, reserve unit. He is the co-author of *Quick Response: A Step-by-Step Guide to Crisis Management for Principals, Counselors, and Teachers.*

SUGGESTED READINGS

Casey, D., & Leger, E. (1996). *Rural emergency response.* Becker, MN: Crisis Management Counseling Consultation Publishing.
  This publication includes a piece regarding CISD for rural emergency responders.

Educational Service District 105, Yakima, WA. (1997). *Quick response: A step-by-step guide to crisis management for principals, counselors, and teachers.* Alexandria, VA: Association for Supervision and Curriculum Development.
  A very practical guide for the management of school crises. For information, please call Randal Town (509) 575-2885.

Gilliland, B. E., & James, R. (1997). *Crisis intervention strategies* (3rd ed.). Pacific Grove, CA: Brooks/Cole Publishing.
  Another good crisis intervention book.

EXIT STAGE LEFT: MY LAST DAYS
OF MIDDLE SCHOOL

CAROLINE BAKER VULGAMORE

It was the middle of May and soothing afternoon sunshine was streaming through my office window. The parent scheduled for an appointment wasn't coming. I had some time to kill before going to my eighth period Student Support Group. This was the last month of nineteen years in this building as a school counselor, as well as a total of thirty-one years with this Colorado Springs area school district. Along with assorted elementary teaching jobs in Phoenix and in rural Indiana, it had been a long haul in public education.

This would be a good time to start attacking the files. Before I knew it, I found myself going through the file drawers adjacent to my desk to begin the gleaning process. From *Alcoholics Anonymous* to *Zebulon Pike Detention Center*, I had accumulated drawer after drawer of reference information over the years. Sure, I had periodically cleaned them out, but never to leave the space completely empty. My replacement had already been hired, and we had discussed her use of my materials. Mostly I needed to create space, to vacate big time. I would never use most of this stuff again. So one file folder after another, out they came, and within a half-hour, I had filled two large wastebaskets. I wasn't even a third of the way through the alphabet when the bell rang.

I stood beside the doorway and watched students darting down the hall, clutching piles of books. Three minutes passing time between classes didn't allow for much distraction. I could feel their energy and the power of their hormones. A group of eighth grade girls squealed as they rounded the corner, a gaggle of greasy skin, braces, enthusiasm, and despair. They lived in the moment. I marveled at huge feet on tiny seventh grade boys and deep voices emanating from ninth grade *men.*

In the weeks that followed, I continued the ritual of packing up and moving on. It was sad, it was funny, and most of all, it felt wonderful. Like tremendous weights being lifted from me and sailing into the universe. The big unit in the conference room with its shelves and drawers was next. By now I had wheeled in the large trash container the custodians used when they emptied wastebaskets in classrooms up and down the halls. A thick volume of articles on family therapy landed in the bin with a resounding clunk. That enormous book had been purchased for $75 back in 1981 as part of a grant I had written on bringing schools and families closer. There were remnants of counseling journals, outdated parenting books, resource directories, flyers from social service agencies, pamphlets on career planning, and everything else teens would ever need to know.

I uncovered vases, plant food, a coffee maker (the ORIGINAL Mr. Coffee), large plastic cups from ice cream float parties, napkins, and T-shirts with conflict mediator logos. There also were attachments for a Mac Classic computer that had been replaced, plastic nametag holders, assorted gift trinkets from kids (a candle holder, artificial flowers, figurines), and greasy accumulations of dust (no, real *grime*) in the corners.

We had agreed the stuffed animals were staying. Four teddy bears, a dog, and a cow had been laundered more or less routinely and now were propped as sentinels on the shelf to monitor this safe little room where so much had happened. Do you know how comforting it feels to hug a teddy bear when you're upset? Especially if you're 13 and no one is looking. The cow was a gift from Daisy, whose dad had died the summer between seventh and eighth grade. She came in to cry on his birthday, Thanksgiving, Christmas, Valentine's Day, and for no special day.

Out went two decades of poster collections. Inexpensive attempts to brighten the drab walls with eye-catching animals and salient messages: *I'm at the End of My Rope, Everyone Needs Friends, It's O.K. to Be You,* and *Stand Your Ground.* Had the sun really faded some of them that much? I examined multiple holes from tacks and the dated look of some of the designs. Some of the current students' parents had attended here when the oldest ones were purchased.

Into the bin went the dog-eared boxes of games, memories of hours spent with kids around the table playing *The Ungame, Dealing with Feelings Card Game,* or *Social Security.* I blew the dust off old tapes and videos on surviving divorce, setting goals, and improving study skills. I sorted out my collection of foam rubber balls. We threw them to each other around the circle to break the ice and stress the importance of learning names. Sometimes kids came in the conference room to just throw them at the wall in anger, so they could settle in and work out what they needed to do.

This room had been the scene of stormy adult meetings, too. Frustrated parents wondered how to improve their teens' grades. Intake workers from Human Services interviewed kids about alleged abuse at home. Sheriff's deputies probed for details about a crime scene. Around this table many special education staffing meetings were held to develop education programs for the learning disabled. Parents met with psychologists, nurses, social workers, and teachers to hear how their student was progressing. In recent years there had been an explosion of those diagnosed with ADD and the use of medications to improve school performance. Now the Counseling Center secretary regularly dispensed powerful prescription drugs.

I kept a separate file of all those meetings, so I could document the key phone numbers, the doctors, the outside therapists, the probation officers, the noncustodial parents, and all the inside information that would not be available in the students' regular cumulative files. There were notes about kids who had gone through the system in foster homes; as victims of neglect, sexual abuse, learning disabilities; kids with consistently failing grades, poor attendance; and all the strategies that we tried. These notes were slowly ground through the shredder.

There was an entire shelf of yearbooks. I mused at all those photos. No matter what the clothing styles were through the years, kids were defining themselves, desperate to be socially adept. The basic T-shirt, jeans, and sneakers uniform had endured, but with constant upgrades. Skater and grunge looks gave way to Michael Jordan and the Bulls, and then John Elway and the Broncos. FUBU® and Tommy Hilfiger® competed with JNCO®. Adidas® never reached the status of Nike®. *Cool.* Back when *Titanic* was so popular, there were students who confided they saw it six times. They wrote me poignant messages on the inside covers of the books: *Thank you for helping me through my dad's heart attack. I'll never forget you. Thank you for being such a great consular. I stayed out of trouble with your help. Thanks for helping me and Vikki with our problem. I hope we can keep in touch. Never forget me! Hope you have many joyable years. Have fun and stay cool. Have fun on your retirement. I know it's what you've always wanted.* These went into the boxes to take home.

What would I do with the note I had crammed between some books on the top shelf? Left on my desk only a few months ago, it was neatly penned in cursive and it read:

Dear Dr. Baker,

I just wanted to say thank you. I'm kinda, really glad you had me call my mom. We had a talk when she got home. She surprised me when she told me she was sorry, and gave me a rose. She told me I could talk to her about anything. It felt really good to hear that and if it weren't for you I don't think I would have heard it.

Thanks a lot,
Stephanie (not her real name)

Her English teacher had marched Stephanie into the Counseling Center just as lunch was beginning. It seems the night before, after a heated argument with her mom, she had inserted a safety pin into her bare abdomen and clasped it shut just above her navel. By now the word had spread throughout the seventh grade locker area. She was the center of attention, having made a new statement in body piercing. The skin all around was inflamed, but who says she couldn't take a dare?

Throughout those final hectic days, as the school year ended, I would continue slipping discards into the wastebaskets. My desk would be the last area to clean out. How did I accumulate so many extra paper clips and staples? The parent letter I had searched for so diligently last fall was crushed in the back of the top drawer! The letting-go was delicious. Bittersweet, yes, but I was not prepared for the ecstasy. I really was being relieved of the day-to-day pressures of being a counselor to seventh, eighth, and ninth graders.

All those years, I had remained professional and kept my boundaries, but inside I had wanted to take many of them home to *fix* things. I had wished I could wave a wand that would make all the hurt go away. It's not fair when your older brother hangs himself in his bedroom, when your mom tells you she is dying of leukemia, when Dad's girlfriend hits you so hard there are welts across your back, when your cerebral palsy imprisons your brain so severely you can't even speak. I wanted to forget the evil kids who manipulated, bullied, and hurt others. Sometimes they were charmers one-on-one, but then they lied, they betrayed, and they could not be trusted. There were many I would never reach.

They all would function—and quite well—without me. I was one small piece in time of a much greater picture. I had learned long ago I could not change the public school system and its meager resources within a materialistic society that was not focused on children's needs. Nor could I alone give moms and dads the energy and commitment to make their young teens their number one priority. Even if parents did have to work overtime, were repairing their own relationships, and/or were still struggling with their identities, I understood they loved their kids. They wanted success too. Would we all as a collective society stop pushing adolescents into being adults before they were ready? Could we improve on protecting them? Let them enjoy a childhood? They needed us to demand that they behave. They cried out for opportunities to shoulder responsibility, to be truly useful to others.

I realized the real value of counseling programs was in the *prevention* we did, not just in the reacting to crisis. All those hours in the classrooms and with small groups talking about improving report cards, managing conflict, making good choices and building healthy lifestyles. That's where we made a difference.

And the teachers! I wished I had more openly shown my support for all their efforts. Sometimes I was too caught up in my own job demands. Over the years there were many in this building who were my heroes. They were themselves role models for their students. They made learning fun. They stayed up to date in their subject areas, at the same time remaining creative. They understood adolescence. They had high expectations and they took an interest in each student. Their sense of humor sustained me.

It was time to say goodbyes. I would let go of all the unfinished projects. I would not miss the early morning commutes, the stacks of phone messages, always playing catch-up, demanding days where I was running all around the school, the things I couldn't change. I knew the day would never arrive when all students would be exemplary in all subjects. The troubleshooting was eternal. At times this job had consumed my being.

I would continue to be an advocate for young mothers and preach to all that listen the importance of BONDING for young infants. I had seen again and again the children who were unable to love, who had no remorse in hurting others, whose anger had made them sociopaths. It was frightening to realize that there were more of them now than in the earlier years.

I would speak from personal experience about the *good* things happening in public education, in spite of fragile family systems and an irresponsible media. For many students, the structure and caring of the school day was the most positive part of their lives. They knew they could count on us. They belonged. Well-run neighborhood schools at all levels of the economic ladder can provide that. No democracy can be successful without a properly educated electorate.

I was turning a new page. The constraints of my career were dissolving. No more demands from this school. Freedom beckoned. I could travel the Earth, read for hours, volunteer my time, hike when I wanted, and even take afternoon naps. Deep down, however, I knew all that I had learned from this world of education was forever written on my soul. When I least expected I would recall a particular student, a final laugh, and a moment of triumph. I chuckled when I remembered what the really cool kids wrote in yearbooks: *2 good 2 be 4 gotten.*

AFTERTHOUGHTS

Beginning counselors sometimes ask how I became the counselor I was. Experience! Beyond learning from mistakes, school counselors can work on some key areas. Understand the age level you are targeting. Besides college courses covering child development, be sure you experience working with kids in that age group so you can quickly establish rapport, gain their trust, and be a resource for parents and teachers in understanding appropriate behavior. Cultivate a mentor, an experienced counselor role model that you can access for support, advice, and inspiration.

Be aware of the power of your building administration. A supportive principal will promote program areas for you to pursue. Through the years, you will need to educate administrators about developmental counseling, that you are there for the entire student body, and that clerical responsibilities limit effectiveness—it helps when you make your principal look good! Defining your role to staff, parents, and students is ongoing. Never underestimate building politics. Be a team player, at the same time empowering your staff to buy into your counseling activities.

Join professional counselor and educational associations and attend conferences and workshops. Read the literature and keep up to date with issues in your field. You can never rest on your laurels; this arena is always changing. Consider LPC and NCC certifications to broaden your base of expertise and credibility. Network with other counselors in your area. Ask for their input when you make tough decisions. Know the community resources in your city, including key names in law enforcement, social services, mental hospitals, private therapists, and career services.

Stay healthy. School counseling requires incredible energy. Develop an exercise routine, good nutrition, adequate sleep, and tools for handling stress. Develop a life away from your job!

My former school has become a seven-eight building (ninth graders are now at the high school) with a new administration. I have not gone back in the traditional sense, but I keep close contact with the counselor who replaced me. We have met for lunch and talked by phone and e-mail. Most recently she wanted information about how I coordinated the end-of-the-year awards assembly. Before that she forwarded a subpoena for me to testify in court for a student who was raped four years ago.

Some students have written to me about happenings at school, especially last fall. I in turn have continued to send notes to former students praising them for accomplishments. This month I sent a congratulatory card to a high school senior from our junior high who received a Phi Delta Kappa education scholarship. I have also met with teachers and our counseling secretary for occasional dinners and they eagerly keep me up to date on their concerns about kids and life at school.

I continue to belong to professional associations and read the literature. I have made guest lecture appearances at local college classes. I volunteer for *First Visitor*, a local program that supports mothers of new babies. I also volunteer as a docent at the Colorado Springs Fine Arts Center, taking school children on tours. My husband Harry and I lead hikes for the Colorado Mountain Club and travel frequently. We have six children and six grandchildren. None of them live in Colorado Springs, but we proactively support their busy lives.

Caroline Baker Vulgamore, Ed.D, LPC, NCC received her BS from Northwestern University, and her MA and Ed.D. from the University of Colorado. Besides elementary and junior high school experiences, she spent ten years as an adjunct professor/counselor educator at the University of Colorado, Colorado Springs. She was region representative for the Colorado School Counselor Association and later president. She was also president of the Colorado Counseling Association.

SUGGESTED READINGS

Center on National Education Policy. (1996). *Do we still need public schools?* Bloomington, Indiana: Phi Delta Kappa.
Good comebacks for those who attack public education.

Elkind, D. (1989). *The hurried child: Growing up too fast too soon.* Reading, MA: Addison-Wesley Publishing Company.
Insight into encouraging healthy development.

Foster-Harrison, E. S. (1994). *More energizers and icebreakers.* Minneapolis, MN: Educational Media Corporation.
All school counselors need a good bag of tricks.

Glenn, H. S. (1987). *Raising children for success.* Fair Oaks, CA: Sunrise Press.
An easy-to-read tool for helping parents of young teens.

Magid, K., & McKelvey, C. (1989). *High risk: Children without conscience.* New York: Bantam Books.
Essential information about bonding and identifying sociopathic behavior.

Myrick, R. D. (1993). *Developmental guidance and counseling: A practical approach.* Minneapolis, MN: Educational Media Corporation.
A real primer for your counseling program!

Piper, M. (1994). *Reviving Ophelia: Saving the selves of adolescent girls.* New York: Ballantine Books.
Pressures on girls that make them prone to depression; strategies to help.

ADVISOR, CONFIDANT, MENTOR, CONFESSOR, SOUNDING BOARD, OGRE, AND FRIEND

JOHN W. BLOOM

'm 55 years old with a thirty-two-year-old love affair with my wife and a second thirty-two-year-old love affair (minus six bad days) with counseling education and the counseling profession. Perhaps I love counselor education because what I do on a daily basis is so much more than just educating counselors. Primarily, I am an educator, but I am also a writer, an advisor, a mentor, a leader, an entertainer, a salesperson, a consultant, and an observer of the group process, a lobbyist, and an administrator. On special days, I'm also a person who remembers that even borderline workaholic counselor educators like me need to climb their mountains, work on their sun tan, or become better acquainted with a glass of fine wine!

My career path started with many twists and turns. Try as I would to find my calling as an undergraduate, all I found was a combination of mediocre grades and a definite lack of direction. I tried the college of business first because my brother had just earned his degree in business. But surprise, surprise, I'm not my brother! I tried systems analysis (precursor of computer science), but couldn't make the simplest of programs run on that day's monster mainframe. I then became an English major because, at least, I had minimal writing skills and loved to read. Both to help assure that I would have a job and that I would minimize the possibility of being drafted into military service, I added teacher certification courses to my program of studies and graduated into the real world as a junior high school English teacher.

Driven by a parent-instilled fear that I would never be able to support a family on a teacher's salary, I quickly began to think about pursuing a master's degree in *something*. Something started out to be curriculum and instruction, but quickly turned to guidance and counseling, upon the suggestion of a highly regarded professor and mentor. Thank goodness for those who are older, wiser, and more observant. That gentle nudge led me into the counseling profession, where I spent short stints totaling six and half years as an elementary, junior high, high school, and college career counselor in three different states. I was a good counselor and hated to leave each assignment, but each leaving meant new beginnings and more valuable experiences that would undergird my years of practice as a counselor educator.

So, what's my existence like as a counselor educator? My assistant professor years were devoted to developing confidence in my ability to tell others how to become that which I had barely become myself. I was barely 30 years old when I started teaching my first counselor education classes. While I had been a counselor for almost seven years, I was very nervous about telling others that I had enough knowledge and experience to teach them my profession. But, you know, I did it and the students responded well. In fact, several from those first classes still keep in touch. One is now chair of the program in which I started my higher education career!

Once I somewhat perfected how I wanted to teach courses like group processes, counseling processes, practicum, and internship, I turned to those other responsibilities that are part and parcel of a professor's responsibilities—research and service. Research first—my university was not a research institution. Thus, it more liberally interpreted and enforced the old *publish-or-perish* dictum. Conference presentations and a few publications (related to those presentations) were sufficient to gain me promotion to the rank of associate professor, with accompanying tenured status.

Mind you, however, that in my case, I had done over 100 presentations on an emerging niche within the counseling profession. Norman Cousins and Leo Buscaglia had had a great impact in the seventies. Cousins taught us about the healing power of laughter and humor, and Buscaglia, dubbed by many as the *Love Doctor,* convinced me to get back in touch with my madness. So I became an entertainer as well as an educator, taking on the persona of *Hearts the Clown* as I went around the country teaching people how to incorporate more Cousins and more Buscaglia into their personal and professional lives. One such appearance as keynote speaker at an ACES luncheon in New York City, with B.F. Skinner in the audience, still stands out in my mind, as I was way outside any box Skinner ever constructed!

As for service, I never did become very involved in campus governance, as many of my colleagues did, to fulfill service obligations. My service was more directed toward service in my professional organizations. I quickly moved through the leadership ranks of my state counseling association and became chair of my region. Ultimately, I was a member of the AACD Governing Council and a candidate for the presidency of the American Association for Counseling and Development. In those roles, I became a lobbyist and a spokesperson for counselor credentialing. I helped found a state counseling certification board and served on that board when it was first established. I still wear my assigned number, *Certified Counselor 2,* proudly.

As a counselor educator and university professor, I have more control over my daily schedule than most K–12 educators and, thus, can arrange my classes. This way, I can meet my teaching obligations while still having time to travel to the state house to testify before a regulatory committee, for example, or fly to a Governing Council meeting on the other side of the country. For me, the only down side of my schedule is having to deal with the perceptions of those who see me only working those hours when my classes are in session. They may mistakenly be believing that, when I'm not teaching, I must be playing golf (or in some other way wasting the taxpayers' or the trustees' money). Actually, my workweek far exceeds the industry standard of forty hours. In fact, as I am writing, it is a beautiful Saturday morning and I'm in the office writing away while my wife and daughters are descending upon a local mall!

So, my associate professor days were spent presenting *Humor of Psychology* or *Psychology of Humor* workshops, lobbying at the legislature, and teaching master's and doctoral level classes. By the way, there are nineteen *Bloom's Doctors*—I am very proud of the accomplishments of all my former doctoral students. The doctoral student–doctoral advisor relationship is like no other in academia. Doctoral students usually spend three years (or more) working closely with their advisor, who is a confidant, mentor, confessor, sounding board, ogre and friend. My "19" are now leaders in the profession. They are deans, professors, private practitioners, directors of guidance, school counselors, and psychologists. Most of them keep in touch on a regular basis and constantly serve as reminders of why I love this profession so much.

I have been a full professor now for more than ten years. I see my teaching responsibilities remaining steady and constant, but see my other duties changing from association and organizational leadership to professional writing. Those skills I learned in Advanced Placement English keep coming in handy! My writing over the last two decades has focused a lot on technology. I chuckle now as I remember being asked to review different software programs for an ERIC/CASS publication in the mid-eighties. I looked forward, with great anticipation, to reviewing the software program that was going to change how we all did our jobs. Little did I know that one of the first programs I would receive was related to assessing personality characteristics via handwriting analysis!

That, however, did pique my interest in technology, and I became a member of various technology task forces. Ultimately, when named to the Board of Directors of the National Board for Certified Counselors (NBCC), I found myself right in the middle of today's technology revolution. One day someone forwarded to me the URL of a website a National Certified Counselor had created. My excitement for one of the world's first Web counselors quickly dampened when I noticed a hotlink to a pornographic site.

Thus, for the last six or seven years, I have continued to examine legal, ethical, and professional counseling practices on the World Wide Web. As more and more counseling websites were brought to our attention, the NBCC board was confronted with having to decide whether to lead, follow, or get out of the way of the technology movement. My colleagues and I on the board felt that, in spite of the many questions that surrounded the practice of counseling, or whatever euphemism Web counselors were calling themselves, it was the responsibility of the board to lead the way.

The decision was made to draft a set of standards for the ethical practice of Web counseling. Despite its imperfections, it is still the industry leader. Since the adoption of these standards in 1998, the American Counseling Association, several of its divisions, and several related behavioral health associations have all adopted similar standards. Counselors who seek to use the Internet as an added dimension of their professional practice now have a starting point for doing so ethically, legally, and professionally.

My typical day as a full professor at a major, regional, private university starts early. This is not because I have to be on campus at the crack of dawn, but because that is when I am most productive—when I don't have to fight traffic and when I can find a parking place. My day starts in front of my computer, the same place where my day sometimes ends! My e-mail system tallies messages I've sent, received, and forwarded. Over the last six months I have been averaging 21.5 e-mails a day, every day, rain or shine, workday or holiday.

Our graduate program is primarily a late afternoon and evening endeavor. This semester, I am on campus every Monday night till almost 10 P.M. One of things I have been doing for almost three decades is listening to or watching videotapes of individual and group counseling sessions. I sometimes shake my head in disbelief at the current emphasis on standards-based teacher education. Ever since I made my first audiotape on that old Wollensak reel-to-reel tape recorder (that was so heavy it doubled as a boat anchor!), I've had to demonstrate my skills, and ever since the inception of the National Counseling Exam, I've had to demonstrate my knowledge. I'm proud that my graduate education has been performance-based and that our current programs will continue to be performance-based!

My two colleagues and I do a lot to support our College of Education that goes unseen by most students in our program. One colleague serves as a *Faculty-in-Residence* in one of the residence halls. As such, he has a *presence* in the residence hall and arranges many social and community based events for the students living therein. My other colleague has been a valued member of the college's Professional Standards Committee and meets regularly to make recommendations to the dean regarding the granting of sabbatical leaves, as well as promotion and tenure.

I serve on a university committee that makes grants to faculty members who want financial support for their research endeavors, want to develop new courses or modify existing ones, or want to present papers at national or international conferences. Hardly a year goes by that we aren't called upon to participate in one or more faculty or administrative searches, as well. When a colleague resigns, in most instances a national search is conducted to find a replacement. These searches are always challenging, as we attempt to find that one individual who can afford to come to my institution, has that unique combination of skills we are seeking, and meets our diversity recruitment goals.

You may have noticed my frequent use of the word *colleague*. In my career, I've had lots of fellow professors, not all of whom I refer to as colleagues. To me, a colleague is someone who is more than just another person on the university's payroll. Like me, a colleague is someone who, by my definition, puts students above all else—above writing, above committee meetings, above professional travel. A colleague is never satisfied with the status quo and works tirelessly to improve the quality of our program. A colleague is an active member of the college and university communities and goes to basketball games and cultural events with me. A colleague helps me when I'm in need, because a family member is sick or because there are boxes or fish tanks to be moved. Strong relationships with colleagues is why I stay at an institution that might not always pay me what I'd like to be paid or isn't always as respectful of my *real* life as I'd like it to be. Colleagues and students are what counselor education is all about.

Oh yes, there is one more aspect of my profession that I must mention. The profession I entered in the late sixties was a European American, male-dominated profession. We had little awareness of what diversity was all about. In fact, we were still of the *melting pot* mentality that suggested we all abandon our uniqueness, so that we could all blend together as one, homogenous stew. I didn't even know that my own German American, Lutheran, Midwestern, monogamous, heterosexual, Protestant work ethnic, wife-and-two-kids upbringing was in any way different than any other person on the face of the earth. My world is no longer that world. My world is one that values diversity and similarity. I love teaching a course by that name. I love the influence of colleagues and friends like Art, Dottie, Virginia, Ade, Levi, Rory, Courtland, Hema, Ramona, Nelson, Betty, and others from diverse cultures have had on my life. I love Mauro, a priest from Ecuador, who just finished his fourth master's degree. I love the woman who completed her first master's degree in her mid-sixties and then went on to complete a doctorate at the Pacific School of Religion in dance! I love Lori, who was just recognized as one of *Ebony* magazine's outstanding *30 under 30*. I love tacos and fortune cookies.

One last point about family. Those humor workshops I presented . . . Susan, Kristi, and Lori all helped me as co-presenters, makeup artists, props persons, greeting card designers, and so on. Those conferences I mentioned . . . whenever possible, they were included in my travels. Those students I talked about . . . Kristi was one of them and received her master's in college student personnel but, unfortunately, she never had the best professor in the program—me—for any of her classes!

Those six bad days I referred to earlier in the chapter—I cannot end without some explanation. They were days when any or all of the following happened: too many meetings, insufficient financial resources, inability to accept my own abundant imperfections, trying to control more than any human should ever control, rain, and to mine own self not being true.

John W. Bloom, PhD, LMHC, NCC, NCSC is a native of Cleveland, Ohio. His bachelor's and master's degrees are from Miami University in Oxford, Ohio, and his doctorate is from Purdue University in West Lafayette, Indiana. He taught for almost two decades at Northern Arizona University before accepting his present counselor educator position at Butler University in Indianapolis, Indiana, in 1996. John helped found the Arizona Board of Behavioral Health Examiners and has served on the board of directors of the American School Counselors Association, the American Counseling Association, and the National Board for Certified Counselors.

SUGGESTED READINGS

Rogers, C. (1969). *Freedom to learn.* Columbus, OH: Merrill.

> Whether you want to teach clients or teach students, Carl Rogers was not only a brilliant counselor, but also a brilliant educator. As readable as all of Rogers' works are, this is a must and if you glean nothing more that the fact that learning is primary and teaching is secondary, you've learned a lot. In fact, Rogers says, *Nothing that is important can be taught, it can only be learned.*

Bloom, J., & Walz, G. (2000*). Cybercounseling and cyberlearning: Strategies and resources for the millennium.* Alexandria, VA: American Counseling Association.

> Recommend reading my own book? Damn right. You've noticed that your professional world is changing, but have you noticed all the ways it is changing? The book can help, and it will recommend hundreds of stimulating websites for your perusal.

Frankl, V. (2000). *Man's search for meaning.* Wilmington, MA: Beacon Press.

> We are all free to choose, and the most important choice of all is the choice of attitude. Frankl's lesson, learned in a World War II concentration camp, served as the basis of my dissertation and a program called Choice Awareness that still shapes the way I view my world. Whether our prison is Auschwitz, a relationship with a significant other (that divorce can't happen quickly enough!), our place of work (God, I hate my major prof!), or our own body (Christopher Reeve, Helen Keller), no prison guard can take away the choice of attitude with which we face every day.

Cousins, N. (1979). *Anatomy of an illness.* New York: Norton.

> This book had a profound impact on me even before Cousins left a dying relative's bedside to meet me in his office at UCLA. While Frankl talked about the choice of attitude, Cousins talked about the choice of one specific attitude—laughter—and its power to heal. The 150 or so humor workshops I did in mid-career helped me and hundreds of others to realize that laughter and play not only heal relationships and heal the soul, but also can heal the body. Zing! There goes another marshmallow! Ha! Ha! I can laugh at myself. Tee hee! There is humor all around us.

The Bible . . .

> Wonderful! Counselor! The Prince of Peace! Why say more?

Grisham, J. (1998). *The street lawyer.* Des Plaines, IL: Bantam.

> Fiction is good and fiction that mirrors reality is even better. Grisham helped me learn so much about life on the streets of our nation's capital! Also consider reading Jean Auer's *Clan of the Cave Bear* series (New York: Crown) . . . Allah and Jondolar—smart and sexy as any person roaming our cyberworld today!

Finally, any book written by someone who is not of my religion, my gender, my sexual orientation, my country, my whatever further helps me appreciate similarity and diversity.

22

FROM JUNIOR HIGH SCHOOL TO COMMUNITY COLLEGE: THE DILEMMA OF A LATINO PROFESSIONAL IN COUNSELING

PEDRO PÉREZ

It was 1990 when I first started my career at Borough of Manhattan Community College. Following a series of individual and committee interviews, I was offered a position with the counseling faculty at this public community college located in downtown Manhattan in New York City. My previous position was in a public junior high school in Washington Heights, NYC. The school was in a community populated predominantly by Dominicans, a growing group of people from the Dominican Republic. Although I had some personal and professional apprehensions making the career transition from intermediate school to higher education, it was a comment made by a colleague that resonated in my mind.

As a young Latino counselor of Puerto Rican descent working in a junior high school whose population was largely Latino, I was faced with making the very difficult decision to leave an environment where young adolescents were in the midst of their own developmental dilemmas. As the only Latino guidance counselor of a staff of five, it was clear that my departure would leave a significant gap. In conducting a literature review on Latinos in education, a number of studies made reference to the concept of role models. That is, studies have shown that Hispanic students adjust better to the academic environment when they can culturally identify with the faculty and counselors. For some, this is a tough concept to grasp. In its simplest form, the phenomenon is one of bonding. Forming a relationship requires time to create and nurture a bond. Cultural similarity—different from language similarity—facilitates the bonding process.

As I was pondering this career change, one of my colleagues whose opinion I highly valued made reference to the *gap* that would be created by the absence of a counseling professional with whom students might be able to easily identify. The question she posed was, *Who will these students turn to when they need help?* Her question led me back to my own reasons for pursuing college.

Coming from a large family with little resources, I had to find a way out of the poverty. I was the seventh child from a family of eight siblings. Together with our parents, there were ten of us living in a three-bedroom apartment. Although we had some great times, we also suffered on various levels. Higher education seemed like the only way that breaking these barriers could be achieved. It seemed that a career in counseling would fulfill at least two particular objectives—personal satisfaction and the opportunity to foster change.

As counselors, we often must broach the very sensitive and difficult area of decision making with our clients. Naturally, I took into consideration variables such as opportunities for growth, professional development, salary, health benefits, and job stability, with the latter being less in vogue these days since career shifts are now viewed as progressive.

As counselors, we also must be clear about our own limitations. We can't be all things to all people. Our expendability, as with most professionals in any other field, is a reality we must accept. So, having given serious contemplation in a short time frame, I marched into the world of higher education. Filled with what some may call naiveté, I optimistically took on the challenges of working in an environment filled with more politics than I had imagined. In just a short period of time it became evident to me that, if I was going to fulfill my ethical duties as a counselor, I needed to be prepared and creative.

Approximately two years later, in response to the resonating question, *Who will these students turn to when they need help?,* I started a student club for Latino students on campus. Having completed some environmental scanning (the new lexicon for specific observations), it was clear to me that there were gaps in support services for Latino students on campus. One way that some of the gaps could be filled, particularly as they relate to cultural adjustment, was through the creation of a student organization where students with similar cultural backgrounds could interact and celebrate their identities.

To put things into perspective, it should be noted that taking on a student organization was an additional function to my already burgeoning caseload responsibilities. I'm certain most counselors could empathize with this reality. Notwithstanding, I had the fortune of having some degree of professional autonomy, where creativity could be exercised. Some of us are not that lucky and others take this for granted. From an administrative angle, the message should be clear—stifling creativity and professional autonomy can have strong negative consequences. Although this is a tangential issue, administrators in organizations should take note: Fostering a climate conducive to creativity is in the best interest and the welfare of both client and employee. This is a premise that can be tested.

Back to the matter at hand, establishing an Aspira Club on campus involved a commitment on my part to help it develop. There were times when I questioned whether the energy involved was worth the time, especially when things just didn't go right. I remember having planned an event in the theater of the college. The invited guest was a disc jockey of a popular Latino radio station. After much work and effort in securing her appearance, the turnout for the event was noticeably poor. There were probably thirty students in a theater that seats over 200. I later learned how to better deal with this issue.

Rather than give up, I knew that I needed to continue my involvement. Staying the course was not only the right thing to do, but it was (as my brother would put it) my duty to put effort into the cause. When I started the club, I wasn't quite up to date with literature on retention. For example, I later learned how forming this group could have positive effects on the students' ability to adapt to the academic environment. Today, almost ten years later, I'm so grateful for the opportunities I've had. I think my feelings can be best understood by a case in point, so here goes.

A young Latino male assigned to my caseload meets with me throughout the semester for counseling. His parents are from Columbia and he was born and raised in New York City. This was a quiet and introverted young man. In counseling he expressed desires to be more social and to make new friends—enter the Aspira Club. We discussed the possibility of getting involved in extracurricular activities by participating in the club. Here he might be able to form new relationships and by extension enhance his social skills. He agreed and the rest of the story is akin to a fairy tale.

In time, the student took on an active role in the club and became a significant, contributing member. During his last semester, he came to me for a letter of recommendation for a scholarship at New York University. His educational goals included pursuance of a baccalaureate degree in English, with plans to go into teaching. In a nutshell, he was accepted into NYU with the partial scholarship. As if this weren't a case of success already, the student recently came back to see me for a visit. I was very happy to see him and learn how well he was doing. It turns out that he was in his last semester at NYU, involved in student teaching, and was approaching graduation. The icing on the cake of this great story was when he asked me if I would be one of his four guests at graduation. Need I say more?

Counselors have a tremendous responsibility. The place where we fulfill our duties as professionals is not accidental. It is my belief that, somehow, through religious calling, destiny, karma, or whatever you want to call it, there is a greater purpose to our actions and the decisions we make. I believe it is a spiritual issue and, when we see how our intervention affects others, a sense of satisfaction and purpose is reinforced.

I think the moral of this story, at least one of them, is that if in our work we are fortunate enough to positively impact the life of just one person, then we have accomplished our duty. The dilemma I pondered regarding a gap possibly caused by my absence in the intermediate school was even more clearly resolved when more than one student at the community college identified themselves as remembering me as their former junior high school counselor.

Pedro Pérez, MS received his Bachelor of Arts in social work from Lehman College and his Master of Science degree in school counseling from Long Island University. He currently serves as a Counselor/Instructor at the Borough of Manhattan

Community College of the City University of New York. In addition to his regular functions at BMCC, he serves on various collegewide committees and is actively involved in student affairs. He is the faculty advisor to the Aspira Club and co-advisor to the Dominican Students Association. Additionally, he acts as the coordinator for a mentor program for Latino students. He has received many awards of recognition and appreciation for his work. Pedro is a member of the IMAGE Wall Street Chapter and the American Counseling Association. He is also a former member of the Latino Coalition for Fair Media. Pedro is currently pursuing his doctorate in higher education from Nova Southeastern University.

SUGGESTED READINGS

Halpin, R. L. (1990). An application of the Tinto model to the analysis of freshman persistence in a community college. *Community College Review, 17* (4), 22–31.
    Halpin studied student persistence or withdrawal at a nonresidential, public, open-door community college in New York. This study applies the Tinto model in analyzing freshman persistence in a community college setting. It compares the experiences of students at traditional four-year institutions to those in nontraditional community colleges. Findings indicate that the students in the former instance leave home to live in a residence hall and study in an unfamiliar environment, while the latter have a life completely extraneous to their new role as students. The need to seek and create a sense of community is greater for the nontraditional student and almost nonexistent for residential students.

Nora, A. (1990, May/June). Campus-based aid programs as determinants of retention among Hispanic community college students. *Journal of Higher Education, 61* (3), 312–330.
    This is the first study of its kind to test persistence models on Hispanic community college students where aspects of financial aid were included. *Hispanic college students are not leaving higher education because of their academic performance but largely because of financial reasons* (p. 326). Nora recommends the development of comprehensive financial aid advisement programs and includes counseling.

Olivas, M. A. (1979). *The dilemma of access.* Washington, DC: Howard University Press.
    An older study that supports the recommendation by Nora and suggests coordination between financial aid officers, remedial programs, and support services. Conclusions: First, two-year college administrators must at least seek to provide adequate surrogates for residential institutions by making available cultural and supportive educational programs; and second, that counseling, academic advising, and financial assistance are essential to nontraditional students in public two-year colleges.

Perez, P. (2000). *Development of a mentor program for Latino students at Borough of Manhattan Community College.* New York. (ERIC Document Reproduction Service No. Ed 439 736)
    In an effort to address a problem regarding lack of services for Latino students at BMCC, a mentor program was developed. Mentors were recruited from within the college community, and in private industry. Students were selected from the College Discovery Program. A literature review and a full appendix containing forms developed to initiate

the program are included. Additionally, data from a pilot implementation is also provided.

President's Advisory Commission on Educational Excellence for Hispanic Americans. (1996, September). *Our nation on the fault line: Hispanic American education.* Washington DC: White House Initiative. www.ed.gov/pubs/FaultLine/

In this very extensive and comprehensive report, a number of critical issues affecting the Hispanic community are raised, especially as they relate to education at all levels. One of the recommendations includes equal and equitable allocation of state and local government resources in schools with large concentrations of Hispanic Americans.

23

STRENGTH-BASED, SOLUTION-FOCUSED CONSULTATION AND EDUCATION

DEBORAH BARLIEB

I am an assistant professor at Kutztown University. I teach students seeking their master's degrees in counseling for careers in schools or agency settings. A typical day for me is very hard to describe because there is not a typical day—every day is different. Some days, I spend twelve hours at the university doing paperwork, preparing for classes or presentations, seeing students and attending department or committee meetings. On other days, I visit students who are doing field practice and I supervise them at their schools, agencies, or wherever they are placed. I also spend one day a week as a consultant for local school districts or an Intermediate Unit—a cooperative special education unit that spans school districts in several counties—to provide services for early intervention programs.

In addition to my teaching and consulting roles, I usually make national, regional, state, and local presentations each year for professional organizations like the American Counseling Association, the Pennsylvania School Counselors Association, and the Eastern Psychological Association. Consequently, I have to spend a lot of time preparing overheads, resource lists, and other materials for presentation. I have such topics as preventing school violence, small group counseling for children of divorce, case conceptualization, and portfolio assessment.

On those days when I spend twelve hours at the office, I typically start by going through my mail, e-mail, and phone messages. Responding to all these can take me more then an hour. Then, I often have papers to grade, class notes to prepare, and publications to read. I like to get students' assignments back to them a week after they are turned in. At least one class each semester is for students doing a supervised field practice in a school or agency setting. Interns have to keep a log or journal of their days on site, and I read those each week to make comments and suggestions or ask questions.

I usually have student appointments when I am in my office. Students have questions about grades, assignments they have turned in, or problems they are having with their internships. I also do one individualized instruction each semester for students who are unable to take a course at night to finish the core requirements. That is usually a lot of fun because it is informal, with two or three students. I design things specifically for them—things they need to learn. It is more of an informal seminar/discussion where we share information on topics and articles in a highly collegial atmosphere.

My classes usually start at 5 or 6 P.M. I teach three nights a week. Classes last two hours and fifty minutes. I really don't lecture because most students in the counseling program are adult learners and nontraditional students. Lecturing is really not the way to go. Adult learners need more participatory activities. We do interactive discussions, seminars, and presentations. I spend a lot of time at home and on the weekends reviewing student logs. I also do a lot of other reading and research while I am off campus. I spend much more time on such things than I had imagined I would.

Some days, before I go to the office, I see students at their intern sites, and that may mean driving an hour or more. I always get where I am going, although I usually get lost. I visit a lot of schools in Pennsylvania and even some in New Jersey and New York. My biggest fear as a professor, sometimes, is that I will forget what it is like to be a counselor in the schools or an agency. Therefore, it really is important to me to see students during their internships and through this stay current with what is happening in the field.

I usually spend time with the on-site supervisor to learn if there are other things that we can be doing at the university to ensure that students are as well prepared as possible. The remainder of the time is spent observing the interns, simply following them around when they are with students, parents, or clients. What I enjoy most is getting a chance to shadow students when they are working in small group counseling. I think the most important advice I give to interns who are working with groups is:

- Encourage everyone in group to participate.
- Construct a safe environment for the group members.
- Listen closely to what group members say rather then be concerned with what you as group facilitator can do or what techniques to use.
- Follow the lead of group members.
- Provide guidance and information when the members are ready.
- Make group relevant and important for group members.
- Help members find the strengths they have within themselves.

One day a week I act as a consultant to early intervention educational programs in Monroe, Northampton, and Pike counties. I provide counseling to the parents and their children and consultation to teachers who might be having difficulty managing children's behavior and deciding what academic programs are appropriate. The children in the early intervention programs have a variety of diagnoses such as autism, Klinefelter's syndrome, and Down syndrome, and many of them have developmental delays. One of the first things I do with the children is observe them in their classroom settings to see what kind of skills they have and determine what they need. Can they communicate? What can they do? How do the classroom structure and teacher meet their needs?

I am not greatly concerned with diagnostic classification because that doesn't give me sufficient information about who each child is or what he or she needs at home and in class. I concentrate on what I am able to see and feel about them. If they scream and yell because they are not getting what they need, we must offer them alternate ways to communicate (e.g., through pictures, signs, and symbols), so they can ask in an appropriate way. I look to see if the child's activities are developmentally appropriate for him or her. No matter the child's age, if his or her skill and functioning level is that of a 10-month-old, we need to give him or her toys for an infant to visually and cognitively stimulate him or her. The children in these programs are probably among the most needy children you will see, dictating a low staff-to-student ratio. It feels great when I do follow-up on a child to find the strategies or the restructuring I suggested were effective. When I revisit the preschool class, I often see a difference in the children's behavior and/or skill level.

One other example of a typical day would include going to public schools, not because I have an intern there, but because I provide consultation as a counselor and counselor educator. I spent a lot of time at a middle school this year working with teaching teams, including the instructional support team (IST). The IST helps students who have academic or behavioral problems overcome their difficulties and move toward success. The teams I worked with were experiencing a lot of frustration because they weren't operating at peak effectiveness. I proposed that they integrate a competency-based or solution-focused approach into their team meetings. This model encourages a person to look for times that the problem does not exist and build upon existing strengths and competencies.

Children can and do find competencies in themselves. Parents and teachers identify what they have done that effectively supports their students. Those strengths, skills, and resources are used to generate strategies that worked in the present and will help shape a better future. All members of the team are empowered and, most importantly, the student feels more positive. When I went back to the middle school, after at least nine visits, I wanted to determine if the team utilized any of the proffered ideas. I was excited to find that several teachers were integrating components of the model into their thinking, resulting in a more positive view where teachers identify what students do right rather then what they do wrong. Other teachers, along with the school counselor, used the redesigned form and structure with a difficult parent whose child was having problems. The parent and child responded well to the new format, resulting in team cooperation and improvement in the child's schoolwork and behavior. The team was able to measure student success.

I think my own particular philosophical orientation began when I first started in the mental health field as a counselor with a community mental health clinic's crisis intervention team. I worked at a mental health agency for approximately five years. The crisis team provided brief therapy using a model that is goal-directed, strength-based, and more time efficient than the long-term therapy model. It looks at helping families and clients who are in crisis to assess their own strengths and environmental resources, whatever they may be, and using those to survive.

That was more than twenty-five years ago. We used to work in teams of two, going to people's homes or scheduling appointments to see clients. Our purpose was to work with families or individuals who were in crisis. We provided brief counseling to help them stabilize after they had suffered some kind of crisis/trauma. Some individuals were able to identify their own strengths and resources, work things through, and move forward on their own. Other clients might be referred to the mental health clinic for ongoing service because they needed additional treatment and support. We helped tie people into the community services that might be available to help meet their needs. Now, crisis services are more of a quick evaluation to determine need for hospitalization or referral.

The team was eventually integrated into the outpatient services milieu at the mental health clinic. I think one of the reasons we were integrated into the outpatient clinic was to produce more income; the stand-alone crisis team did not charge clients for any services. Following the change, I acted as a liaison with the county's Children and Youth agency, consulting on cases where children were being reintegrated into their homes after being removed because of abuse. We helped parents develop and use more appropriate parenting skills, including discipline and time management. We taught them to understand how children develop and we connected them with other community resources.

During that time I also started to establish some liaisons with local schools. I was the contact person for school-age children in need of mental health services, something that had not previously been addressed. Members of the crisis team also offered preventive programs to some districts. I remember offering a program entitled *Who am I?* to senior high school students. Our aim was to help them look at the different roles they play, determine their areas of interest and skills, and encourage them to find some kind of direction for themselves. I wanted to work with school-age children. I initially got my master's degree in school counseling because of my desire to be a counselor in the schools. After all, the majority of children go through the public school system. The school district was a place to see children who were developing normally, as well as those who had some problems.

When I had the opportunity to go to the Intermediate Unit (IU) as a school psychiatric social worker in the Carbon County area, I went for several years. The area might be considered disadvantaged because some of the families had significant financial need. In Carbon County I dressed casually and was low-key. After all, I was asking people to let me come into their homes. Some homes had wallpaper made out of newspaper or no plumbing. I accepted children and families as they were and provided whatever assistance and referrals they needed. I worked closely with the schools and special education services.

I decided to obtain additional academic training and certification to work more effectively in the schools. While on maternity leave from the IU, I moved up to Penn State with my 6-month-old son to enroll in a doctoral program in School Psychology. I studied before my son woke up and after he went to sleep at night. We did not have much of a social life. I was able to make it in the program with support from my husband, family, and a few really close friends who actually lived in State College. After completing the residency portion of the program, I rejoined my husband in the Lehigh Valley area to finish an internship at the Intermediate Unit and begin work on my dissertation. I subsequently left the IU to work with school districts in the dual role of school counselor/ psychologist for the next fifteen years.

My first full-time position in the dual role of school counselor/psychologist was with a suburban middle school. When I arrived, the school was not actually following middle school philosophy, although it was called a middle school. Over a ten-year period, I was fortunate to be part of the evolutionary process to transform the school into a model middle school. The team concept evolved. At times, it was difficult for staff to accept children who were a little bit different, didn't have as much money, or needed help to survive in school academically or because of personal concerns. Students had problems ranging from suicidal ideation, to the kid next door *looked at me funny,* to the kid next door *sexually abused me.*

My main job was coordination of services, assuring availability of small group and individual counseling services, and consulting regarding both individual students and curriculum. I worked with the health teacher to revamp the curriculum to address the developmental needs of middle level students. It was a mental health curriculum to meet the needs of the entire student population, not just individual students at risk. I believe the role of the school counselor is to advocate for all children, not just those children deemed at risk. I believe all children are at risk—it is just a matter of degree.

One of the more difficult things to deal with is the death of a staff member or child. I was part of the response team to such crises. Fortunately, I had materials, scripts, and a coordinated plan ready to implement and felt we offered a smooth transition to support. Every school must have a crisis response plan that addresses public relations, coordination of support services, available school resources, what exactly to tell students, what exactly to tell parents, and so on.

I subsequently took employment at another school with a more diverse population, supposedly to offer me more challenge. I got to work with a greater age range of students and assisted in the coordination of services for kindergarten to grade 12. I was then afforded the opportunity to teach at the university level on a full-time basis, thanks to the variety of opportunities and experiences that I had in education and agency settings.

Probably the thing I find most challenging at the university is trying to find a way to balance all the expectations and responsibilities placed upon me. I am going into my fifth year at the university. Many people may have the perception that being a university professor is a relatively easy job, but I found that is not true at all. It can be overwhelming because I am not only expected to be an excellent teacher, but also to stay current in the field; publish; research; provide consultation; serve on committees in the department, university, and the community; supervise interns; and on and on. Probably the biggest challenge is to balance all those responsibilities and do a decent job at all of them. I try to make time for a two- to three-mile walk through the farm fields each morning, or do some other quiet activity, in order to preserve my own mental health. It gives me time to both reflect and organize my thoughts for the day.

I think what is most important to me is to try to provide my students with what they need—the skills and background to be good counselors. Teaching means finding ways to objectify what makes a good counselor, so I can evaluate students' skills and abilities and help them to fill the voids. The research has found that the most important variable in determining the effectiveness of counseling is the client–counselor relationship. I try to emphasize that for students. Maybe it also turns out that the most important relationship in graduate school is that of student to professor and, through that relationship, you generate or encourage the development of appropriate skills and knowledge.

The other challenge for me is to keep growing as a counselor, because I think that will help me be a more effective teacher and consultant. I am hoping I will be able to do some counseling at the college counseling center so that I can continue to refine my skills and do some research on the solution-focused model. I worked for a year at the university's counseling center when I was on maternity leave from the school district. I enjoyed the university setting that afforded the opportunity to work with students with both personal and academic concerns.

The university students reminded me of middle school students in that they were in a transition period of their lives. I believe that my interest in the solution-focused model originates with my training in brief therapeutic crisis intervention. The solution-focused theory stresses the importance and discussion of nonproblem data when solving a problem. The theory also emphasizes nonpathology rather than pathology or mental health rather then mental illness.

The solution-focused model promotes finding solutions that are generated by exploring client/student strengths and competencies, as opposed to solving problems by identifying limitations or analyzing the problem. The past is explored merely to recall a time when the problem presented did not exist. These times of exception to problem behavior indicate resources used to create and maintain the exceptions. The goal is to identify, rename, or possibly reframe behaviors and beliefs as strengths that will facilitate a move to solutions. The counselor must concentrate on the client-counselor relationship rather than technique. Any techniques/interventions used are generated from client preferences for treatment or treatment style. The model assumes that:

- Nonjudgmental focus and positive expectation exist.
- Unique, individualized solutions evolve through conversation.
- Exceptions lead to solutions and support.
- People are resourceful and resilient.
- Change occurs all the time.
- Small change leads to larger changes.

These guiding concepts impact on the counseling process by defining it as collaborative, strength-focused, and goal-directed. The process is more time efficient and productive.

In my teaching, the greatest reward is to feel that I have imparted some knowledge and that the students have gained something from me, as well as my gaining knowledge from them. I love when superintendents call looking for me to recommend one of our students to be a school counselor for the school district. It is wonderful when students come back to me and say they thought I was a good teacher and that they learned from me. And it's great when previous students or clients for whom I was a counselor let me know that they remember something special I did with them.

Deborah Barlieb, PhD is an Assistant Professor for the Department of Counseling and Human Services at Kutztown University of Pennsylvania. She received her Doctor of Philosophy degree from Pennsylvania State University in 1985. Her dissertation topic was communication skills training with a nonclinical population of sixth graders. She received a Master's of Education from University of Virginia in Secondary School Counseling in 1974. She holds national certification as a counselor and school psychologist, as well as state certification in the areas of secondary school counseling, school psychology, pupil personnel supervision, and home/school visitor. She has at least twenty-five years field experience in educational and agency settings as a mental health counselor, school counselor/psychologist, and teacher/professor.

SUGGESTED READINGS

Bonnington, S. B. (1993). Solution focused brief therapy: Helpful interventions for school counselors. *School Counselor, 41* (2), 126–128.

Matthews, W. J. (1999). Brief therapy: A problem solving model of change. *The Counselor,* 29–32.

Metcalf, L. (1995). *Counseling towards solutions.* West Nyack, NY: The Center for Applied Research in Education.

Peller, J. E., & Walter, J. L. (1992). *Becoming solution focused in brief therapy.* New York: Brunner/Mazel Publishers.

The works cited all refer to solution-focused counseling. The article by Bonnington and book by Metcalf specifically look at the application of this model within the school setting. The other sources look at this model, offering some basic descriptive information and material on its applicability/use within the field of counseling.

MY PRIVILEGED AND FULFILLING LIFE AS A COUNSELOR EDUCATOR

MARK S. KISELICA

I often reflect upon the fact that I live a very privileged and fulfilling life. I am Associate Professor and Chairperson of the Department of Counselor Education at The College of New Jersey (TCNJ), as well as a licensed professional counselor and licensed psychologist. This chapter is an account of December 7, 1999, a typical day in my professional life, and of how I attained my current positions as an academician, teaching graduate students, and as a practitioner, providing counseling services through my work in private practice.

I live in beautiful Bucks County, Pennsylvania, in a historic town located just a few miles away from the spot where George Washington and his troops crossed the Delaware River on Christmas to defeat the Hessians at the famous Battle of Trenton during the Revolutionary War. Today, like most days, as I drive across the Delaware in route to TCNJ, which is located in Ewing, New Jersey, I gaze northward and southward and notice the scenic forests that line the shores of the Delaware. I think about how fortunate I am to live in such a beautiful area and to travel across the Delaware each day to and from a job I enjoy very much. More importantly, I say a prayer of thanks for the blessing of beginning and ending each day in the comfort of my home with my wife, Sandi, and our two precious sons, Andrew, 12, and Christian, 8. Thinking about my family, my home, and my job is just one of the many pleasures that I will experience today.

My mind is filled with these thoughts of gratitude as my car approaches the college. TCNJ has a beautiful campus, adorned with two small lakes, numerous tall oak and maple trees, and many reddish brick buildings designed in Georgian architectural style. The centerpiece of our college is Green Hall, which is noted for its prominent white clock tower, the tallest and most visible landmark on campus. As I make the turn onto the campus and drive along its main road, I gaze across one of the lakes at the white gazebo located on the western shoreline. Then, I glance eastward across Quimby's Prairie, the great lawn in front of Green Hall, where a flock of geese is nibbling on the frost-encrusted grass. Today, the surface of the lake is like a sheet of glass and, at this early hour in the day, the campus is quiet and peaceful. Walking from my car to my office in Forcina Hall, I take deep breaths of the cold, crisp air and try to absorb the serenity of the campus before the hustle and bustle of the day begins.

By the time I arrive at my office on the third floor of Forcina, it is about 8:20 A.M. I unlock the door to my office, flip on the lights, hang up my coat, and turn on my computer. After placing my lunch in the department's refrigerator in the room next door to my office, I sit in front of my desk and organize my thoughts for the day, which is going to be a busy one. In ten minutes, three outstanding graduate students—Theresa Bonnano, Shannon O'Brien, and Kim Onichowsky—will arrive for supervision of their work as teaching assistants in my Introduction to Counseling class, which runs from 9:30 until noon. I will hold office hours for my students from noon to 1 P.M. From 1 P.M. to 2 P.M., I will conduct individual supervision with a practicum student. From 2 P.M. to 5 P.M., I will attend to a variety of duties associated with my work as chairperson of the department, researcher and scholar, and volunteer.

Afterwards, I will head home, eat a quick dinner and then drive my boys to a karate class conducted at our local health club. I will jog for a bit on the treadmill and do some weightlifting while the boys learn the techniques of Shotokan karate. After returning the boys home, we will share a snack together, I will read books to each of them, tuck them into their beds, kiss them on their foreheads and bid them *sweet dreams* for the night. While Sandi stays home with the boys, I will drive two miles away to my private practice, where I will meet a client from 9 until 10 P.M. and try to help him sort out some relationship difficulties he has experienced in his life. Once back home, I will relax and talk with Sandi about our respective days, watch a little TV, and fall to sleep between 11 and 11:30 P.M., ending my day in the comfort of my home with my precious family.

As you can see, I have a pretty hectic schedule filled with my responsibilities as a husband, father, counselor educator, and counselor. I must confess that I am usually pretty worn out by the time Fridays roll around, and my responsibilities as a family man and professional don't end once the weekend arrives. But I do manage to slow down a bit during the weekends, which permits me to recharge my batteries sufficiently enough that I can face the demands of the week to come. These demands are quite similar to those that I have just described, although they vary slightly according to the day or season of the year.

What are these variations? Perhaps I can best answer this question by explaining more fully what I do as a counselor educator, counselor, and family man. Although these could be construed as separate spheres of my life, they overlap and connect in ways that give my life much meaning and personal satisfaction.

I feel very privileged to be an academician, especially a counselor educator. This feeling stems from the fact that I train graduate students who are interested in careers as counselors. On the whole, people seeking careers in counseling are compassionate individuals who care deeply about the well-being of others. Since our master's degree programs in school and community counseling are accredited by the Council for the Accreditation of Counseling and Related Educational Programs (CACREP), and since TCNJ is recognized as one of the finest schools in the country, we tend to attract to our counseling programs students who are not only compassionate but are also highly talented and committed to their studies. As a counselor educator, I am in the enviable position of training these well-rounded individuals.

My greatest pleasure as a counselor educator is working with our students at TCNJ. Although I have taught a variety of classes throughout my career—including courses in counseling theory, psychological testing, school counseling, statistics and research, practicum, and internship—I currently am responsible for teaching sections of the Introduction to Counseling course at TCNJ. This course has several purposes: to orient the students to the counseling profession, to teach the students how to write a term paper in counseling according to the conventions of the *Publication Manual of the American Psychological Association* (American Psychological Association, 1994), and to teach the students the micro skills of counseling (e.g., open-ended questions, reflections of feelings, etc.).

I consider it a privilege and responsibility to teach the Introduction to Counseling course. It is a privilege because I get to teach such fine people and to share in their educational experience. It is an important responsibility because the information I provide is likely to affect how my students view the profession. So, I consider it a duty to keep abreast of current trends in counseling and to convey this information to my students so that they have an up-to-date and accurate sense of the profession. I also have a duty to be a skilled clinician myself so that I can teach counseling skills to my students competently.

In order to fulfill these responsibilities, I engage in many activities that inform me about the profession and refine my skills as a counselor. I am a member of numerous professional organizations: the American Counseling Association, the Association for Multicultural Counseling and Development, the American School Counselor Association, the American Mental Health Counselors Association, the Association for Counselor Education and Supervision, Counselors for Social Justice, and the American Psychological Association. As a member of these organizations, I receive numerous newsletters and journals in counseling and psychology, most of which I read on a regular basis to keep myself informed about what's happening in the field. I also attend many state and national conferences in counseling and psychology, where I make presentations on subjects that are of interest to me, observe presentations by other professionals, and participate in meetings associated with committees and journals in counseling. As a result of these activities, I am usually aware of the hottest developments in the field and learn new skills to facilitate my work as an educator and a counselor. I make it a point to infuse this knowledge into my class lectures, my supervision of students, and my work as a practitioner.

In addition to learning about what others are doing in the field, I have tried to help shape and define the direction of the profession through a variety of professional activities. I am an active scholar and conduct research on a wide variety of topics, particularly the subjects of teenage pregnancy (most especially teen fathers, who have been greatly overlooked by society), counseling boys and men, and the process of confronting prejudice. As of this writing, I have completed forty-nine presentations at professional conferences and thirty-five *juried publications* (including three books, several book chapters, and numerous articles) on these and other subjects. Juried publications are manuscripts that are subjected to review by other professionals in the field before the manuscripts can be accepted for publication. By publishing juried publications, I contribute to the knowledge base of the profession. Doing so is very gratifying! I still get excited when I see my work published and I am especially proud of my three books: *Multicultural Counseling with Teenage Fathers* (Kiselica, 1995), *Confronting Prejudice and Racism during Multicultural Training* (Kiselica, 1999a), and *Handbook of Counseling Boys and Adolescent Males* (Horne & Kiselica, 1999).

Another way I try to contribute to and influence the profession is through several service and leadership roles. For example, I have served on the editorial boards of the following journals: *Journal of Counseling and Development, Journal of Mental Health Counseling, The School Counselor, Professional School Counseling,* and *Psychology of Men and Masculinity.* As an editorial board member, I read and critique manuscripts that have been submitted for publication. Through this work, I help to assure that manuscripts published by these journals meet high standards of scholarship, research methodology, and composition.

I also have held several leadership roles in professional organizations that have an interest in helping children and adolescents. For example, in 1992 I started the American School Counselor Association Professional Interest Network on Teenage Parents and served as its coordinator from 1992 through 1998. In this position, I wrote numerous columns on counseling teenage mothers and fathers for *The ASCA Counselor,* the national newsletter of the American School Counselor Association, and served as a resource on adolescent parenthood for school counselors in the United States.

One final example of leadership—in 1999 I served as president of the Society for the Psychological Study of Men and Masculinity: Division 51 of the American Psychological Association. As president, I wrote quarterly columns focused on psychotherapeutic work with boys and men for *SPSMM Bulletin,* the newsletter of the division; helped to organize the division's national convention program pertaining to the psychology of boys, men, and masculinity; and I gave an invited presidential address at the 1999 Annual Convention of the American Psychological Association (APA), which was held in Boston, Massachusetts.

I would like to say a few things about my presidential address (Kiselica, 1999, August) at APA because doing so illustrates a point I had made earlier: that my professional work and personal life are linked in important and meaningful ways. My presidential address was entitled *On Being a Son, a Parent, and a Mentor of Teen Fathers.* Through this talk I described how much of my life is centered on fatherhood, the gist of which I will reiterate here. I am the son of a truly heroic man, Otto Kiselica, who overcame poverty and numerous hardships to become the most loving father any son could ever ask for. My father has been a tremendous influence on me throughout my life and I am certain that my research and counseling with teen fathers and troubled boys and men stems from my love for my father and his love for me. My father has also influenced who I am as a parent. I begin and end each day with the most precious of all experiences I could have in life: being a father to my dear sons, Andrew and Christian. Often when I relate to my sons, I am guided by the example my father set for me. So, my personal life and my professional life are greatly intertwined around issues pertaining to fatherhood. How fortunate I am!

It is very common for me to express these positive feelings in my work as a counselor educator. I am always excited whenever I enter the classroom, and I tend to be very passionate, animated, and enthused as I lecture and facilitate classroom discussions. I consider my students, my administrative support staff—Gloria Valeri and Debbie Caroselli—and my faculty colleagues in the Department of Counselor Education—Charleen Alderfer, Marion Cavallaro, Bill Fassbender, Mary Lou Ramsey, Roland Worthington, and Mark Wood Ford—to be a part of my extended family. I enjoy sharing lunch with my students and co-workers, talking about our personal lives, discussing the goings-on in the Department, and exploring topics related to our profession. I like it when current and former students stop by my office to say hi or visit me and my family in my home. I enjoy everyone's company so much that I host an annual potluck dinner in my home for our entire department. Typically, over sixty people participate in this event, which adds to the fellowship that defines our department. My co-workers and I also celebrate the Christmas and Hanukkah season with a special holiday party where we enjoy a meal together, exchange gifts, sing holiday songs, and perform little skits through which we roast each other.

These cheerful events make the more difficult aspects of my work more tolerable, and believe me, there are some very tricky challenges to deal with in my work as an academician and counselor. For example, it's tough adjusting to the many variations in my schedule. Although I am able to work a fairly predictable 9 to 5 schedule during the summer months, my schedule is really crazy during the fall and spring semesters, which are referred to in higher educational circles as *the academic year*. Some days during the academic year are like the one I described earlier—filled with work at TCNJ during the daytime and family and private practice responsibilities at night. Usually, my schedule is slightly different one or two days per week: I rush home from work in order to pick up my sons from school, help them with their homework, cook dinner, clean the table and dishes with their assistance, wrestle and play with them (What fun!), and end the day by reading with them at bedtime. On other days, I may spend the entire day on campus attending meetings, teach a three-hour evening class and not arrive home until after 11:30 P.M. I surely don't relish this odd and tiring schedule! I must confess that I don't look forward to many of the administrative and committee meetings I am obliged to attend as a function of my roles as a faculty member and chairperson. Also, it takes a great deal of patience, persistence, and dedication to grade a huge stack of term papers at the end of the semester, especially considering that I am committed to giving each student extensive feedback regarding the strengths and shortcomings of the papers.

In addition to these mundane tasks, I often have to respond to a variety of crises that can occur unexpectedly at any time. Some students might need special administrative permission to enroll in courses that have already reached their enrollment capacity. Other students might be seeking my advice about some personal dilemma and its ramifications for their continued study in a particular course or graduate program. Conflicts arise between individuals that require me to serve as a mediator. New college policies might require immediate action by me as chair. Political tensions might erupt between my department and other departments on campus. I recognize that responding to these types of crises is a part of my job and I give them my complete attention and energy until they are resolved. This activity usually leaves me feeling satisfied, though emotionally and physically drained. So, I am grateful that other aspects of my work are more enjoyable and less taxing on me and that I am blessed with a family whose affection and understanding soothe me when I have had a bad day.

Because I have been blessed in so many ways—a wonderful family, good colleagues and students to work with, a job I enjoy a great deal, a comfortable living—I try to give back to my community in many ways. For example, I participate as a volunteer in several organizations dedicated to promoting peace and tolerance while combating prejudice and racism. I provide pro bono services to numerous organizations whose mission is to prevent adolescent pregnancy and to assist teen parents with the transition to parenthood. I counsel numerous clients free or for greatly reduced fees. I volunteer at my sons' school and at my church. I coach my sons and many of their peers in soccer and basketball.

I am glad that I have achieved such a wonderful lifestyle at the age of 42. It has not always been this way. As a young boy, my family didn't have much money. My parents, especially my dear mother, Winnie Kiselica, explained to me at an early age that none of my ancestors had ever been able to afford going to college and that this lack of education had hurt our family financially for many generations. Just to make ends meet, both of my parents worked outside of the home, and my father often worked two jobs. They urged us to get a good education so that we would not have to struggle economically as they and their parents had. My parents were determined that I and my two brothers and two sisters should go to college. They told us that they would do everything they could to help us acquire a higher education but that their finances were limited. So, they expected us children to work hard in school and to find ways to support our family financially. They knew it wouldn't be easy for any of us, but my parents also had faith that we could all succeed with this dream if we pulled together.

So, I began studying dutifully at a very early age, inspired by the vision that I would obtain an advanced education that would afford me the opportunities my ancestors could only dream of. I also worked numerous jobs during my late childhood and adolescence to help my parents with my living and educational expenses. At ages 12 through 14, I had numerous odd jobs, such as cutting lawns, raking leaves, and shoveling snow. At age 14, when I was old enough to be formally employed, I worked as a gas station attendant pumping gas and as a librarian's assistant shelving books after school and on weekends. I continued to work these jobs throughout my high school years and also worked as an assistant janitor toward the end of my high school days. I studied diligently throughout grade school and high school so that I could earn a scholarship to college. In 1975 I was awarded that scholarship I had worked so hard to attain: a full, four-year academic/ leadership scholarship to Saint Vincent College, where I earned my bachelor's degree in psychology.

Throughout my college years I studied day and night, was employed in many on-campus jobs, and labored in several different factories during the summer months to help pay for my room and board and living expenses at college. After completing college, I was employed for two years as a mental health worker on an in-patient, adolescent unit in a private psychiatric hospital where I gained valuable experience working with emotionally disturbed teenagers. I often worked sixteen-hour shifts during that two-year period so that I could save as much money as possible for graduate school. From 1981 to 1987, I attended graduate school, first at Bucknell University, where I earned a master's degree in psychology, and then at The Pennsylvania State University, where I completed my doctorate in counseling psychology. Throughout those seven years, I was always exhausted from the demands of full-time graduate study and employment in numerous counseling and noncounseling jobs that paid me just enough money to meet my educational and living expenses.

All of those years of studying on a daily basis, working in all kinds of settings, and living on a shoestring budget were definitely worth it. By the time I was awarded my doctorate in 1987, I was qualified to seek full-time employment as a counselor, psychologist, or academician. After working a few years as a clinician at the University of Medicine and Dentistry of New Jersey and then at the New Jersey Department of Corrections, I realized that I would be most fulfilled working as a counselor educator. So, in 1990 I accepted a position as an assistant professor in the Department of Counseling Psychology and Guidance Services at Ball State University, where I eventually became director of the master's programs in counseling and earned a license as a psychologist in Indiana. Desiring to move closer to my native state of New Jersey, in 1994 I accepted a position at TCNJ, where I have been employed ever since. After moving back to the east coast, I have become a licensed professional counselor in New Jersey and a licensed psychologist in Pennsylvania, credentials that have enabled me to work in a small private practice where I counsel my own clients and supervise the work of other practitioners.

Whenever I think about the fact that I am an academician and a licensed counselor and psychologist, I am filled with a profound sense of gratitude to my mother and father for instilling in me an appreciation for education and hard work and for making many sacrifices to help me achieve the lifestyle that I now enjoy. They are my heroes and I am pleased to know that I have made them feel proud of me.

I hope that this account of what I do and how I got to where I am in life is helpful to students contemplating a career as a counselor educator. Although it takes many years of sacrifice and hard work to earn the credentials required for employment as a counselor educator, I can think of no other career that is as satisfying or rewarding as mine is. I live a stimulating life, work with wonderful people, contribute to the well-being of others, and find fulfillment and meaning in what I do. Although I could certainly earn more money in a different career, I know that I have found the life that is right for me and my family. What more could a man want?

Mark S. Kiselica, Ph.D, NCC, LPC is Associate Professor and Chairperson of the Department of Counselor Education at The College of New Jersey. He has conducted fifty juried convention presentations and is the author or editor of forty juried publications, including *Multicultural Counseling with Teenage Fathers: A Practical Guide* (Sage Publications, 1995), *Confronting Prejudice and Racism during Multicultural Training* (American Counseling Association, 1999), and *Handbook of Counseling Boys and Adolescent Males: A Practitioner's Guide* (Sage Publications, 1999). He is a former consulting scholar to the Clinton Administration's Federal Fatherhood Initiative and the immediate past president of the Society for the Psychological Study of Men and Masculinity: Division 51, American Psychological Association. Dr. Kiselica was named Counselor Educator of the Year (1996–1997) by the American Mental Health Counselors Association and was the recipient of the Publication in Counselor Education and Supervision Award for 1999–2000.

SUGGESTED READINGS

American Psychological Association. (1994). *Publication manual of the American Psychological Association* (4th ed.). Washington, DC: Author.
>   This book contains the writing conventions of the American Psychological Association and is used by counselors, psychologists, educators, and other professionals writing professional manuscripts. Perusing this book will provide readers with a sense for how counselors prepare papers for publication.

Horne, A. M., & Kiselica, M. S. (Eds.). (1999). *Handbook of counseling boys and adolescent males: A practitioner's guide.* Thousand Oaks, CA: Sage.
>   This book is the most comprehensive volume on counseling boys that has ever been published. It consists of twenty chapters that were written by thirty-three mental health professionals from the United States and New Zealand who are authorities on understanding and helping boys. It provides the reader with practical suggestions for addressing the developmental, socialization, and clinical issues of boys.

Kiselica, M. S. (1995). *Multicultural counseling with teenage fathers: A practical guide.* Thousand Oaks, CA: Sage.
>   In this book, I explain how teenage fathers have been misunderstood and neglected by society. I also examine teenage fatherhood from various cultural perspectives. Readers of this book will get a flavor for one of my lines of scholarly inquiry and the development of my thinking about teen fathers through my work as a practitioner, scholar, and social activist.

Kiselica, M. S. (Ed.). (1999). *Confronting prejudice and racism during multicultural training.* Alexandria, VA: American Counseling Association.
>   Consisting of twelve chapters written by numerous authorities on multicultural training, this book attempts to provide the reader with an understanding of the complex

challenge of helping counseling students to confront their cultural biases while developing an appreciation for diversity.

Kiselica, M. S. (1999, August). Division 51 Presidential Address: *On being a son, a parent, and a mentor of teen fathers.* Symposium conducted at the Annual Convention of the American Psychological Association, Boston, MA.

In 1999 I served as the president of the Society for the Psychological Study of Men and Masculinity, which is Division 51 of the American Psychological Association. One of the privileges of being president is that I had the honor of giving an invited presidential address at the Annual Convention of the American Psychological Association, which was held in Boston in 1999. In my address, I explained how my life is centered on fatherhood through the influence of my own wonderful father, my role as a parent of two precious sons, and my work as a counselor and advocate for teen fathers, and I suggested an agenda for how the mental health professions can better serve boys and men.

TO BE OR NOT TO BE: A MULTICULTURAL COUNSELOR EDUCATOR'S PERSPECTIVE

ROGER D. HERRING

I am a still-evolving individual, the product of diverse influences, including a small degree of megalomania. In order to understand who I am becoming involves a long history with numerous career and personal twists. My story begins with my birth during the last days of World War II. For the purposes of consistency and coherence, my story will be divided into chapters. A concluding section of each chapter will address some potential implications for graduate students in counselor education, or other areas for that matter.

CHAPTER ONE: SURVIVAL (BIRTH TO AGE 16)

My life consisted of turbulent experiences from birth to 16. I was reared in southeastern North Carolina, as the second child of a Native American Indian mother (who rejected her heritage) and a very authoritarian European American father. Four school systems existed in that area: one for Blacks, one for Whites, one for Native American Indians, and one for those who could not identify their ethnicity due to interbreeding. My mother insisted that I attend the White schools to protect me from being labeled a half-breed. My parents were tenant farmers who decided to work in the textile mills in order to obtain a more steady income. The entire family continued to help out selected farmers to earn extra income (e.g., picking cotton and cropping tobacco).

I finished high school due largely to the persistent encouragement of my mother. She realized that education was essential if I were to escape the low socioeconomic status (SES) and misery of textile mill and farm work. However, on the negative side, I spent my adolescence being treated as a little adult and being compared to my sibling's excellent academic accomplishments. Also, I never could attend extracurricular events because I had job responsibilities after school hours, beginning at age 10. Yet, I managed to survive the obstacles and challenges of growing up and staying in school. In fact, I graduated before my seventeenth birthday.

Implications: The experiential base of the formative years of individuals will drive many, if not all, of their later life and career decisions. Counselor educators would serve their students well if the professionals stress how to use early experiences in positive and beneficial ways. Being a victim of varying degrees of oppression and discrimination will often serve as valuable learning experiences. Graduate students from such backgrounds have a wealth of experiences from which to draw and to renew their life and career goals.

CHAPTER TWO: BEATING THE ODDS (AGES 17 TO 21)

For a child of textile mill workers living across the tracks to graduate from high school was indeed an accomplishment. For this child to be accepted to college was even more incredulous. Both accomplishments certainly represented beating the odds. This chapter included my matriculation at a nearby college that had been created for the Native American Indian students of the area. Again, I probably overachieved and completed my undergraduate education within three years. Incidentally, during this chapter, my parents finally managed to build a house with indoor plumbing. This event increased my self-esteem and ego tremendously.

After graduating, I was offered a teaching position at the high school that had served as my student teaching site. This opportunity softened my transition from school to work. This particular high school served predominately Native American Indian students. Being trained to become a social studies teacher, my first year's teaching assignments were challenging: one world cultures class, two English 10 classes, one basic math class, and one study hall. Welcome to the real world, I thought. Nevertheless, I endured that first year to the degree that I decided I needed a master's degree to increase my salary. I applied and was accepted into graduate school. This acceptance represented several benchmarks. Not only was I the first in both parents' families to attend college, the first to attend graduate school, but this would also be the first time I had spent overnight away from my family.

During this chapter of my life, I also began to think very carefully about my Native American Indian heritage. I would ask questions but rarely received any useful information. I had been passing as White throughout these experiences. I began a quiet process to learn more about my heritage and eventually self-identified as Native American Indian.

Implications: Graduate students need to become aware of who they are ethnically. Historical antecedents may cast doubts on one's ethnic identity. Multiple or ambiguous ethnic ancestries may result in students' self-denial or even self-hatred of their ethnic heritage. Simply stated, one can never help others until one accepts self. Individuals who have attained graduate student status certainly need to be confident of who they are prior to working with other individuals who are confused regarding their ethnic identity.

CHAPTER THREE: SUCCESS—I THOUGHT (AGES 21 TO 30)

Chapter Three represents a perception of being a success. I had overcome many hurdles and had witnessed some positive experiences as a classroom teacher. I had my master's and thought that I enjoyed my career choice. Of course, teachers' salaries in the 1960s and 1970s were not what they are today. Most teachers could not survive financially without having summer jobs to supplement their incomes. I acquired many vocational experiences during those summer months when I was not in graduate school.

I worked as a corn detassling crew chief, a service station manager, a clothing store clerk, a stockperson in a pillow factory, a produce stand manager, and in sundry other jobs. Nevertheless, I began to rethink my perceptions of being a success. These thoughts began to have their effect on my long-term goals and short-term satisfactions.

This chapter of my life witnessed the forced integration of schools and faculties. Each day brought a new series of difficulties. During the midst of this transition, I was assigned to halftime as the school counselor at the junior high school. I recall one day in particular. That day was spent erasing or removing any negative comments that had been placed in students' cumulative records. Also, this frustrating assignment was frequently interrupted by physical confrontations between ethnically dissimilar students in the hallways.

Implications: The lesson of this chapter for graduate students is to not be afraid or reluctant to acquire diverse work experiences. One of the best reasons that I know to teach CNSL 7203: Orientation to Industries or similar courses is to observe graduate students' vicariously experiencing different work settings and career options. In this same vein, job shadowing has proven to be one of the most popular and rewarding class assignments for many graduate students.

CHAPTER FOUR: DISENCHANTMENT (AGES 31 TO 42)

Chapter Four developed into a period of boredom and redundancy. I was transferred to another school and returned to the classroom full time. Teaching became a monotonous, forced routine, and the change in schools did not improve my attitude. I eventually decided to resign and search for another source of employment. Fortunately, with hindsight, the principal asked me to become the school counselor and see how that would work. I got rejuvenated and decided to obtain certification as a school counselor. In addition, I continued to research my mother's ancestry when time permitted.

The days in the life of a school counselor do not resemble those of a classroom teacher. Each day brings different students with diverse presenting problems. These problems can range from superficial boy/girlfriend disagreements to serious inappropriate acting out behaviors. Some only required minor intervention, whereas others needed referrals to a mental health specialist. The worst day in my school counseling experience involved trying to help a tenth grade male student who was hallucinating about being possessed by Satan. In the midst of the long session, he rose abruptly, dashed into the hall, and rammed his hand through a glass door. Suffice it to tell, he was taken to the hospital for medical and psychiatric treatment.

In 1984, I took a leave of absence and returned to graduate school to further my psychological and mental health knowledge. I concurrently earned another master's (Psychology) and an Ed.S. (Secondary School Counseling). I also reached closure with my heritage and was enrolled in the Lumbee Tribe although my ancestry was Catawba/Cherew. In fact, my graduate education was partly funded by a Native American Indian Fellowship through the Office of Indian Education and Department of Interior.

I returned to my school counseling position with a renewed passion. I thought that I could solve any problem presented by students or faculty. I was wrong and began to have negative interactions with other school counselors. I was trying to impart some of my recent content and process knowledge to them. Things got worse and, once again, I became disenchanted. I was especially perturbed by other school counselors' refusal to adopt new (to them) ethnically appropriate interventions. The multicultural movement was just getting started and I bought into it—hook, line, and sinker. I decided that my best method to make a change in the lives of students would be at the counselor education level, so I enrolled in a doctoral program.

The proverbial straw that broke the camel's back occurred during the in-service days before the students came. The school system's central office staff decided to offer an in-service workshop on learning style differences. By this time, I was commuting 200 miles twice a week to take doctoral courses, which probably influenced my attitude. I had already been exposed to this topic and had given learning style inventories to faculties at several different schools, not to mention numerous students at my school. I did not think that I needed this workshop and could better use my time remaining at school and preparing for school opening events.

Alas, the telephone rang and the principal informed me that every faculty member must attend the workshop and to get there post haste. I was highly irritated by this form of coercion. However, I went and nonchalantly went through the motions. I contacted my doctoral advisor and mentor that night and explained my distress. He understood my reactions and informed me that he could arrange a graduate assistantship if I decided to become a full-time student. I discussed my discomfort with my principal the next morning. He understood my thinking, but could not overrule the superintendent regarding workshop attendance. The events of that day remain very fresh in my memory. I resigned effective at the end of the month and became a full-time student.

Implications: Graduate students will have days with failures. Many may begin to reflect on their expectations in counseling. Counselor educators, on the other hand, can alleviate most of these doubts through such activities as mentoring and personal reflection. Over 200 Native American Indian tribal languages still exist in the United States. The term *mental health* or *mental illness* is not found in any of them. Most Native American Indian nations and tribes interpret mental health as being in or out of balance with nature and self. Graduate students need to realize that they are not going to save every student; regrettably, some will be lost. But, we must continue to try. Moments and periods of imbalance will occur. Knowing that beforehand can ease the frustrations and disenchanting moments. By recognizing out-of-balance conditions, graduate students can begin to search for what is causing their imbalance.

CHAPTER FIVE: I HAVE ARRIVED (AGE 43 TO PRESENT)

In 1989, I was hired as a counselor educator and began the most fulfilling period of my career path. I became aware of my knack for writing during the process of adapting to higher education's demand for teaching, research, and service contributions. I have been blessed to have had some success in these areas and have received numerous awards at the local, state, regional, and national levels. I have received positive feedback from students and colleagues that I do have something worthwhile to give to the training of school counselors and other helping professionals.

Each day brings telephone calls, e-mails, snail mails, and interpersonal dialogues with students, former students, and colleagues. Some are minor and some are stress-producing. These exchanges frequently are superseded by the demands of service, teaching, and research. In addition, days of a counselor educator are often controlled by such negative events as drive-by shootings, acts of school violence, lifestyle conflicts, student suicide, suicidal ideations, and other acts of personal injury. I think that when all variables are considered and analyzed, any objective individual would conclude that I have arrived.

In my attempt to appropriately train school counselors and other helping professionals, I have endeavored to write ethnically appropriate literature for that training. Over fifty articles can be accessed through various sources. Chapters in over ten edited works are available. Several resources are presented at the end of this discussion for the reader's perusal. If they meet your needs and expectations, use them; if not, offer some suggestions that may enhance these works for the training of school counselors and other helping professionals.

Implications: For many graduate students, the road to success may be long and filled with obstacles. For others, less time will be needed. Graduate students must persevere and prioritize their goals. Addressing obstacles one by one is certainly more advantageous than several at one time. Graduate students also must understand that career goals may change as time passes and one's expectations may also undergo revisions.

CHAPTER SIX: THE FUTURE

I am sure that many counselor educators and other individuals have faced the question *To be or not to be*. I am also confident that most of these professionals made career and educational decisions that resulted in more positive self and career identities. I look forward to whatever the future has to offer to me professionally and personally. To that end, the story of my life will continue to be enriched and to be guided by continual revisits with *To be or not to be*.

Implications: Graduate students will serve themselves well if they seek and find a reliable mentor. I recall several mentors from my graduate student days. They remain approachable today, even though we are now colleagues. One of the best pieces of advice that I received was to get an early start on a research agenda. The first years after graduation will be dominated by learning the ropes of your career choice. Graduate students can achieve this by focusing their research assignment in graduate courses on their intended area of research. Many class assignments can be publishable with appropriate mentoring. For example, my first publication and national presentation was in 1988, one year before I graduated. The excitement of seeing one's name in print can increase one's determination and perseverance during the down moments. I spend many hours mentoring students, both gradu-ate and undergraduate. It is very rewarding to see students improve in their areas of need.

CASE STUDY

The following case study exemplifies the need to incorporate understanding of a client's culture into the counseling process. The Jacobs, a bi-ethnic (Cherokee/English) family who relocated to a large urban area and were practicing Christians, had two children—Judith (17) and Daniel (16). The children were enrolled in a Christian parochial school system with a large Native American Indian population. The family was referred to a local therapist by the school counselor because Daniel was having numerous negative interactions with other students. Daniel was reacting to other students labeling him as a half-breed. After initially feeling that things were going well, the therapist began to sense that the family had become resistant, particularly after Daniel was placed in detention for another episode of fighting. The therapist had instructed the parents to have Daniel remain there so that he could really experience the consequences of his actions. Without notifying the therapist, the family had him released and brought back to the reservation to stay with an aunt and uncle. When the therapist contacted the parents about this, they scheduled an appointment but did not show up. When Daniel returned to school, the family resumed therapy, only to have the same pattern repeat itself.

The Jacobs family had brought their son home to be with an uncle, a person who traditionally plays an important role in a son's upbringing. They also used the services of a medicine man and were involved in the Native American Church. They were reluctant to discuss these involvements with the therapist, feeling she would not understand their decision and would reject their traditional approach, so they tried to avoid her. Instead of presuming the family was rejecting treatment, the therapist began to explore why the family had chosen another path. Gradually, she began to integrate some of their Native health methods into therapy. After two years of experiencing this integrated therapy, Daniel had accepted his Native heritage and had begun training to become a *fancy dancer* in ceremonies and rituals on the reservation.

Roger D. Herring, Ed.D, NCC, NCSC received his BA from Pembroke State College (now the University of North Carolina-Pembroke), two MAs and an Ed.S from Appalachian State University, and his Ed.D from North Carolina State University. He is a Professor of Counselor Education in the Department of Counselor, Adult, and Rehabilitation Education at the University of Arkansas-Little Rock. He has written four texts, one book of poetry, over fifty articles, and over ten chapters in edited texts. He is a member of the American Counseling Association and its divisions of AMCD, ACES, ASGW, AHEAD, and its affiliate Counselors for Social Justice. He is also a member of the regional and state levels of these professional organizations.

SUGGESTED READINGS

Herring, R. D. (1997). *Multicultural counseling in schools: A synergetic approach.* Alexandria, VA: American Counseling Association.
> This text provides direction for working with ethnic minority and ethnic majority students' worldviews and identifies synergetic and developmental interventions that meet their needs. The book discusses the relationship of changing school demographics to socioeconomic and psychoeducational imperatives, the balance between universalism and cultural pluralism within the schools, the resilience of ethnic/cultural student groups, and ethnic and cultural status as stressors on the normal development of youth. Each chapter concludes with experiential activities that inspire ideas on how to ensure a multicultural environment to your school.

Herring, R. D. (1998). *Career counseling in schools: Multicultural and developmental perspectives.* Alexandria, VA: American Counseling Association.
> This handbook presents explicit interventions, assessment techniques, and information services for successful career counseling with diverse school-aged populations. The book addresses the unique career concerns of immigrant students; gay, lesbian, and bisexual students; and students with physical, mental, or medical challenges. Each chapter contains experiential activities that can be adapted to various ages, grades levels, and learning styles.

Herring, R. D. (1999). *Counseling with Native American Indians and Alaska Natives: Strategies for helping professionals* (Multicultural Aspects of Counseling Series 14). Thousand Oaks, CA: Sage Publications.

This book provides practitioners with key cultural information, as well as practical guidance that will enhance their credibility when helping Native clients. It addresses key questions relevant to providing services to this population, including: What are the developmental challenges of Native clients? How can Native clients achieve a mature and healthy sense of themselves in relation to others? What are the specific cultural and ethnic issues on helping Native clients? What are the effective methods for establishing rapport and intervening with diverse Native populations, especially those concerns that were historically ignored by society?

Herring, R. D. (1997). *Counseling diverse ethnic youth: Synergetic strategies and interventions for school counselors.* Fort Worth, TX: Harcourt Brace.

This book is an attempt to bring together, in one volume, new directions for counseling practice with culturally and ethnically diverse school populations in this nation. Theoretical, clinical, and empirical evidence is presented in an attempt to increase the reader's understanding of the complex barriers faced by today's ethnic and cultural minority youth, both in school and society. Content material and counseling strategies are followed by experiential activities, integrating this information in a practical and applicable manner for the school counselor.

26

COUNSELORS ADVOCATING FOR ACADEMIC SUCCESS AND EQUITY IN THE BRONX

STUART F. CHEN-HAYES

Recently, a group of my school and community counseling students started internship class, as usual, with a check-in. The first counselor trainee shared she had successfully stopped a suicidal adolescent who was putting a rope around her neck and threatening to kill herself at her school counseling internship site. The next student stated she had been working during the past week at her school counseling internship site with a school community coping with a multiple murder tragedy that included members of one family murdered in three different locations nearby, one of which was a murdered student who had attended her school. The next student's week as a school counselor intern included counseling and advocating for four students in his school just placed with a neighbor after witnessing a parent murder another person in their home. A fourth student shared she was working with a recent murder involving a family at her school as well.

In seven years of teaching internship, this class was the most challenging I had had in terms of anger, pain, sadness, and shock related to the violence outside school affecting students, families, school counselors, teachers, and administrators inside schools. After sharing strategies for coping and providing violence, trauma, grief, and loss interventions for students, families, teachers, and ourselves, we reflected on what it meant to deal with so much violence and so few resources as Bronx-based professional school, community, and family counselors.

Having spent a year working to transform how school counselor education is taught as a companion institution partnered with the Education Trust's Transforming School Counseling Initiative, we were prepared. However, as an internship class we didn't focus exclusively on the mental health issues related to suicide and homicide and their effects on students and families in each school. Instead, after covering some basics about the aftereffects of trauma, PTSD, and working with teachers, parents, and outside referral sources, we shifted focus to our central mission—ensuring academic success for all students, including those affected by violence in or outside school and the importance of monitoring changes in behavior, grades, and the learning process in the wake of the violence.

Initially, having been trained as a community and family counselor, I resisted this shift of focus toward academic success as most important in school counseling. I changed my mind, however, in seeing the state of disarray that school counseling is in throughout New York City public schools, particularly in the Bronx. School counseling currently has little voice or visibility in the public schools. It is one of several professions under control of various *student support service* administrators at each district level, but few people have time or energy to focus on school counseling when teaching is under political attack from many sides.

In order for school counselors to be seen, heard, and respected as leaders in the schools, we must play a central role in developing academic success. School counseling needs to shift to a primary focus on academic success for all students, particularly students of color and poor and working class students, who traditionally have had little or no access to a comprehensive developmental school counseling program in Bronx public schools. Instead of focusing our limited time and energy on crises, we can instead focus our energy on ensuring that all students receive the academic and preventive resources they need. This includes school counselors' offering information about careers, college choices, high school admissions, study skills; ensuring high expectations and high standards are being utilized by all teachers; and minimizing the time used for noncounseling activities such as discipline and programming. School counselors can continue to deliver career and interpersonal counseling services, but the mission of both is clearly related to academic success and learning.

Yet, many teachers in schools are unaware of school counselors' old roles in schools, let alone that we are changing. I recently addressed the sabbatical teachers in the Bronx and I asked them what they saw as the role of professional school counselors. Their responses? The top three were discipline, crisis intervention, and programming. I was most appreciative of the teachers' honesty, because it indicated the importance of counselor educators', teacher educators', and district administrative staffs' working collaboratively to ensure that pre-service teachers and counselors work together toward academic success, our shared goal.

It is this set of beliefs—that academic success for all students and closing the achievement gap for poor and working class children and youth of color—that is the primary road for school counselors to travel. The fact that it is achievable in collaboration with the few resources that we do have—parents, teachers, and students—helps to keep me motivated in spite of my own lack of resources. This past year, my full-time counselor education colleague went on sabbatical. I was left with one colleague assigned part-time to the counseling program and a group of mostly new adjuncts to support a program of well over 100 graduate students. Lehman, like all New York City public schools at all levels, has yet to recover from ongoing cuts to full-time teaching staffs that have seriously affected the quality of teaching and counseling at all grade levels.

Yet, I kept my own sense of humor and maintained my excitement about the possibilities for true systemic change as I continued to learn and teach the Education

Trust transforming school counseling model to my students and to school counselors in the Bronx. We are the only ones who can change school counselor education, if it is to remain a viable profession. We must shift away from primarily individual, crisis-driven, mental health models toward group and family counseling approaches that are preventive and focus on academic, career, and interpersonal success for all students. As Fred Bemak (2000) has eloquently stated, school counselors must be leaders and collaborative change agents with teachers, parents, and administrators in order to ensure academic success for all students in the school setting.

Through classroom group work and in small groups in specific areas, we need to give all students a set of critical skills—bereavement, antiviolence, conflict resolution, critical thinking, and anti-oppression/social justice skills. This, as Ruth Johnson (1996) has powerfully argued, is in addition to ensuring that all students receive the coursework they need for success prior to college entrance and that all students receive a college preparatory curriculum—ending the role of school counselors as gatekeepers and moving toward counselors as advocates for the academic success of all students.

Students in our school and community counseling program, like many of the K–12 students in the Bronx, are primarily from poor or working class backgrounds and identify primarily as Latina or Latino, Dominican, Puerto Rican, or Caribbean, African, African American or Black, and Afra-Caribbean. Our students in the school and community-counseling program reflect the cultural diversity of Latino and African populations in the Bronx. They are overwhelmingly women, and most are first-generation immigrants who have English as a second language. Some students identify as lesbian, bisexual, gay, and transgendered; some are open and others are not, due to cultural variations. Some students have disabilities. The median age for students in the program is late thirties. Most of the students have at least one child and are working full-time as teachers or in other positions in the community. The spiritual diversity of students is broad and includes Jewish, Protestant, Catholic, indigenous, agnostic, and atheist traditions. While the students and families in the Bronx are quite diverse, I concur with Sonia Nieto's (1999) assessment of the multicultural education movement: that we need to focus our efforts on student learning and academic success for all students. Anything less is window dressing for the students who can least afford it.

BRONX-BASED SCHOOL AND COMMUNITY COUNSELING STUDENT STRENGTHS

After having taught for two years as a counselor educator in the Bronx, the following strengths have emerged from our school and community counseling students and their efforts in New York City public schools:

- Caring.
- Resilience.

- Ability to use humor appropriately, even in situations of extreme oppression and violence.
- Willingness to stay in city schools when salaries in the suburbs are 25 percent higher.
- Commitment to their ethnic/racial communities (If we don't give back, then who will?).
- Fear about how dominant culture institutions' control and dominate poor and working-class children and adolescents of color (NYPD and Board of Education over diagnoses of special education, poor bilingual education).
- Interest in challenging the lack of role models of color in leadership positions—particularly counselors, teachers, and administrators—in Bronx schools and agencies.
- Firm belief in the importance of getting information out about academic success, career options, financial aid, and how to get into and stay in college as essential for every Bronx child, youth, and family from elementary school through high school.
- Equally firm belief that the school counselor's current job description is so amorphous that school counselors are often at the mercy of whatever a building principal tells them to do and that, for real change to occur, counselors, teachers, and administrators alike must learn about the new function of school counselors as agents advocating for academic success for all students.

School counselors are wasted in schools when they are only used for crisis intervention, discipline, and programming. With huge immigrant and English as a second-language populations, lack of access to accurate information about the college search process, financial aid, what courses are needed for success in college, and ensuring high aspirations and expectations are all critical areas for school counselor intervention with students and families at all grade levels.

MY OWN JOURNEY

With eighteen years experience in counseling, and seven years as a counselor educator, I've worked in community agency, private practice, couples and family, sexuality, college, and middle school counseling settings and as a counselor educator in community and school counseling programs. I'm currently co-coordinating the graduate program in counseling at Lehman College of the City University of New York. With my interest in culturally competent work with families, I have shifted from an interest in mental health work to a systemic focus on school counselors as academic success advocates for all students and their families. I am especially indebted to the work of Patricia Martin, Reese House, and the other school counseling programs and school districts who have worked so tirelessly with the Education Trust's Transforming School Counseling Initiative to show how to turn school counseling services into advocacy and equity-based skills especially for students and families of color and poor and working class students and families in rural and urban areas.

I have realized—watching what *mangled* care does to mental health services, agencies, staff, and otherwise—that the future of counseling is probably not in agencies. It is instead in schools, where ironically, counselor education began. My current joy is working with students, staff, counselors, teachers, and families and doing intensive community and family-supportive school counseling that ensures equity and access to information and academic resources for all students. Here in the Bronx, one of the poorest urban school systems in the country, the monetary and other resources are slim. Institutional racism and classism ensure that most students in the Bronx get a poor public education compared to their privileged suburban and private school peers. So, the resources that we do have to work with are (1) the data that we can find in our schools as something we can use to ensure that all teachers and counselors teach to high standards; (2) believing that every child and adolescent can and will learn at high standards; (3) that all students potentially can and will go on to college or other post-secondary education; and (4) that school counselors are central leaders for advocating for change and equity in schools alongside parents, guardians, teachers, and administrators.

This past year, having partnered with the Education Trust's Transforming School Counseling initiative, we have worked collaboratively to change how school counseling is taught and implemented. Our program partnered with the Bronx Educational Alliance's Gear-Up grant to provide academic and career counseling success to 1,600 poor and working-class children and youth of color in seven Bronx middle schools over a five-year longitudinal grant. The program, when we realized that our students lacked liability insurance, asked all students to become student members of either the American Counseling Association or the American School Counselor Association to increase professional visibility, identity, and to ensure liability coverage. We increased the number of hours needed for internship. We created a new group admissions process for prospective students, involving current students and school and community counselors as part of the interviewing process. In conjunction with other Lehman education faculty and Bronx-based school and community counselors, we transformed the curriculum readying for national accreditation from the Council on the Accreditation of Counseling and Related Programs (CACREP).

Best Aspects

The best aspects and joys of the job as a Bronx-based counselor educator are:

- Feeling needed and appreciated by most students and staff (but not everyone is open to change; some have deeply resented the need to change).
- Getting the word out about professional counselors, especially in schools, and about the changing role of school counselors to academic success advocates as well as the role of community counselors as advocates for change in agencies and schools.
- Reconfiguring how school and community counseling is taught in New York City.

- Infusing social justice advocacy and multicultural perspectives and teaching anti-oppression skills.
- Teaching critical thinking and how to challenge institutions and systems that keep students and their families down and out.
- Anti-oppression work with primarily first-generation immigrant and ESL students from the Caribbean, Africa, and Central and South America and how to advocate against individual, cultural, and systemic racism, classism, ableism, heterosexism, and so on.
- Freshening a graduate counseling program to align with CACREP accreditation standards.
- Coordinating school counseling services for a Gear-Up grant in the Bronx with poor and working-class children, youth of color, and a wide variety of counselors in seven Bronx middle schools, one in each Bronx school district.
- Spreading the news that the *g-word* is dead—professional school counselors deliver a variety of services. The old word, *guidance,* is something that all adults do, but it's not a profession—it is instead a dated term for career counseling or developmental school counseling lessons that are provided in classroom settings.
- Teaching counselors and teachers to be culturally competent and comfortable working with families of nondominant economic, ethnic/racial, and other cultural identities.
- Writing on sexuality, gender, and social justice advocacy issues.
- Presenting on counseling-related issues at local, state, and national conferences both alone and with counselor education students and colleagues in school and community counseling.

Frustrations

My frustrations as a Bronx counselor educator this past year include:

- Lack of resources throughout the public school system for elementary, middle, high schools, and colleges and universities in New York City.
- Climate of institutional and family violence targeting especially poor and working-class persons of color in NYC.
- Not enough time.
- Not enough full-time faculty to cover the graduate counseling program.
- Little done to promote professional school and community counseling in the Bronx.
- Multiple educational bureaucracies.
- Turf wars.
- Outside interference in this current political climate from the mayor and other politicians bent on unhelpful reforms to education.
- Chronic understaffing and underfunding for counselor education and school and community counseling programs.
- Lack of recognition/appreciation for school and community counselors.

Risks?

The Bronx is one of the poorest counties in the country. Yet, I feel quite safe there. I recognize that because of White privilege and my own anti-racism work, as a White person I am safer in neighborhoods of color than most people of color are. Property crime is an issue for all of us, and the levels of police brutality, criminalization of poor people of color, violent reactions to oppression, and lack of resources in schools and agencies are major risks for all members of our community.

Specialized skills that counselors and counselor educators in the Bronx need to hone and practice include advocacy, equity, social justice, multicultural skills; organizational change and leadership skills; public relations; and learning how to collect data to work in partnership with teachers, families, and administrators to ensure academic success for all children and youth. If people don't believe that all children and youth of color who are poor and working class can and will learn to higher standards, then they need to find work outside of the Bronx.

Because the Bronx community is so poor, we rely heavily on our practicum and internship students to staff our schools and agencies with competent school and community counseling students who know how to act as advocates for change and support and members of the community. Staff turnover and reluctance to change have been issues in many Bronx schools and agencies and our students learn firsthand about how to intervene in situations with few resources.

How I have survived and how I suggest my students and colleagues survive and thrive include having a network of friends; maintaining a commitment to social justice work; keeping in contact with professional colleagues locally and around the country; and having a loving partner, family of origin, and family of choice. I also enjoy gardening, travel, working out, the arts, and meditation. I'm always looking for something fun or humorous in the midst of chaos and learning to let go of what won't change overnight.

Being a counselor educator in the Bronx is without dull moments. The best part of the job is how much I learn about the importance of working with and supporting students' and families' multiple cultural identities to challenge the violence that accosts students, families, and community members in the Bronx. I will always be a family counselor first, but I've fallen in love with teaching how to do counseling in schools and communities to ensure equity and academic success for all students. This is particularly the case with persons of color and of poor and working-class backgrounds who lack the financial resources to achieve equity compared to their economically privileged peers. Be open to many possibilities in your counseling career; you never know when another door will open onto a full range of opportunities and challenges.

Stuart F. Chen-Hayes, PhD, NCC is Assistant Professor and Coordinator of the graduate counseling program in the Specialized Services in Education department at Lehman College of the City University of New York, Bronx, NY. His Ph.D. is from Kent State University and he has an Ms.Ed. and B.A. from Indiana University. He is co-chair of ACA's Public Awareness and Support Committee, Treasurer of

Counselors for Social Justice, and a member of ASCA, ACES, AGLBIC, IAMFC, and AMCD.

SUGGESTED READINGS

Adams, M., Bell, L. A., & Griffin, P. (Eds.). (1997). *Teaching for diversity and social justice: A sourcebook.* New York: Routledge.
An outstanding resource for learning how to teach anti-oppression work in classrooms for all ages. Excellent exercises, resources, and curriculum development guidelines to challenge racism, heterosexism, classism, ableism, sexism, and anti-Semitism.

Andrzejewski, J. (Ed.). (1996). *Oppression and social justice: Critical frameworks.* Needham Heights, MA: Simon & Schuster.
A powerful reader on issues of advocacy and oppression in school-based settings that includes articles written by a diverse cadre of writers on equity issues in education.

Bemak, F. (2000). Transforming the role of the counselor to provide leadership in education reform through collaboration. *Professional School Counseling, 3* (5), 323–331.
An important article that argues the importance of school counselors' working collaboratively with other educators, students, and family members to ensure academic success and equity for all students.

Chen-Hayes, S. F. (in press). The social justice advocacy readiness questionnaire. *Journal of Lesbian and Gay Social Services.*
The author has designed this qualitative consultation tool as a method to assess personal and organizational social justice advocacy readiness in schools and community agencies.

Helms, J. (1992). *A race is a nice thing to have: A guide to being a white person or understanding the white persons in your life.* Topeka, KS: Content Communications.
An easy-to-read and powerful book on anti-racist white identity development written by one of counseling's most cited authors on ethnic and racial identity development models. Brief chapters and interesting, provoking exercises.

Herring, R. D. (1997). *Counseling diverse ethnic youth: Synergetic strategies and interventions for school counselors.* Upper Saddle River, NJ: Harcourt College.
Written by a practicing school counselor educator and former school counselor, this book sets the standard for how to intervene effectively with diverse students of various ethnic and racial identities in school counseling settings.

House, R. M., & Martin, P. J. (1998). Advocating for better futures for all students: A new vision for school counselors. *Education, 119* (2), 284–291.
One of the first articles written to describe the new vision of school counselors as academic success advocates, directly challenging the old model of school counselors as mental health workers. House, a former counselor educator and school counselor and Martin, a former school administrator and school counselor, are staff members with the Education Trust's Transforming School Counseling Initiative.

Johnson, R. S. (1996). *Setting our sights: Measuring equity in school change.* Los Angeles, CA: The Achievement Council.
A powerful book of how to change schools for equity and academic success based on developing collaborative leadership teams in schools that focus on collecting, analyzing,

presenting, and using data for equitable educational change. Easy-to-understand graphs, charts, exercises, and guidelines for getting started.

Lee, C. C., & Walz, G. R. (Eds.). (1998). *Social action: A mandate for counselors.* Alexandria, VA: American Counseling Association and ERIC/CASS.
An edited volume full of interesting chapters about how counselors need to become advocates in schools and agencies.

Lewis, J., & Bradley, L. (Eds.). (2000). *Advocacy in counseling: Counselors, clients, and community.* Greensboro, NC: Caps Publications (ERIC/CASS).
An edited volume that includes various chapters on advocacy in communities of color, for gender and sexual orientation issues, and concerning lifespan issues.

Lewis, J. A., Lewis, M. D., Daniels, J. A., & D'Andrea, M. J. (1998). *Community counseling: Empowerment strategies for a diverse society* (2nd ed.). Pacific Grove, CA: Brooks/Cole.
An excellent set of tools for change in school and community settings related to systems change, leadership, change agentry, advocacy, and so forth.

Nieto, S. (1999). *The light in their eyes: Creating multicultural learning communities.* New York: Teachers College Press.
One of the top multicultural education experts argues that multicultural education needs to devote its resources exclusively to the academic success and learning needs of all students in all schools.

CRISIS INTERVENTION COUNSELING

TROY R. HANSEN

I am a crisis intervention counselor. There really is no such thing as a typical day for someone who works in crisis intervention. In general, I work with the chronically mentally ill, but, in practical terms, my clients can be anyone who chooses to access our services. If a person has called our hotline and is in need of immediate intervention and assessment, the hotline contacts an on-call worker (in this case, me). I then go and meet the client at a home, at a jail, a shelter, or wherever he or she happens to be located at the time.

Today, for example, my client was a woman who probably was suffering from undiagnosed Bipolar I Disorder. She was psychotic, experiencing both delusions and hallucinations, and she was in the midst of a manic episode. When we arrived, she was seated on the floor of her kitchen, surrounded by pots and pans, as well as other utensils and miscellaneous items. She stated that she was in the process of creating a bomb, which was to bring about the apocalypse. The bomb, as far as we could see, consisted of a stick of butter (on its dish) that resembled a pincushion—impaled with pencils and pen caps. Apparently, the pot lids were part of the device as well.

The woman claimed to have the ability to see 10,000 years into the future and had received special messages from God, whose child she was to bear in a day or so, though she was not visibly pregnant. She was clearly out of touch with reality and refused to answer even the most basic questions or consider any help whatsoever. At one point, she became very agitated and yelled at us, demanding that we leave her alone.

While my partner and I spoke with a family member, she took the opportunity to get several kitchen knives, unbeknownst to us. When we returned to the kitchen, her behavior had escalated and she began to make threatening gestures toward herself and us with the knives. We attempted to calm her and convince her to put down the knives, but she remained so out of touch with reality that she refused to believe that we were not allied against her. At this point, I called 911 and police and an ambulance responded. Before they arrived, however, the client had held the knives to her throat, wrist, and eyes at different times, and we actually witnessed her making a significant cut on her wrist.

The result was that the client was transported to the hospital. Based upon our information, she was involuntarily committed. First, she received medical treatment for her wounds, which were not as serious as they had first appeared. The outcome was stressful, time consuming, and difficult, but it was a positive one. The client got the help that she needed, despite the fact that she was not even aware of that need.

When I received my master's degree in Counseling Psychology, I was not prepared adequately for days like that one. Like many counselors, I expected to be hired on with a counseling agency, to provide therapy to willing clients with problems of depression and anxiety. Instead, I found myself working with persons who were chronically mentally ill. Most do not have any insurance and many that need help the most will refuse it. Like all counselors, I ultimately became a counselor in order to help others. From high school, I had been interested in psychology. I was fascinated by the workings of the mind and the behaviors that those thoughts produced. However, it was not until my undergraduate program that I realized that what I wanted, and I believe was called to do, was counseling. As far as my current job is concerned, I did have a graduate class in crisis intervention, but I had no plans to pursue that area as a specialty. It was simply the best job offer I received after completing my master's program. I discovered, to my surprise, that I genuinely enjoyed crisis intervention.

While it is stressful and often difficult, it is also greatly rewarding. The rewards are less tangible at times and nonexistent at others, but, overall, it is fun, exciting work. Crisis intervention, by definition, is a short-term process. We simply meet the clients right where they are at that particular point in time, de-escalate tension, build trust and empathy quickly, and then help them explore options and solutions to their particular crises. Much of the time, this entails assisting them in arranging more long-term services. When this is complete, we leave the clients, satisfied that they will get the ongoing help that they need, and we move on to the next crisis.

The level of stress in crisis intervention is by no means consistent. There are often periods of down time where I am involved in other more mundane activities. There are also weeks where I scarcely get a break, and I feel like I am going from a difficult case to an even worse one. Part of getting through the busy times is to take advantage of the slow times—to relish the days when I am not called to do a crisis intervention assessment and can use the time instead for self-renewal and professional development. Another key to minimizing stress is to walk away from the pager. When my on-call shift ends, the pager is turned off. It is as simple as that. I am given paid time off for one reason—to use it! I try to plan at least one day off each month for my own mental health, along with one or two more significant breaks a year. As with most of us in this field, a primary way in which I deal with stress is by utilizing my support system—my family and friends.

Those of us who work in crisis intervention also understand the need to process and debrief after particularly stressful/traumatic cases. As a result, there is always a manager at our office who is on call and available to debrief any staff members who may need that. Probably the best way that we deal with the stress of crisis intervention is never to lose our sense of humor. Joking and laughter are very effective ways of dealing with the stress of crisis intervention and with the awful and disturbing situations that confront us almost daily.

Probably the best and the worst part of crisis intervention is the fact that it is extremely short-term, usually several hours at the longest. For those of us who crave variety and a sense of excitement, this is positive. I never know what the next call will be or what kind of situation I will be walking into. It is somewhat nice to go in, help the client with an immediate need, and then leave. However, for those of us in counseling, part of the reason we went into the field in the first place is the fact that counseling, primarily, is about a relationship. The classic I-Thou—the relationship between the counselor and the client—is the heart of the vocation. This is what is missing from crisis intervention.

Definitely, I have to be able to join with the clients where they are and build empathy and understanding quickly, but the deeper, long-term counseling relationship is not there. With some difficult clients, it is easy to walk away, but with others, I often think *I could really see myself doing therapy with this person.* Nevertheless, for the crisis intervention counselor, that is not an option and, in fact, can be an obstacle to good crisis intervention. I often have to instruct fellow counselors that we are not here to do therapy with clients. We are here to assess and intervene in the midst of the crisis. There is always a degree of *unlearning* that occurs with counselors, and it certainly did with me. We are trained to do therapy, and sometimes it is difficult to change that way of viewing a client.

Another day I was called to assess a middle-aged woman in a small, neatly kept apartment. She was very depressed and had experienced fleeting thoughts of suicide, with no plan or intent to act on those thoughts. She was tearful throughout the assessment and had to stop speaking several times to regain her composure. Her symptoms were almost verbatim from the DSM-IV diagnostic criteria for a Major Depressive Episode: difficulty sleeping, poor appetite, lack of interest in activities that had formerly been enjoyable to her, indecisiveness, problems concentrating, and feelings of hopelessness. She had experienced significant losses within her support system within the last year and recently had begun to have problems at her workplace.

Ultimately, we arranged an appointment for the woman at a community mental health center for the next day. There she would have an evaluation for psychiatric treatment and ongoing counseling. We provided some telephone numbers to depression and grief/loss support groups and educated her about these issues as well. In the end, what made the most difference was simply that we came to speak with her—the fact that there were people who cared enough to actually come into others' homes to speak with them at a time when they were experiencing a crisis. Most of all, the client was touched by the fact that we came to her home and listened to her. We were able to empathize with her and explore solutions to her crisis.

The two most common groups of professionals working in crisis intervention are, not surprisingly, counselors and social workers, although I have worked with several psychiatric nurses as well. There is very much an overlap in crisis intervention, and that lends itself fairly easily to either social work or counseling. There are aspects of crisis intervention that are very much counseling-related in nature and others that are routine social work practice. The most common issue for counselors when entering the area of crisis intervention is the fact that we must adjust our thinking for the differences in crisis intervention versus psychotherapy. The counselor needs to work quickly to build rapport and a good working relationship with the client, doing so in 15 minutes, not in two 50-minute sessions. In addition, we as counselors have to get to the point of being able to let go of a client when the crisis has been averted and appropriate follow-up has been made. Unlike ongoing counseling, we finish most of the work in about two hours, not eight to ten sessions.

Social workers tend to have a better knowledge of community resources, but counselors learn the best resources rapidly, so this difference in preparation is hardly noticeable. Even social workers and psychiatric nurses see the value in counseling and do not hesitate to connect a client to a counseling center if needed. Most of the time, the only interaction we have with various hospitals or ERs is when we have a client who needs inpatient treatment. The most we can do is make a recommendation to the ER physician or psychiatrist—we cannot guarantee admission. This is the same regarding involuntary commitment. We will complete affidavits and help facilitate transport to the hospital, usually via ambulance, but it is ultimately the hospital's decision to commit someone or not. Our documentation and affidavits do carry weight with many ERs, but we do not have the power to involuntarily commit a client, only to make recommendations and facilitate the process as far as the ER.

Crisis intervention is definitely not for everyone. It is demanding, draining, and unpredictable. It is often ambiguous, frequently lacking satisfactory closure, and, some of the time, it is difficult to know if we have been successful or not. It is also among the most rewarding experiences in which I have ever participated. I cannot count the number of times a client has said *Thank you! It has helped so much just to be able to talk to someone.* This fact alone, I think, does the most good for our clients. In the midst of a crisis, they often cannot see any solution or muster any hope that things will improve. We come into the situation, despite the crisis, and help them realize a solution. This is our primary function in crisis intervention, and as counselors in general—to instill hope in our clients. One of my professors in graduate school told me this, and I have never forgotten it. Crises provide a unique, if difficult, opportunity for clients to change. If we can intervene and provide hope to them during the crisis, then perhaps they will come out of the current crisis having learned something and having grown as people. It is experiences like these that make crisis intervention counseling an exciting and rewarding niche in the wider field of mental health and counseling.

Troy Hansen, LPC, NCC received his BS in Psychology from Texas Christian University in Fort Worth, Texas and his MA in Counseling Psychology from Oklahoma City University. He served as the Clinical Manager of the CISM Department (Critical Incident Stress Management) at Behavioral Health Response, Inc. in

St. Louis, Missouri for the past two years. Behavioral Health Response (BHR) is a private, nonprofit corporation that provides telephone crisis intervention to three-fourths of the state of Missouri and face-to-face assessment and crisis intervention in the eastern region of the state. Troy was employed at BHR for $4\frac{1}{4}$ years, working as a Crisis Intervention Counselor (on the phone) and a Mobile Outreach Team Member before becoming the Manager of the CISM Dept. BHR's Crisis Management Services include face-to-face evaluation and crisis intervention, as well as Critical Incident Stress Debriefing. Recently, Troy has left the world of crisis intervention and is engaged in counseling in a group private practice setting. He is a member of the American Association of Christian Counselors. His main areas of professional interest are depression and suicide among the elderly and geriatric counseling in general, couples/marital counseling, and spiritual issues in counseling. Outside counseling, Troy is an avid reader and aspiring fiction writer. He also enjoys outdoor activities and serves as a Deacon at Memorial Presbyterian Church (PCA). He lives in St. Louis with his wife Sarah and their son, Ian.

SUGGESTED READINGS

Beck, A. T. (1976). *Cognitive therapy and the emotional disorders.* New York: Meridian.
    A classic in the field and one that influenced me significantly as a counselor.

Corey, G. (1977). *Theory and practice of counseling and psychotherapy.* Belmont, CA: Wadsworth.
    An excellent overview of the major counseling theories and techniques and a valuable reference.

Slaikeu, K. A. (1984). *Crisis intervention: A handbook for practice and research.* Boston: Allyn and Bacon.
    A thorough and practical look at crisis intervention—what it is, the theories behind it, and the various methods and techniques of crisis intervention.

CRISES COUNSELING AT HOPE HOUSE

CYNDEE L. HILL

L et me begin by saying it's not a spelling error or a typo. I am employed as a crisis counselor, but what I do is really *crises* counseling. I'm never dealing with just one crisis; it's always many crises at the same time. I work in a short-term, residential, psychiatric crisis center. It is a ranch-style house with five bedrooms (six beds) situated in a nice suburban neighborhood. We accept adults (18 and over) for a five- to ten-day stay to help them stabilize emotionally and/or psychiatrically. The work I do is both interesting and challenging.

I have not been a counselor for a very long time, but I do have a few years of experience. I graduated from college in 1991 with a bachelor's degree in psychology. I soon found a job as a foster care caseworker and found the work to be draining, yet energizing at the same time. I didn't really enjoy the case management aspects of the job; I much preferred the direct contact with the children and families on my caseload. While I tried to be a *miniature counselor* with my bachelor's degree, I knew I wanted to go back to school so I could follow my heart's desire to become a therapist. I continued to work full time (although at different jobs), and several years later (1998), I finally obtained my master's degree in counseling.

Just when it appeared that everything had fallen into place and I could pursue the career I had always dreamed of, my life circumstances changed. I was pregnant and my first child was going to be born just four months after I graduated. The funny thing about the passage of time is that you tend to get older! When I started graduate school, I didn't realize I'd be 29 by the time I graduated, and my husband and I didn't want to wait much longer than that to start a family. So here I was, struggling with every mother's dilemma: career or family?

I was determined to make the most of what I'd achieved, and I have been able to make things work for me. I stay home with my child during the week, and I work at the crisis center on weekends, when my husband is home and able to care for our child. I think I have the best of both worlds and I am definitely satisfied that I am keeping up with my career, learning new things, as well as taking care of my family.

So let's get back to my job. Crisis counseling wasn't really something that I had envisioned myself doing when I was in graduate school. I thought I would be sitting in a nice office, working for myself, and primarily counseling people who were having a hard time dealing with some simple, well-defined problems. Nice dream, but I don't think that job exists in reality. My state (Pennsylvania) is just now implementing licensure for master's level counselors, so there goes the idea of working for myself. And clients with simple, well-defined problems—I haven't met one yet! So I stumble upon an ad in the paper that says an employer is looking for crisis workers to fill weekend shifts. Perfect! I interview and the job is mine.

Now what exactly do I do? Many, many things. First of all, let me explain the setup of the house and staffing. It is run somewhat like a hospital, with three shifts every day; it is always staffed with at least two people. If we have a full house, the ratio is three consumers to one staff person. We also have a nurse and a psychiatrist who put in several hours each week. On weekdays, office personnel and management are also onsite during the day. I was required to participate as a third staff person for several shifts as a way to receive hands-on training and learn about how the program is run.

I mentioned earlier that I considered myself experienced. After all, I had worked in the field of human services for eight years before getting this job. However, as a counselor, I had never worked with someone with a chronic mental illness, and I certainly never worked side by side with a psychiatrist before. Needless to say, I was a little intimidated, but I had to get over that pretty quickly to make this job work for me. By the time my shifts of training were over, I felt ready to do the job as part of a two-member team.

On any given day at the crisis residence, many things are happening at once. Consumers need to be observed taking their medications several times a day, meals need to be planned and prepared (usually by the consumers themselves), household chores need to be completed (e.g., laundry, dishes, vacuuming, shopping), and appointments need to be attended. Each staff person is also responsible for taking referrals for new consumers as they come in. All referrals must come through the county emergency services division, and since the nature of this work is crisis, we are responsible for making a decision about acceptance within thirty minutes of receiving the referral.

Consumers are almost always accepted (when beds are available), unless there is a medical emergency or drug and alcohol detoxification needs to take place. Once admitted, a brief intake interview is conducted, which includes identifying, psychosocial, and drug and alcohol history. A treatment plan is also developed to help consumers focus on one or two achievable goals during their stay. During the regular workweek, case management services are provided to link and refer consumers for any appropriate social or aftercare services.

Of course, while all this is going on, counseling is also taking place. Consumers are free to approach staff at any time if they want individual counseling. Additionally, three formal counseling groups are held each day, and consumers are expected to attend and participate. Since this is a short-term program (5 to 10 days maximum), consumers are strongly encouraged to utilize all services available to them as a way to achieve stabilization and future direction.

The types of counseling issues consumers raise are varied. Some examples of situations I have encountered include panic attacks (*I have to get out of here; I feel like I'm having a heart attack;* and *I can't breathe*); depression (*I hate myself; I know I'll be dead at my own hand in a few months; I feel lower than an ant; Why does God hate me so much?;* and *I just want to sleep . . . forever*); and schizophrenia (*The devil wants my soul; Make the voices stop; The spirits are pounding on my chest and raping me; I'm really from another earth;* and *The bugs are crawling all over me*). There have also been episodes of mania during which the sufferer may not sleep but a few minutes a day, incidents of angry outbursts, persons with eating disorders, obsessive-compulsive behaviors, and struggles with the ever-so-needy borderline personalities.

Counseling is primarily focused on assessing and assuring the safety of each individual, redirecting and testing reality, providing ongoing support, goal planning, and educating consumers regarding medications. Group counseling serves to provide peer support and psychoeducation on topics such as self-esteem, anger management, anxiety, relaxation techniques, and/or healthy relationships. Since I only work on weekends, I am usually faced with a completely new group of individuals every time I start a new shift. I find counseling in this type of environment to be refreshing.

There is not much time to spend on building relationships or delving into long-standing issues. I usually build rapport by exploring the presenting crisis and working backwards from there, helping the consumer identify one small, achievable goal to focus on while stabilizing from the crisis. My unique role as a weekend-only staff person sometimes seems to give me the advantage of being *anonymous.* Consumers seem to use individual counseling with me in the same manner one might call a hotline—seeking support for problems with no strings attached for any further relationship. While ongoing counseling has often been needed and recommended for consumers to deal with their underlying problems following the crisis, such practice is neither realistic nor appropriate in a short-term crisis residence. It is that unique role as an anonymous counselor that has been refreshing to me.

An example of a typical counseling session follows. The consumer's name and some details have been changed to protect confidentiality. I remember working with Lila for the greater part of one shift. She was a middle-aged woman reeling from the recent breakup of a long-term relationship. Her history included alcoholic parents, sexual abuse, bipolar disorder, and multiple suicide attempts. She was on a variety of medications and had been receiving psychiatric treatment for many years. She had also been to the crisis center a few times before.

When I met with her this particular shift, it was to provide medication. She appeared calm and serene and had been socializing with staff and peers in an appropriate manner. She was scheduled for discharge the next day, having been at the residence for nine days for medication adjustments. As I asked her how she was feeling that day, she calmly said that she was now feeling as poorly as when she had come in, and she didn't think there was anything else we (or anyone) could do to help her. Medication only helps for so long, she said, and then she returns to a deep depression. She said she was tired of the routine. I asked her if she was thinking about hurting herself. She smiled and said yes, but not now. She said she was safe here, she had signed a safety contract and would abide by it, and she didn't need to go to the hospital because she wasn't actively suicidal. But one day, she said, probably months in the future, she was sure she would kill herself.

My goal in this session was to keep her talking, let her get everything out, and help her see that she needed further treatment. Having her committed involuntarily would not work because she was not currently suicidal. We talked about her painful childhood and the traumas she had suffered. We talked about the good things in her life and all that she had to live for. We talked about her past suicide attempts and the fact that she had always notified someone of what she did (overdosing) so that she could be saved. I tried to help her see the value of her life. As my shift was coming to a close, she was able to say that maybe she could try some longer-term treatment; she wasn't sure, she had to think about it. I reminded her of her safety contract and she went to her room. I passed all the information on to the new staff coming in for change of shift so that they could follow up with her. My job was done and all I could do was hope for the best. The next week I learned that Lila was discharged the next day, but she did not go home. She had agreed to go to an inpatient program for further treatment.

The best aspects of this job for me are that it is very fast-paced, it is a casual homelike setting, and I can work hours that suit my needs. I am able to counsel a large number of individuals with various needs and issues, and I have also learned to love the fact that daily notes must be completed by the end of each shift. This, for me, brings closure to each workday and allows me to go home without feeling like something is still hanging over my head.

In addition to the above, I have enjoyed the fact that I am able to gain insight from co-workers who possess various skills and training within the mental health field. For example, our psychiatric nurse has taught me a great deal about the medical side of mental illness, how medications can affect one's physical functioning, and how health can affect one's mental illness. I have also witnessed the immense power and authority that a psychiatrist holds in the eyes of many consumers. I have seen consumers change their presentation for the doctor in order to (try to) get what they want, and I have seen psychotic individuals maintain composure to avoid negative consequences with the doctor. I have learned some basic sign language from another social worker. (Ironically, we have worked with two deaf individuals who are schizophrenic and hear voices.) I feel that each staff person at our residence is unique and each has a lot to offer consumers and peers in regard to treating mental illness.

The worst aspects of this job for me involve the upkeep and maintenance chores of the house (e.g., cleaning the bathrooms), counting medications (done at the start and finish of each shift), and dealing with inconsistencies in procedures between different staff members. For example, when some staff are viewed as flexible and others as rigid, consumers often attempt to use this to their advantage or try to split staff to get what they want.

I have valued my experiences as a crisis counselor. It seems to me that I have gained more varied experience in the months that I have held this position than I could have in another, more traditional counseling role. I have had the opportunity to encounter a vast array of psychiatric diagnoses, I have learned and observed the effects of various psychopharmacological medications, and I have had to be quick on my feet and problem solve under a variety of crisis situations. I have also learned to look for and appreciate the small achievements that we sometimes take for granted. Crises counseling has helped me grow as a counselor and as a person.

Cyndee L. (Vallone) Hill, MA received her BA degree in psychology from Allentown College of St. Francis de Sales, Center Valley, PA. She received her MA in counseling from Kutztown University, Kutztown, PA. This article is based on her position as a crisis counselor with Hope House, a division of Resources for Human Development based out of Philadelphia, PA.

SUGGESTED READINGS

Gorman, J. M. (1997). *The essential guide to psychiatric drugs* (3rd ed.). New York: St. Martin's Griffin.
This book helped me familiarize myself with the different medications, their uses, and their side effects. It was also a helpful guide to use with consumers in educating them about their medications.

Reid, W. H. (1989). *The treatment of psychiatric disorders*. New York: Brunner/Mazel Publishers. This book is a simple guide that I used whenever I found myself working with consumers presenting a diagnosis that was new to me. It describes medical treatment, which helped me understand how and why our psychiatrist made his decisions. It also provides information about counseling techniques used to treat consumers with various diagnoses.

29

WHAT I GET FROM GIVING: VOLUNTEERING FOR THE AMERICAN RED CROSS

ROBERT L. DINGMAN

started working when I was 10 years old. I liked it. I liked every one of the almost fifty jobs I held during my lifetime. I have had five factory assembly line summer jobs, three newspaper delivery jobs, many retail business jobs, and a long list of part-time jobs such as babysitting, lawn mowing, and so on. The ones that might have become boring I turned interesting by creating a new way of looking at them, finding a way to learn in the process, or emphasizing the relationships I developed in them. Mostly, though, I learned that the jobs with people were the most enjoyable. The ones where I could give a service were the ones I liked most. By finding a way to give to others, I found that I got the most reward.

Now I am retired from a forty-three-year, full-time employment history that includes twenty-eight years as a college professor at Marshall University, and thirty-six years as a counselor. But even in retirement, I find that I get the most from giving. The most consistently rewarding work I have done is when I have volunteered for the American Red Cross (ARC).

I have worked as a volunteer in seventy-plus disasters for the Red Cross and taught more than seventy classes for them. I have been involved in the writing of many of the materials developed for the Disaster Mental Health Services (DMHS) program for them. I have spent about 150 days a year, since my retirement four years ago, in those volunteer activities.

I loved teaching counseling courses, consulting with organizations such as Head Start, professional presentations, professional writing, plus activity with local, state, regional, and national professional organizations. I was proud of my work in my part-time private practice. I enjoyed almost every minute of the time spent with professional activities.

My family time has always been important to me. My children are now spread over the country and even overseas. We stay in contact regularly. I spend wonderful hours with my wife, who supports me in all my diverse activities. She is a counselor, too, so she helps debrief me, provides consultation, and loves me.

Of all the wonderful experiences life has offered me, I will choose the work I do with the American Red Cross to exemplify the days in my life as a counselor. I began in 1981 as a disaster volunteer for the ARC. For ten years I volunteered for the local chapter and went to about twenty disasters, many of which were within 100 miles of my home in flood-prone West Virginia. I worked mostly as a Family Service interviewer, which was the nearest thing to counseling offered by ARC during that time. I was promoted to Family Service Coordinator in the national disaster system and served as the Family Service Officer on one occasion. I also served on the local Disaster Action Team, in Damage Assessment, Mass Care, and often as the catchall titled Worker-in-Charge. I often spent 100 days a year volunteering, in addition to my teaching, private practice, consultation, and professional organization activities. I stopped all my summer teaching and suspended my private practice each spring in order to provide for my time to volunteer during the summer.

In 1991 I became active in the development of a new program in ARC disaster services, which became the Disaster Mental Health Services function. Since then I have continued in the development of materials for DMHS, worked about fifty more disasters, and taught the DMHS and DMHS supervision courses all over the country. I have trained about 1,000 mental health professionals in disaster mental health. The experience is the most memorable and rewarding of my career.

A very interesting aspect of Red Cross mental health is its multidisciplinary perspective. There are counselors, social workers, psychiatric nurses, psychiatrists, marriage and family therapists, and psychologists who work in ARC mental health. Leadership comes from all of the disciplines and in no specific order. Once mental health professionals qualify for service, their particular discipline is no longer important. All of us start at the entry level, and those who want to do so can progress through training and experience to the higher levels. Counselors and nurses often hold the higher leadership positions, as do the other professions. Often no one is even aware of who is from what profession.

I will focus on one of those disaster experiences that was among the most rewarding and memorable. I was the DMHS Officer for the Alaska Airline crash in January 2000. As a member of the ARC Aviation Incident Response (AIR) Team, I was on call for February. I heard of the crash about 6:30 P.M. on January 31 and said to my wife Janet that I had just missed another air crash, because my month didn't start for several more hours. At 6:40 I received a call from ARC HQ that the February team was being activated. Thus began my volunteer work on one of the most stressful of the disasters an ARC volunteer can do.

We are required to be prepared to travel within four hours of activation, so I was already packed, except for the two sets of clothes (one for summer and one for winter) that were hanging in the closet of my home office—California, so it would be the summer ones. Flight arrangements couldn't be completed for an evening flight, so I left at 4:30 A.M. for the airport, arriving before noon in Los Angeles.

Once there, plans had already been changed. Instead of renting a car and traveling north of LA about 100 miles to a city near the crash site, we were to set up headquarters near the LA airport. The crash site area did not have the facilities to support an activity as large as most air crashes. At headquarters I met the rest of my leadership team. Five other mental health professional leaders from the DMHS AIR Team were present or on their way. Local mental health professionals trained as ARC DMHS workers were already present and had been since about an hour after the crash.

Before it was all over, more than 100 DMHS workers worked for me on the mental health team. All of them were from California; almost all from three counties in the LA area. The leadership team members were from CA, CT, HI, NY, VA, and VT. We joined and became an efficient unit within hours. Training and preparedness gave us the opportunity to begin immediately to deliver service to the friends and family, as well as the workers, who were affected by the crash. Job descriptions (with one exception that will be discussed later) and AIR Team training helped us to know what to do and what others were doing as well.

Mental health workers providing service in aircraft incidents need skills beyond those who provide service in most other disasters. The stresses are magnified. Everyone is intense. Exposure to the death, mourning, tension, and possible gory details of the crash create a highly stressful environment all of the time. Mental health workers who can deliver quality service under these trying circumstances are selected for service in air crashes. In fact, workers in all parts of the Red Cross services for air disasters must be able to deliver services under these stressful circumstances.

The Los Angeles area Red Cross mental health people were invaluable. They were fully prepared for such a disaster. Throughout the United States, Red Cross chapters are expected to have a plan developed so that they can respond immediately if a disaster occurs in their jurisdiction. The LA chapter was particularly thorough in its plan for air disasters. When we arrived, hotels were already identified, workers were already working, and materials were already available. Their response was impressive.

The Red Cross disaster headquarters was located in one hotel and the Family and Friends assistance center was located in another hotel nearby. At ARC HQ there were about forty people also trained for AIR Team membership. They were the leaders and workers of several other ARC functions necessary for response to transportation accidents. They too came together and efficiently provided the services for which they were trained.

At the Family Assistance Center (FAC) workers were available for the support of the families and friends of the crash victims. ARC DMHS provided crisis intervention as needed, for workers as well as the family and friends who chose to come to the area of the crash site. Many other groups provided services, including city, county, and state law enforcement personnel; airlines officials; and many airline workers trained to support the loved ones of the crash victims.

One of the demanding jobs my leadership team had was working with the media. An air disaster is a large media event and this one was no exception. The media representatives are competing with each other for the best stories they can find. Too often their activities can interfere with the needs of the friends and families of victims and with the delivery of the needed services. Thus, it is important for a mental health person to provide the media people with what they need without their interference in the needs of the friends, families, and other persons providing service. One of my team members was assigned as the media liaison. That was the one job for which neither he nor I had a description. We did, however, very successfully deliver that service by determining the responsibilities between us.

As the officer in charge of the mental health function, I spent much of my time at HQ with management activities. One of the parts of my job that I find is most rewarding is the mentoring of other mental health people. Not only do I get a lot from teaching others about the job, but they also get a great deal from it in learning the skills needed for moving up to the next level in the Red Cross. I believe training others to do my job is very important to the overall development of DMHS in the Red Cross.

While I do spend a large amount of time at headquarters, I feel it is important for me to have enough contact with the activities in the field that I can make appropriate decisions. It also helps me to feel I am a mental health worker as well as an administrator. Mental health workers in the field find satisfaction in showing their bosses around their work area. Thus I participate in some on the scene mental health activities. Here are some examples:

- The second day on the job, I was informed that an airline vice president requested a mental health person assist in the selection of a location for a site visit. I decided I should be there and I spent most of the third day assisting in that process. It involved representatives of the National Transportation Safety Board, California Highway Patrol, the Ventura County Sheriff's Department, Los Angeles police, Alaska airlines, the U.S. Navy and the U.S. Coast Guard. Participating in the process of choosing a site location for a family and friends visit was fascinating. Safety, privacy, and mental health considerations were uppermost. The site chosen was on a naval base near the crash site where media would be minimally intrusive, the water could be patrolled by the Coast Guard easily, and the families and friends would have a maximum of privacy for their mourning. Providing escort for the families and friends while traveling from the hotel to the site was the role of the CHP. The unstructured nature of the visit was an important dimension of the activity.

- Another activity I participated in was observing the operations of the FAC. I shared a meal with a family and their Alaska Airline support people on one occasion. On another occasion I sat in on one of the briefings done by NTSB. I also visited with some workers—ARC and others—to help in determining the morale of the work force.

- I supervised the Childcare Aviation Incident Response (CAIR) Team and the Spiritual Care Aviation Incident Response (SAIR) Team. Both groups were new members of the AIR team and each had important roles in the mental health support of the families and friends. Since neither group had people experienced in ARC disaster work, it was decided that the DMHS officer would be responsible for the administrative portions of their tasks. This provided me with several interesting new experiences. Helping to develop materials for the memorial service, managing of the childcare centers, and educating the ARC people (and others) about those two groups were among the valuable new experiences I gained from this assignment.

- I was pleased to be one of the mental health workers who traveled to the memorial service on a bus with family and friends and their Alaska Airlines support people. Normally, I would have remained at HQ, but so many groups of families and friends arrived for the memorial service that every available mental health person was needed. We traveled to the service in a thirty-five-vehicle caravan that was the largest ever in the LA area.
- The memorial service was extremely powerful. The site was Pepperdine University's field house, overlooking the Pacific Ocean. The ARC SAIR team officer was the host. Additionally, many religions were represented, each offering a prayer. After the service, eighty-eight white doves (one for each victim) were released. They circled the area for several minutes before flying off in the direction of the crash site. Flowers were placed by family and friends in baskets, which were loaded on helicopters, flown to the crash site, and released at the exact minute of the day when the crash occurred. All contributed to a very powerful service.
- The next few days following the memorial service proved the value of the service. Families and friends began leaving LA almost immediately. By the third day after the memorial, only three families remained. We felt that the memorial service brought appropriate closure for families and friends, doing so completely enough that they could return to their homes to continue their mourning.

The cooperation of the many organizations, and more importantly, their people, created an atmosphere in which people could begin the recovery process. The feeling of making a contribution to an immensely difficult ordeal, and the relief of being able to leave it behind, were powerful. I have never had so much positive feedback about helping mental health clients as when I participate in disaster mental health with the American Red Cross.

If you enjoy giving, if you can work with a minimum of structure, if you are skillful in thinking on your feet, if you can handle stressful work, if you get great rewards from giving to others, then you would be fulfilled in doing volunteer work for the American Red Cross through the Disaster Mental Health Services function. You don't have to be retired to be active as an ARC mental health worker. You just need to recognize how valuable the experience will be for you as well as the people to whom you give and then be creative in how to make room for it in your schedule.

Robert L. Dingman EdD, LPC (WV), NCC, CCMHC received his Bachelor of Science degree from Central Michigan University, his master's and doctoral degrees from Wayne State University. He began his counseling experience as a junior high school counselor in Hazel Park, Michigan after having been a mathematics teacher and football, baseball, and wrestling coach in the same school district for five years. He spent several years as a high school counselor in Livonia, Michigan, where he was counseling department chairperson, director of research, and part-time night school counselor. He then spent twenty-eight years in the counseling department at Marshall University in Huntington, West Virginia. For twenty-six of those years he also had a part-time private practice. He has been active in the profession organizations of counseling since 1962. He was the president of the American Association of State Counseling Boards in 1990–1991 and has received honors from Marshall University, the West Virginia Counseling Association, the American Mental Health Counselors Association, and the American Counseling Association.

SUGGESTED READINGS

Dingman, R. L. (Ed.). (1995). Disasters and crises: A mental health counseling perspective. [Special Issue]. *Journal of Mental Health Counseling, 17* (3).
    This special issue has several articles related to Red Cross Mental Health, as well as articles from a variety of other settings.

Greenstone, J. L., & Leviton, S. C. (1993). *Elements of crisis intervention: Crises and how to respond to them.* Pacific Grove, CA: Brooks/Cole.
    This book is an excellent quick reference for many areas of crisis intervention.

Weaver, J. D. (1995). *Disasters: Mental health interventions.* Sarasota, FL: Professional Resource Press.
    Excellent reference book. About half is related to Red Cross; the other half is general crisis intervention information. Weaver is donating half of the royalties to the ARC Disaster Relief Fund and his publisher is matching the donations.

COUNSELING IN ZIMBABWE— AFRICA'S HOUSE OF STONE

KIMBERLY RICHARDS

Hi, I am Kimberly! How I became a counselor is a bit odd. I received a degree in Wildlife Science in 1980 and I expected to have a long and wonderful career as an ecologist in one of Zimbabwe's national wildlife parks. However, due to civil strife in Zimbabwe in the early 1980s, I wound up teaching because the guerillas would use the game parks as a source of food and a place to hide. Though my career as a wildlife biologist was like a dream come true and was something I had dreamed about since the age of 8, I did not think it was worth possibly sacrificing my life. Instead, I went into teaching. Although I was not trained as a teacher, there was a great need for science educators in Zimbabwe at the time, so individuals with degrees in science were taken into the teaching force. I taught chemistry, biology, physics, general science, and mathematics. The students seemed to be able to talk to me, and I became an unofficial counselor. In 1985, I was transferred to a school in Harare (Zimbabwe's capital) and that is when my career as a counselor officially started. All teachers are assigned afterschool activities, and I was assigned to career guidance as my after-school activity.

Zimbabwe became independent from the colonial Rhodesian regime in 1980. The Rhodesian government had built few schools for non-White students, and the few they did build were inferior in terms of resources, building construction, course work, and activities, when compared to the ones built for White students. Guidance and counseling had not been a priority of the Ministry of Education of Rhodesia, or the new Zimbabwe. Although *guidance/careers* was provided occasionally as an afternoon activity in the former White students only schools, it was mainly used as a way of correcting students seen as having behavior problems, and it provided limited career information to students. The individuals providing the guidance were mainly trained teachers, not trained counselors. School guidance in Rhodesia was used as a tool of the colonial regime in that it helped to maintain the regime by propagating the construct of White supremacy. School guidance in South Africa even provided a platform for the apartheid security forces, and, on closer inspection, one may find a similar relationship in Rhodesia, apartheid's sister state.

As far as I know, there was not any school with a Ministry of Education–supported guidance and counseling department. There are now a few schools with guidance departments in Zimbabwe, but I only know of one that is a full-fledged department (Prince Edward School). I thought that since our schools could benefit from well-rounded guidance and counseling programs, I should study for a degree in counseling, so I went back to school in 1987. I first took a qualification in management because I thought that would be important in establishing and running counseling programs. Then I started work on a master's degree in counseling in 1989. I was very lucky to wind up in a counseling program run by Ken Norem at the University of North Alabama, because Ken is very professional, professionally active, and also very supportive of his students and their views. Thanks to Ken's encouragement, I had my first paper published while a master's student, and that gave me a lot of confidence. I learned a lot in addition to what I was taught from the curriculum, and I took it all back with to me to Zimbabwe.

When I returned home, I was assigned to Prince Edward School (PE), an all-boys' high school, as a science teacher. I joined the National Guidance and Counseling Association of Zimbabwe. I eventually wound up being the Chairperson of the Harare Chapter and served on the executive committee of the Association. PE had a careers department that offered occasional career lectures, some shop floor activities (where they were required to work and job shadow at an organization for two weeks), and useful volunteer activities for some students in the community. I thought it had a good base upon which to expand. When the person running the department decided to leave, I took over the department. At that point, my duties as a science teacher lessened, which provided me the opportunity to get a more comprehensive guidance program established.

I developed a written plan for the department, as it had none, and turned the plan into action. The plan included working not only with students, but also with teachers, school and Ministry administrators, parents, and the community—all the stakeholders. I revived the *education for living* classes, which had not been taught for some time. The school provided me with some teachers for this and I now had a department with a staff of five. The PE headmaster (Mr. Barnes) sent me to a child counseling and development course and then to a course in family counseling. I found the specializations useful to my duties as a school counselor. I started providing personal counseling as well as career and academic forms of counseling. I also began to initiate activities like education day and careers days and got many speakers to come in to talk about their careers and/or the services their organizations provided the community. I held workshops for parents, staff, and students.

I also planned activities with the University of Zimbabwe and local industry. Students went on shop floor activities. They would attend a class of interest at the university and visit different departments to see what they offered. I managed to get publicity in the local media around various activities that were put on by the department, and this helped alter perceptions of this program. Others soon viewed it as relevant and desirable. This was important because many people involved did not initially see the need for a full-time guidance and counseling department.

Somehow I had managed to run the program with almost no budget, which I don't think is so unusual for most school counselors around the world.

I collaborated with the school librarian on various AIDS projects, and we accomplished a lot at the school in that area. We managed to get a lot of literature and textbooks on the subject and had our students involved in AIDS dramas, art contests, and many other activities. We had speakers come in and talk about AIDS, caring for AIDS patients, AIDS counseling, and human sexuality. We did this with no budget whatsoever, just a lot of networking and resource sharing with individuals and organizations outside of the school community. The Headmaster, who is really a person of vision, saw the value of this (and of a full guidance and counseling program) and would provide us with school transportation and other ways of supporting our AIDS activities. He did all he could to make sure the projects were a success, though the Ministry of Education and the school itself could not provide us with a budget for our AIDS projects.

About a year after we started the AIDS project, the Ministry of Education made it mandatory that every student in Zimbabwe's schools had AIDS education classes once a week (Zimbabwe has one of the highest AIDS infection rates in the world, with at least one in four Zimbabweans infected). The Ministry first trained two staff members at every school in AIDS education. Those two would, in turn, train all the form teachers (something like homeroom teachers) in how to provide AIDS education. The librarian and myself were sent to this training. When I returned, I was told that this program would be run under my department, but the Ministry would not provide any money for the program. Well, next thing I knew, I had a staff of about 40 and no budget to run the program. Most of my staff did not want to teach about AIDS. They cited moral, religious, and cultural reasons as to why they would not do it. Some saw it as a Black problem and objected on those grounds; others saw it as a gay problem and objected on those grounds. I really did not know what to do. It was obviously a problem for everyone to address, but it seemed some just could not (or were not yet ready to) try.

I had been given this directive, which I thought was even a good one, but most teachers were adamant about not teaching AIDS education classes. Fortunately, a handful of teachers were so concerned over the issue that they were willing to take on the workload of those who refused to teach their AIDS education class. We wrote syllabi for the different forms (grades), we planned activities, and we got the program organized. This was all very stressful, at times, yet it was also very elating. For example, I started receiving anonymous threatening letters in my mailbox from a couple of staff members. I had shouting, hang-up phone calls from parents who objected to their sons being taught about human sexuality. The other females involved and I now had to talk about sexuality with high school boys and teach them how to use condoms (though we advocated abstinence)—something most of us female teachers did not know how to do. We helped each other cope as we taught each other things we did not know. We learned to talk about sexuality by doing it with each other. We quelled each other's temper when we would come under verbal attack from staff members about the AIDS classes. We shared our experiences both inside and outside the classroom and started to socialize together, which most people in this group had not done before.

I occasionally taught classes in counseling theory and practice at the University of Zimbabwe (UZ). Eventually, I was taken on full-time at the university as a counselor in the distance education program, and I continued to teach part-time classes in other departments as well. I reluctantly resigned my position at PE, as I really enjoyed that job despite the complications of the AIDS education program. At that time, the UZ distance education program had about 3,000 students spread all over the entire country. Somehow the other counselor and I had to service all of those students. It was really an impossible task for us.

I thought it would be a good idea to organize a basic-skills training workshop for our tutors and coordinators in the ten regions. The director of the program agreed. I managed to line up speakers from all over Zimbabwe and one from Canada who had been associated with counseling in Zimbabwe on previous occasions. I thought this training would be of some help in providing counseling services to the students. Likewise, I spent a year writing a student resource guide that covered the whole country. This guide identified places where students could go for help for various problems and where they could get inexpensive accommodations when they came for lectures or exams. I found it frustrating to have such an enormous task to carry out—to develop and service a counseling program that was spread out over the entire country when I had so little resources.

Everything I did (or wanted to do) had to be approved by the distance education director because our department did not have a budget. This required lots of paperwork and presentations to the director, but I was committed to its success. I was also a little frustrated with other staff, most of whom saw little value in having student-counseling services. I felt like the counseling department always had to prove its worth, unlike other departments. I wound up working more than the required hours, but others did too. We really wanted the distance education program to be a success. It was a new program, and we did not want it to falter.

Things got even more complicated when the other counselor was put in an administrative position and I had the entire program to run myself. I found I was constantly traveling. Instead of trips twice a month, I found I was on the road, in the air, or staring back at hotel room walls most of the time now. At first it was kind of boring, especially the lonely nights in hotel rooms. I quickly decided I would just have to get out and do things alone that I never would have done before, like go to movies, concerts, plays, and other entertainment spots. This really helped me grow as a person. I developed confidence and increased my social skills. I wound up making friends from all over the country that I would then visit with when I went out to the region again.

It was pretty stressful to be responsible for all of those students, with so many different problems. When I would get to the regional center, I would see student after student all day and sometimes see others in the evening as well, because some students had classes all day. It was a real stress reducer to be able to go and have fun and just let go of all the issues the students would bring to me. With AIDS so rampant, death was a frequent issue for students. I found that to be the most difficult issue for which I would have to provide counseling. I am glad that I tried to overcome my discomfort with doing unescorted activities in the evenings; otherwise I think I would have just burned out on it all. Eventually, I became desensitized about the death and grieving of my clients (and myself), which in itself is sad, but death by AIDS becomes almost an expected or *normal* part of life.

While working at the university, I started the Southern African Counseling Association (SACA). I wanted to link up counselors from all over Southern Africa. Not long after starting to develop this organization, I was also accepted into a Ph.D. counselor education program in the United States. The organization grew rapidly and SACA quickly had 200 members, but we had not the time to have first elections before I had to leave. After I left, the elections were never carried out, and the organization in time collapsed. I was pretty sad about that.

At the writing of this chapter, I am now a Ph.D. student and I will be having my written and oral exams soon. Though I am a student, I remain professionally active and involved in community service as well. I have worked with several AIDS organizations, as a journal reviewer, and with the Red Cross drive for flood relief in Southern Africa. I have written articles for publication, both academic and nonacademic, and I have formed the African Counseling Network. Now I want to connect counselors from all over Africa, not just Southern Africa. The Network has been pretty successful and it provides me with moral support and understanding from professionals back home as well. They have supported my advancement as a professional and I am grateful for that. The Network has a Web page: http://www.geocities.com/Athens/Crete/1919. In fact, it was through an e-mail message to this Web site that I first learned of the call for manuscripts that led to this chapter. The Network has a listserv as well.

Being a student has really been exhausting. Sometimes I would work my assistantship and two other jobs as well, besides being a single parent and full-time student. I have a good support system with a few other students. We help each other as much as we can to maintain balance, get through all the work, and keep from just quitting! We listen to each other, go bowling, and engage in other activities together. We provide help when we can, such as rides when cars break down, babysitting, cash advances, and we are as emotionally supportive as we can. I also have several people who are well established in the counseling profession and are sort of like mentors. I have never met them, but we chat via e-mail and on the phone. That has been a great help to me—having others believe in my ideas (and me). I think one of the best ways to maintain a sense of self and wellness is not to become isolated, though that is so easy to do.

After I receive my Ph.D., I am not sure where in the world I will wind up. That depends on the opportunities that come my way and, of course, the needs of my children as well. I look forward to all of the possibilities with eagerness. I do know, though, that my commitment to the ACN and counseling in Africa will remain. I would like to see the ACN become a more powerful organization. By that, I mean, for example, for ACN to get involved with the Organization of African Unity (OAU) and United Nations' programs. I plan to remain professionally active, and I have a keen interest in the development of new counseling models, the relationship between psychology and oppression, and in research epistemology and alternative research practice.

In Africa there is a critical shortage of mental health professionals, be they practitioners, school counselors/psychologists, counselor/psychologist supervisors, or counseling/psychology educators. I also think there is a great need for helping professionals in other parts of the world to collaborate with their professional counterparts in Africa and help them as they can. Knowing the warmth and vitality of the African people, I think any counseling professional would be welcomed as a partner in the development of counseling in Africa—there is so much to be done! However, it would be important for these helpers to understand that counseling in Africa can look very different from the United States. Instead of trying to change the way it is, the helper would need to work with counseling as it is practiced in Africa and view it as legitimate practice, even if there are ethical dilemmas the helpers would have to face in that process. What may be considered ethical in one country and/or culture may be considered unethical in another. Africa knows what is best for Africa and, if the helper understands that, all help will be welcomed with praises and encouragement.

There are many ways of helping in Africa that do not even require counselors to leave their own countries! Providing highly reduced price journal/association subscriptions to African subscribers/members would be important—my subscription to ACA in Zimbabwe represented two+ months of my salary! Things like twinning help too. For example, if the Oregon State University counseling department twins with the University of Zimbabwe to provide textbooks or journals, that would be an enormous help. Many educational institutions and counseling organizations in Africa are in need of equipment like computers, fax machines, VCRs, tape recorders, and video cameras. If organizations like ACA would provide free or reduced conference fees to professionals and students from Africa, this would all help. Providing scholarships for counseling students from Africa, offering help with the time-consuming tasks of building the ACN (or other professional counseling organizations in Africa), and mentoring would all help provide a voice for African counselors.

Kimberly Richards is a Ph.D. candidate in the Counselor Education program at Oregon State University. She has an AA in Liberal Arts from Massasoit Community College, a BS in Wildlife Science from Oregon State University, and a MA in Community Counseling from the University of North Alabama. She also holds a Certificate in AIDS Education, Zimbabwe Ministry of Education; a Certificate in Child Counseling and Development, Zimbabwe Institute of Systemic Therapy; and a Certificate in Family Counseling, Zimbabwe Institute of Systemic Therapy. She is currently the manager of the African Counseling Network. She is a guest reviewer for the *International Journal for the Advancement of Counselling* and co-chairperson of the Corvallis NAACP Youth Awards Program. Richards is a past president of the Zimbabwe chapter for the African Network for the Prevention and Protection Against Child Abuse and Neglect, and a former Harare branch Chairperson for National Guidance and Counseling Association of Zimbabwe. She has worked as a consultant with the Zimbabwe Ministry of Education, Musasa Project, and the Zimbabwe/United Kingdom AIDS Network.

SUGGESTED READINGS

Nicholas, L. (1993). *Psychology and oppression: Critiques and proposals.* Braamfontein, South Africa: Skotville Publishers.
   This book is a collection of writings from counselors and psychologists from Africa. The writers examine the relationship between psychology and oppression in Africa and how this relationship between psychology and oppression may impact people of African descent worldwide.

Nasamenang, A. B. (1997). Towards an Afrocentric perspective in developmental psychology. *Ife Psychologia: An International Journal, 5* (1), 127–139.
   Nasamenang presents an Afrocecentric perspective toward developmental psychology and development psychology research.

Richards, K. A. M. (2000). Counselor supervision in Zimbabwe: A new direction. *International Journal for the Advancement of Counselling, 22* (2), 143–155.
   Richards discusses the factors that would impact on the counselor supervision process in Zimbabwe and provides recommendations and practical ideas for improving counselor supervision practice in Zimbabwe.

31

COCONUT HEAVEN
LEIGH FOX

It's 4:45 A.M. and my alarm clock rings. Time to begin another day in the public school system on the island. *Hafa Adai* (Greetings) *from Guam, Where America's Day Begins.* I'm a school counselor in the tropics, located at 13 degrees north of the Equator—between Japan and Australia.

How did I end up here? One day in the midst of a cold Montana February blizzard, I decided that I was through with snow and ice. The next day, I was idly scanning the notices on the faculty bulletin board when I read a small advertisement warmly inviting me to *Teach in the Tropics.* I mailed my resume and transcripts immediately and received a phone call from Guam's Department of Education Personnel Office a month later. *Miss Fox? We'd like to hire you.* And that's all it took. I taught art on the island for the next nine years before returning to the States for my master's in Counseling.

After a wake-up shower and cup of coffee, I munch my bran cereal and fresh mango as I scan the daily paper. The clock hands have slid around to 6 A.M. and it's time to leave. My school is ten miles away from the little cottage I rent on the beach, but I don't mind the curving drive—it's on the prettiest stretch of roadway on our island. I see the ocean on my left and a majestic range of jungle green mountains on my right. Tropical flowers bloom in colorful profusion along the highway.

Twenty minutes later, I'm in my office. (My hours are 6:45 A.M. to 1:15 P.M., but I like to arrive early.) Also, Shane will be there. He's my 11-year-old assistant, you see. Shane volunteers his thirty minutes before school time, as well as his daily lunch hour, to run errands, fill my coffee maker with water, or get me caught up on his weekend adventures. It was all his idea. I suspect he likes the air conditioning. Whatever the reason, I'm grateful!

Today I have some birthday notes that need delivering to some of Shane's classmates, and he assures me that he'll leave early to drop them off on his way to Home Base. He departs with notes in hand and I glance at my daily calendar. It looks like the usual . . . another full day.

Before I can jump into it, our attendance clerk informs me that we have two new students. I welcome the kids and their father into my pale pink, English Victorian-style office. The father declines a cup of coffee and the teddy-bear tea party at the small lace-covered table seems to enchant both sister and brother. They smile shyly and visibly relax. These children are from the Marshall Islands. Most of my students are either local Chamorros or Filipinos. We have some from the outer Micronesian islands, too.

I complete their class schedules and arrange for one of our student counseling aides to take them on a short tour of the campus while I converse with their dad. They return soon and dad takes off, leaving them in our care. I walk the kids to their classrooms and the teachers are gracious about the interruption. I quickly ask who belongs to *Welcome Wagon* (WW) and several hands fly up. I know my new kids will be fine. We began WW at the beginning of the school year and it's easy to belong. You just wait for a new student to be assigned to one of your classes, then you *shower* the newcomer with kindness—say *Hello* or *Welcome,* ask that person to lunch, show off the campus, walk her or him to PE class, or even spring for ice cream at our Student Store. WW has ended the fighting between newcomers and veterans.

I have the entire group of sixth graders this year as my caseload—about 200 kids. Our school has three counselors, one per grade level. We then follow our groups through each year of middle school—grades six, seven, and eight. I'm now counseling my second bunch of students and this is my fourth year as a counselor. I've learned from several of these students that I was their older brother or sister's counselor. They seem to like that.

Each grade level also has its own principal. We are a school within a school. The students are placed in teams. Sixth graders have six team teachers while seventh and eighth have five. *Today is Team Meeting Day,* my principal cheerfully reminds me as she hustles by. I return to my office to finish up work on the classroom lesson I'll be teaching Team A students (the Dragons). I dash off a reminder note to their science teacher to confirm that I'll be spending tomorrow with him, teaching all five of his classes. In two days, I'll repeat the same procedure with the Silver Knights (Team B). Then I can check off *Exploring Careers* on my lesson plan list for sixth graders. I note that I've taught a total of 28 days, 14 lessons per team this school year.

Making sure that I have enough materials for tomorrow's lesson, I pick up my phone when the intercom buzzes. *Line one for you, Miss Fox.* Joaquin's mom has called to let me know he'll be out for a few days and can I please let his teachers know? And, while I'm at it, could I pick up his homework assignments, too? I inform her that I am just about to meet with Joaquin's teachers in our weekly meeting. She's called at the right time. I promise to call when the assignments have all been turned in and are ready for pick-up.

Our weekly session with the teaching team and sixth grade principal goes well. She always starts the meetings and I end them. Having everyone there together saves time and prevents miscommunication. All are clear about the upcoming field trip, the date that academic progress reports are due, and the myriad other details that educators have to wade through.

It's nearly time for *Lunch Bunch* in my office, so I make a dash for the restroom then check my mailbox on the way back up. I find something needing immediate attention. Glancing at the clock, I see that the kids are due to arrive in ten minutes. Looks like the paperwork required isn't too complicated. I finish up just as they burst into my office, drinks and food in hand with book bags slung over their shoulders.

I don't know who looks forward to Lunch Bunch more—the kids or me. Once a week, up to four students are allowed to bring their lunches and eat inside my office. We kick back, relax, and tell silly jokes. My Lunch Bunch clipboard is filled out months in advance. I am humbled that they want to share their time and friends with me. I stifle a giggle when I hear them come into the counseling reception area and grandly announce, *We have reservations for lunch with our counselor.*

Forty minutes of fun and laughs have flown by. The kids depart, thanking me. *No,* I say. *I'm the one who should be thanking you for rescuing me from paperwork.* They grin and skip out, leaving a trail of energy and optimism in their wake.

Time now for computer work. Last week the kids preregistered on paper for their seventh grade elective classes, so I've got to input that information into the computer by pulling up each individual's schedule and entering the data. Our school's computer program automatically schedules the academic classes, but electives have to be entered one at a time.

Our counseling department secretary pops in to remind me that our monthly faculty meeting is today after school. Luckily, it's not our department's turn to serve refreshments! I think our month is June. Better check on that, so I write myself a note to do so and tape it where I'll see it.

I return to inputting the students' electives and a teacher taps on my door. *Leigh,* she calls, *are you busy?* She looks upset and I gesture for her to come in. I use a pencil to mark where I left off and turn to face her. She's worried because one of the students has missed several days of class. We pull up the child's attendance record on the screen and, yes, she's missed a lot of school. I flip to demographics and jot down her home phone number.

We make the phone call and the mother's home. We learn that our girl has to have surgery so we ask what we can do to help. Mom assures us that she'd been planning to call but had been caught up in all the off-island hospital arrangements. *Don't worry,* we assure her, *just let us know what you need from us.* She sighs gratefully and says she'll keep us posted on her daughter's progress.

The bell rings and the teacher is off to class. She calls out a *thanks* as I dive into my file drawer. I just know I stashed some get-well cards there. Here they are. I'll catch the girl's teaching team tomorrow and have them all sign before mailing it. Back to scheduling. I've completed about 15 more when three kids walk into my office, hand me a corridor pass, and ask if I'm busy. *Not at all,* I assure them, *how can I help? It's our friend,* they begin. *We're not getting along. You look kinda mad. What's up?* I query. *Well, we're in the same Science Fair group and he won't go along with our project.*

They give me more details before I present them with some options. They elect for a group mediation session, so I send a pass for him to come to my office. He doesn't seem all that surprised to see his science group in there. I review confidentiality rights and mediation rules before giving everyone an equal chance to speak. I ask what they want and then ask if they'd like to work on a solution. They all say yes. I invite each to say one or two things that might help the situation.

The original three seem amazed to hear that the fourth member has feelings, too. The group arrives at a workable resolution and I ask for an update tomorrow at lunchtime. They promise to let me know how it's working out. They depart, arms-in-arms, friends again.

Back to the schedules. Well, not quite. The principal pages and asks me to pop down into her office. A problem has come up between two students and she wants to refer them to me. I tell her I'd like to see the kids separately. She gives me some background information. It's nearly the end of the day, so I'll see them tomorrow. We don't want students confusing discipline with counseling. A day after the occurring incident, both parties should be cooled down enough to have a more comfortable chat with me.

Back up to my office to input more scheduling data. I'm about one-third through. It's nearly 1 P.M. and I look at tomorrow's calendar. Another busy day. Hmmm, maybe I'll just dig in my heels and stay here until I finish these schedules. The dismissal bell rings and the school buses arrive to whisk the kids home. I realize that I can get more paperwork done in one solitary hour after school than in an entire school day.

Our attendance clerk peeks in at 2:30. *Leigh, are you still here? I'll be locking up and leaving soon.* That's right. She starts work at 6:00 A.M. and her workday is over. I exit out of the computer program and am gratified to see that I have about twenty-five schedules left. *After all,* I counsel myself, *tomorrow is another day.* We walk out together into the sultry sunshine.

Got to gas up and get groceries before leaving town. Living on the beach is great but the amenities aren't close. The mail contains my *Counseling Today* publication and I glance at the headlines. It's a great resource for one who lives surrounded by the Pacific Ocean, 9,000 miles away from my alma mater.

The drive winds me down. I absolutely love my job but, let's face it, work is work and home is home! I put the groceries away and drop my mail on the table. That gorgeous blue water is calling. Changing out of my usual school attire (shorts, school tee shirt and athletic shoes), I pull on my swimsuit and grab my snorkel, mask, and fins.

The spinner dolphins are out, but they are elusive and shy. The closest I've come is about ten yards away. I respect their space and luxuriate in other underwater delights—stunningly colorful fish, beautifully textured corals, interesting cavern-like features of the reef. No noise, phones, schedules, or computers. Just that dreamy, turquoise water. I float on my belly and reflect on the shoreline, rimmed by coconut palms. After twelve years in the tropics, I never tire of its exotic beauty.

The sun is beginning its nightly descent and I reluctantly leave the bay. Using the outdoor shower to rinse myself and my equipment off, I watch sunbeams swash flaming colors across the sky. Darkness is a half-hour off and my stomach starts clamoring for dinner.

After a quickly prepared meal, I settle down to read. No TV at my house! Scanning the counseling newspaper, I make note of the *Families in Crisis* editorial. I think I'll bring this up at our weekly counselors' meeting next week.

I take a peek outside and the stars pop out in brilliant clarity. They shine brightly here on the beach, with few streetlights to deflect their radiant glory. Sitting on the front step, I search for Orion.

Back inside as bedtime looms. Have to be asleep by 9. My 4:45 wake-up alarm is set. I'm reading *Chicken Soup for the Kids' Soul* and I tuck in a few bookmarks here and there—stories I think the students will like, if I read them aloud as part of my next classroom lesson. Time to close the book and get some sleep. *I am lucky,* I think as I drift off. *I'm a school counselor in Coconut Heaven.*

Leigh Fox, M.Ed is a school counselor for the government of Guam, Department of Education. She received her BA in History, English, and Science, and a BS in Art Education and Social Studies, from the University of Montana–Western. She received her first M.Ed. in Secondary Education from the University of Guam and a second M.Ed. in Counseling and Development from Montana State University–Northern. She is a Certified School Counselor in Guam and Montana. She is also a member of ASCA and ACA.

SUGGESTED READINGS

Fox, L. (1997). The reality of using informed consent, kid style. *The International Journal of Reality Therapy, 17* (1), 60–62.
   Explaining confidential rights to minor children in an understandable way can help to facilitate further counseling sessions.
Glasser, W. (1998). *Choice theory.* New York: Harper Collins.
   Teaching kids that they are in control of their choices can help them to manage school and personal problems.
Somers-Flanagan, J., & Somers-Flanagan, R. (1997). *Tough kids, cool counseling.* Alexandria, VA: ACA.
   Adopting a kid-friendly office and *dressing down* are a few visual ways to let kids see that counselors are not only advocates who care but who also know how to relate to children.

32

COUNSELING: A VIEW FROM AN ASSOCIATION MANAGEMENT PERSPECTIVE

HOWARD B. SMITH

I am what some would call an *experienced* professional counselor, having earned my master's degree over twenty-five years ago. During my career, I have held local, state, regional, and national offices, both elected and appointed, within professional counseling associations. In addition, I have been a private practitioner, a counselor educator, and an academic department head. I am currently serving as the Senior Director for Professional Affairs with the American Counseling Association.

During my career I have held positions that have afforded me the opportunities to see the counseling profession from many different vantage points. I have worked directly and indirectly with clients (as practitioner and then as counselor educator). I have worked directly and indirectly with counseling students (as faculty member and then as an academic department head). And now I work directly and indirectly with members of the profession (providing ethical and professional consultation to members and supervising the public policy and legislative efforts and the continuing education programs for the American Counseling Association). I mention these things not to impress the reader but rather to say that I have paid my dues in the profession and continue to do so as an association executive.

So what is a person like me doing in Association work as a senior level staff member? It is my hope that upon reading this chapter it will become obvious that everyone's professional journey must be crafted individually and allowed to evolve with a delicate balance of internal and external influences. Much of what has occurred within the profession has occurred because of where the profession has been in relationship to other mental health care providing professions. During my career, the focus of the profession has been on developing standards and a professional identity. Some things have occurred by luck, others as the result of long hard work of several members. I have heard it said that luck is where opportunity and preparedness meet. Counseling, as a profession, has had a lot of luck in its development. However, if it had not been prepared to move when the opportunities presented themselves, we would not be where we are today. It has been the job of my contemporaries and me to keep the profession prepared for those opportunities when they arrived.

Throughout my career I have been driven by a strong belief in the inherent value of humankind and a strong sense of amazement at the resilience of human nature. This belief was present at entry to the profession, as a master's level practitioner, and now, when I occasionally find myself thinking about retirement. People can, and do, change. Occasionally, they need a little help in doing so, whether that help comes from friends, professionals, or from the wonders of modern science and medical research. Simple suffering can also prompt individuals to engage in self-motivated change that has a significant therapeutic value as well. The real essence of professional counseling, then, is the knowledge and ability to know when professional help is needed, when to refer to the medical community, when to rely on friends to be of assistance, and when to allow simple suffering to be the agent of change.

Other writers in this book have addressed the profession from their unique perspectives. I will attempt to do the same from my current position as a senior level association staff person. To do that, let me begin by describing my position. Then, I will share with you a typical day's activities. As Senior Director for Professional Affairs with the American Counseling Association, I supervise two Departments within ACA Headquarters. These two departments, the Professional Learning and Resources Department (PLR) and the Public Policy and Legislative Department (PPL), are comprised of a total of nine staff members.

The PLR Department consists of several programs. First, to address the *learning* part of the responsibilities, there are the continuing education (CE) products that we produce for members who need CE credit for credential renewal. Supervision is the operative word here, as there is involvement by members and other staff in both preparing and submitting proposed courses and the ultimate selection of the courses. These courses are offered through Learning Institutes or Content Sessions for the Annual Conference, plus Home Study and Online courses that are offered by ACA throughout the year. In a sense, I am somewhat like a public school principal in that I need to secure a well-qualified faculty to teach the courses and work with the other staff members in the department to see to it that the courses are, in fact, offered in the best way possible. Also, I do not operate independently. The elected leaders of ACA make the final decisions regarding what we will offer. To carry the analogy a bit further, they might be seen as the Board of Education. I must also be aware of the needs of the profession to do this job effectively and, therefore, conduct surveys or needs analyses from time to time in order to provide direction to these learning services.

While the ACA Library is small by most standards, in its inventory there is every issue of every publication ACA has produced from Volume 1 (1) to the current issue. There is also an impressive collection of books regarding the profession that are used in preparing professional bibliographies, which are sold to members at cost. It is not a lending library but nonetheless plays a vital role in *resourcing* the profession. My involvement in the library consists primarily of offering suggestions, from time to time, on whether I feel we need a particular book. The ACA librarian does all of the daily work and responds directly to members.

The second program within the PLR Department is that of providing professional resources in the form of ethical and professional consultation and promoting research in various areas of the profession. We receive an average of ten to twelve calls per day from members who want to utilize the ethics consultation services. It is important to understand that we do not provide ethical advice, but rather offer assistance to the members in making their own ethical decisions, much the same as a colleague would do when asked to help. In that sense, what we do is not that much different from the counseling process in which our members engage. We attempt to help the members see the issues from a more comprehensive perspective. To do that, we encourage the callers to draw on their own understanding of right and wrong, in terms of the Code, and offer suggestions and insights to help the callers develop a more total picture of the options and issues they face. We occasionally find ourselves arguing both sides of the issue to assist the members in developing a more complete picture of the ethical dilemmas in which they find themselves.

For example, after nearly ten years of being in private practice, a counselor had just received her first subpoena. Her first instinct was not to comply. A colleague of hers had told her that she could be in legal trouble if she did not provide the requested information. In her mind, she saw a subpoena and a judge's order as being mandates. All she needed was some encouragement to contact an attorney and see about getting the subpoena quashed.

We also receive ten to twelve calls per day from members on a variety of professional issues. The issues might be reimbursement by third party payers, licensure questions, testing privileges, dealing with their school administration around the issues of the role and task of a school counselor, starting a private practice, closing a private practice, or getting on approved provider panels by managed care organizations. Perhaps the most frustrating of these calls is the call that wants to know if Licensed Professional Counselors can bill insurance companies. A simple, straightforward question with a very complex answer, given the state of recognition of LPCs as approved providers.

We occasionally get calls from people who are considering entering the counseling profession and want to know what to look for in a graduate program and what they might expect to earn in the profession. Many of these calls are from people in their late 30s or 40s who are looking for a career change. Others come from high school students who do not understand the difference between an undergraduate and a graduate degree.

The PPL Department is a bit more specialized and focused. The focus here is on advocacy for various client populations and for the profession itself. While we attempt to work on issues that present themselves at both the state and federal levels, in point of fact, we are poorly equipped to deal effectively with some state issues, due to the variation in state statutes. And, the geographic realities of being located near the federal government also dictates that we need to focus on the issues before Congress. The state issues are primarily scope of practice issues, whereas the federal issues deal with recognition in a broader sense. We also know from experience that, with the constraints of limited human and financial resources, we serve more members by focusing primarily on federal issues.

We divide the staff assignments into clinical practice issues, education issues, and rehabilitation issues. We certainly cover other issues on an as-needed basis, but these three areas constitute our primary focus. In addition to the lobbying efforts for specific legislation, the ACA staff offers assistance to congressional delegation staff members in preparation of position statements that are invited by, or offered to, the particular representative or senator, as he or she formulates his or her stance on the issues.

There is a very strong education component in this department as well. We conduct legislative training each year for a select group of members who come to Washington, receive two days of training, and follow this training with visits to Capitol Hill to meet with staff and members of Congress to lobby for client populations and the counseling profession. We also have a listserv that is maintained and being updated on a regular basis to keep the membership informed of various legislative issues involving our efforts or when we need their support.

As the Senior Director for Professional Affairs, I supervise the staff members who carry out these tasks and develop new programs in concert with the volunteer leadership. To that end, in the short time I have been on staff, we have developed a Practice Research Network (PRN) made possible through a subcontract we have with a research consulting corporation (the Lewin Group, Inc.), which has a contract with the federal government (Center for Substance Abuse Treatment). This program offers ACA an opportunity to conduct outcomes or efficacy research directly from clients of professional counselors. In this day of accountability, it is essential that we know that what we do gets results.

A second major project on which I have worked with the leadership is to expand the continuing education or professional development programs. We have developed six online courses that will make it possible for members to earn continuing education credit in the comforts of their home or office. We have also developed a course offered in an Independent Study format. The purpose here is to make the professional development that is required by credentialing bodies for renewal more available through capitalizing on state-of-the-art technology.

After describing what appears to be a broad range of responsibilities, let me share with you the typical activities. As is true of any position that consists of many tasks, it is difficult to predict what I will be doing an hour from now, let alone planning a week or more in advance. However, that is part of the job that I like; the variety of activities. Not just once in a while but every day. In any particular day I will be involved with some aspect of seven to ten of these areas just described. For example, I usually arrive at work between 6:30 and 7:00 A.M., because early morning is the most productive time of the day and has the least interruptions. I have more control over how I spend my time early in the day. I use this time to respond to member inquiries in written form and to complete the unfinished business of the previous day.

The calls and e-mail messages from members requesting ethical or professional consultation begin to come in around 9:00 A.M. and the flow will increase to peaking early- to mid-afternoon and then begin to subside on toward 5:00 to 6:00 P.M. Being located on the east coast makes it difficult for members who live in the western part of the nation to have access to an office that closes at 5:00 EDT (which means 2:00 PDT). Depending on the nature and complexity of the call, I will spend up to half an hour with the member. In order to accommodate a total of twenty to twenty-five calls per day, ranging from a very brief response to one that takes up to thirty minutes, you can see that the segments between calls is usually very brief, making it difficult to have long periods of concentration on other tasks. This, I would admit, is the most frustrating aspect of the job. While I enjoy the variety, the lack of extended time to concentrate, due to the frequent interruptions, makes it frustrating at times when deadlines for projects are approaching all too rapidly. This is where having a strong and supportive staff is essential. I delegate as much as is appropriate to the staff.

The calls come from professional counselors who have several years of experience all the way to those individuals who are thinking about a mid-life career change and want to talk about the profession from that perspective. While this adds to the richness of the experience, it can be a bit disconcerting at times. For example, I might have a call or an e-mail request from a high school student who found his or her way to the ACA Web page and who wants me to provide him or her with *all the information we have* about being a counselor. I would attempt to give this person a fairly accurate picture of the virtues of the profession and encourage him or her to give it serious consideration. Within five minutes of that call, one comes to me from a counselor who has been in practice for twenty-five years and has just received his or her first subpoena and wants some guidance on how to handle the situation. Persons such as these are anxious and upset, often somewhat embarrassed to be calling and asking for assistance. Some even refuse to give their names.

A few months ago, I received a call from the receptionist who sits at the front door of the building and notifies ACA staff members when they have a guest. Since I was not expecting anyone (and we rarely have members who just walk in), I was somewhat surprised when I was told that someone needed to see me. Apparently, this person, who had been drinking, just walked in off the street and began telling the receptionist that he was going to commit suicide and wanted to talk to someone. Since I was the only LPC on staff, and even though I do not provide services directly to the public, the situation required action.

I believe that the uniqueness of this perspective is part of what makes it so challenging. Other members in the profession provide a very vital service to their clients, to their communities, and to society as a whole, by providing state-of-the-art mental health care services to them in an ethical and professional fashion. I see my role as providing support to my colleagues, fellow professional counselors, by helping them stay current in the profession through the continuing education courses and by offering ethical and professional consultation when they request it. In that sense, it is incumbent upon me to keep my finger on the pulse of the profession, to stay in touch with practicing counselors in all of the specialties of the profession, and to be a worthy consultant when any colleague requests consultation.

It really is not the kind of position that lends itself to having a counseling student do an internship in one of the departments I supervise due to the lack of clinical opportunity. However, it would provide an excellent introduction to certain aspects of the profession. I am currently considering seeing if the leadership would consider having a student do an independent study project where he or she would come to work for a semester or summer session, during which time ACA could provide an opportunity and exposure across a broad spectrum of the profession. Another possibility would be to provide sabbatical experiences for counselor educators where they could come and conduct research in the ACA Library, gain some exposure to the post-degree continuing education needs of people in the profession, and also do some legislative work on an issue of their choice.

I hope that what I have described here has generated within the reader the excitement I feel for the position. It is stressful to be sure, which necessitates developing some survival skills. I have developed at least two that are very effective for me and very different from each other. The first is that I like to take long motorcycle trips. This gets me completely away from dealing with people and the profession. When I ride, I do my best to just be another motorcycle enthusiast.

The other is volunteer work that I do for the American Red Cross in its Disaster Mental Health Services following a national disaster. This activity throws me in the other direction—directly into contact with people who are either impacted by the disaster itself or who are trying to provide relief to those who have been impacted through their own efforts as a volunteer. I am also an instructor for the Disaster Mental Health Services course. These activities sometimes cost me my annual leave, but I have yet to feel as though I have been cheated by going out on a relief operation as opposed to going on vacation. The change of pace, the change of duties, and the change of scenery all contribute to the attraction this holds for me. The biggest attraction of all, however, is the satisfaction I get from knowing that I made a contribution toward helping individuals in crisis.

Howard B. Smith, Ed.D, NCC, CCMHC, LPC received his doctoral degree in Educational Psychology and Counseling from the University of South Dakota in 1980. He is a Past President of the American Mental Health Counselors Association, past Chair of the American Counseling Association Public Policy and Legislation Committee, past Chair of the Professionalization Committee, and has served as Parliamentarian of the American Counseling Association Governing Council. He has held offices in state and regional professional associations as well. He has twenty years of experience as a counselor educator and department head.

SUGGESTED READINGS

American Counseling Association. (1995). *The ACA code of ethics and standards of practice.* Alexandria, VA: The American Counseling Association.
  This document is absolutely essential for every counselor. It should be consulted any time there is an issue. It will provide guidance in the decision making on practice issues as well as ethical concerns.

Bernstein, B. E., & Hartsell, T. L. Jr. (1998). *The portable lawyer for mental health professionals: An A–Z guide to protecting your clients, your practice, and yourself.* New York: Wiley.
  This is a handy guide for private practitioners in easy-to-use format. It includes sample forms for a variety of situations in which counselors may find themselves.

Browning, C. H., & Browning, B. J. (1996). *How to partner with managed care: A "do-it-yourself kit" for building working relationships and getting steady referrals.* New York: Wiley.
  This book has a plethora of ideas on working with managed care organizations and offers suggestions that are practical and effective.

Frager, S. (2000). *Managing managed care: Secrets from a former case manager.* New York: Wiley.
  Frager takes an interesting stance on many of the most irritating issues faced by counselors when attempting to work with managed care organizations. She helps alleviate some of the frustration with simple, straightforward explanations from an insider's perspective.

Lawless, L. L. (1997). *How to build and market your mental health practice.* New York: Wiley.
  This book is chock full of useful ideas and suggestions for building and maintaining a private practice. The author has a clear writing style that leads the reader through the steps.

Richards, D. L. (1990). *Building and maintaining your private practice.* Alexandria, VA: American Association for Counseling and Development (now the American Counseling Association).
  This book is a classic. Richards does more than provide information. He discusses key issues faced by a counselor who is considering private practice and takes the reader through the emotional preparedness for this venture.

LIFE AS AN EDITOR:
THE *TAO* OF WRITING, REVIEW,
REJECTION, AND REVISION

EARL J. GINTER

Being asked to describe what one does for work is similar to being asked to pause and focus on some autonomic nervous system function that is self-governing. I still remember when I first took notice, as a child, that I was breathing and almost simultaneously realized that something so natural was inexplicable. I also noticed that the more I focused attention on my breathing, the more it seemed to require effort to maintain this process. It appears that paying attention to something that is typically taken for granted sometimes makes it less automatic and even more difficult to understand—one of the dangers involved in self-reflection.

Difficulties aside, as I focused on identifying what aspects of being an editor are important to identify and discuss, I realized for the first time there are several concepts from Eastern philosophy that I could borrow to capture the essence of what it means to be an editor. These concepts provide meaningful metaphors for the process of becoming and serving as an editor. The concepts are *Tao, te,* and *satori,* three ideas that also provide the three subheadings found in this chapter. (Note: The term *concept* is not fully applicable to what I have borrowed from Eastern philosophy since *Tao, te,* and *satori* are viewed as transcending both written and spoken language.) Specifically, I provide a summary of what (the *te*) led up to my current position as editor for the *Journal of Counseling & Development,* followed by a description of a day in the life of an editor (the *Tao* of editorship). I conclude with several of the things that I have learned (*satori*) as an editor.

WRITER, RESEARCHER, AND EDITORIAL BOARD MEMBER:
ALLOWING THE *TE* TO UNFOLD AND DEVELOP

While philosophical concepts possess layers of meanings, one meaning of *te* is the innate strength or energy that resides in each person and enables each person to achieve his or her unique way of interacting with the world. Meaningful work is one manifestation of *te*. If the work is not meaningful, that is, congruent with a person's potentiality, then one's *te* is not flowing correctly and the person may even experience a type of condition that in Western philosophy has been equated with *existential anxiety*. The primary lesson of *te* is to be true to one's self.

Shortly after receiving my doctorate at The University of Georgia, I accepted a teaching position at Nicholls State University in Thibodaux, Louisiana, the same university where I had received my master's. Nicholls was a commuters' university that emphasized teaching over research and publishing. I was assigned five different courses to teach my first semester. I found myself working until 10 P.M. on Fridays to pull together my lectures for the wide mix of undergraduate and graduate courses I was assigned. Following the initial shock of being assigned five different courses, I was able to turn my attention to other activities. A prevailing interest of mine was writing. In spite of the heavy teaching load, the university's inconsistency in rewarding faculty members who published, and the many different demands placed on a new member of a counseling/psychology department, I always found energy to write, and write, and write.

I wrote manuscripts and proposals for conference presentations. During this stage in my journey toward becoming an editor, I learned what it meant to devote time and effort to a scholarly product, only to discover submitting a manuscript or proposal was no guarantee of acceptance by reviewers. In spite of the frustration, I persisted and gradually learned how to organize and present my thoughts to gain acceptance by reviewers. *Negative, nonproductive energy* was replaced by *productive energy* when I recognized that the reviewers and editors rejecting my early efforts were not rejecting *me*, but rather were rejecting a manuscript. Their comments almost always displayed considerable thought. I soon understood that their comments could serve as a very useful guide to strengthen a manuscript or proposal for submission elsewhere. I also realized that frustration itself possessed neither a negative nor a positive quality; rather, frustration was a sign that some potential avenue of meaningful experience was blocked. One area of frustration resulted from having to depend on others for data analysis and recommendations about research procedures. Energy was freed up for a higher level of productivity when I acquired research skills (statistics/research methodology was my minor area of study during my doctoral program).

In addition to acquiring research skills and continuing to write and submit manuscripts and proposals, during 1985 I applied for a position on the editorial board of *Counselor Education and Supervision*; Richard W. Bradley was editor. I was accepted as a member of the review board and, soon after, I started reviewing articles submitted for blind review. Reviewing and commenting on the work of others contributed greatly to further developing my own writing and research knowledge and ultimately placed me in a better position to serve as an editor. Subsequent to this editorial board position I served in the following roles: editorial board member for *The Professional Reader* and the *Record in Educational Administration and Supervision*, contributing editor for the *National Association of Rehabilitation Professionals in the Private Sector*, chair of the American Mental Health Counselors Association's Publication Committee, associate editor for the *Journal of Mental Health*

Counseling, member of the American Counseling Association's (ACA) Editorial Advisory Board, editor for the *Journal of Mental Health Counseling*, co-chair then chair of the ACA's Media Committee, and interim editor of the *Journal of Counseling & Development*.

All of these experiences contributed to amassing a group of skills that allow me to currently serve as editor for the *Journal of Counseling & Development* (JCD), a journal read by approximately 50,000 professionals (not counting the readers at various institutions around the world that subscribe). *JCD* is a journal that has undergone many changes over many decades and can be directly traced back to the beginnings of the counseling field in the United States (personal communication, Sylvia Nisenoff, July 6, 1999). Listening to and following the lead of what energizes us (i.e., *te*) has both surprising and personally fulfilling results, especially in light of the starting point marked by that first step taken to start on a personal journey fueled by one's *te*.

A DAY IN THE LIFE OF AN EDITOR: THE *TAO* OF EDITORSHIP

If the *te* is the energy that enables us to follow a certain path, the *Tao* of editorship is the *path* itself—a more literal translation is *the way*. Paraphrasing one Chinese philosopher, Lao Tzu, the essence of publishing resembles the empty space inside the hub of a wheel. The empty space *supports* the axle (editor) and wheel (journal) as they turn to reach an end point (published issue of the journal). In *JCD*'s case a myriad of elements come together to fill the void—in addition to the editor, there are associate editors, statistical consultants, an editorial consultant, editorial assistants, 139 editorial board members and ad hoc reviewers evaluating manuscripts, and, of course, the authors submitting manuscripts. The following represents a typical day in the life of this editor (times noted are starting times for a series of related activities).

Monday—3:30 A.M.

The alarm goes off. My first thought, semi-coherent I admit, is that it is Monday and *I must get up or fall behind on journal stuff.* After three cups of coffee, two slices of dark toast, two ounces of peach jam, and 30 minutes of early morning television (avoiding infomercials), I remove three manuscripts from my briefcase. These manuscripts are ones I will not send off to an associate editor for a recommendation. Instead, I will make a decision on each. Reviewers' evaluations (ratings and comments) and my own evaluation of each manuscript's merits result in a decision of rejection for two of the manuscripts. The immediate task now is to compose two rejection letters. A yellow sticky note on each manuscript will remind me to copy the written comments to attach to each letter that I typed on my laptop computer.

4:45 A.M.

I return to the third manuscript. The manuscript is a revision that was sent out to reviewers for a second round of evaluations. The same reviewers who reviewed the original version reviewed the revision (along with the revised manuscript, each reviewer received a copy of prior reviews and my letter requesting a revision). The second evaluation results in both reviewers recommending *acceptance, after minor changes/corrections.* I read the manuscript, the most recent reviews, past reviews, my letter requesting a revision, and the author's cover letter that she had sent with the revised manuscript (a letter that outlines changes made and two requested changes that were not made along with justifications for not making them). I agree with both reviewers' recommendation, but I have a concern that requires contacting one on the journal's statistical consultants. Again, a yellow sticky note placed on the manuscript will later remind me to phone Joseph Wisenbaker, one of *JCD*'s statistical consultants, to obtain an answer to what appears to be a misuse of technical language.

5:55 A.M.

Another cup of coffee and then thirty minutes on the treadmill. I shower, wake the kids, and prepare lunch for my oldest son, who is waiting for his friend to provide him a ride to high school. I drop my other two sons off at their respective schools.

7:45 A.M.

I enter the *JCD* office housed in the College of Education. My primary work site is across campus in the Division of Academic Assistance—I am a full professor working as a counselor and teacher. At the *JCD* office I check for phone messages compiled by John Petrocelli, one of *JCD*'s editor assistants. These messages usually pertain to questions from authors or potential authors interested in obtaining information before submitting a manuscript. I also leave a message for John. The message informs John that I have decided to send a certified letter to one of *JCD*'s editorial board members who has not completed three reviews in a row and has not responded to John's voice mail messages about the missing reviews, John's letter of inquiry, or John's e-mail messages. I then review the manuscript files and pull several to be sent to one of the associate editors for an evaluation. Finally, I review the editorial assistants' worksheets (sheets outlining what was done and the amount of time devoted to each task). The sheets outline the time devoted to logging manuscripts, notifying authors of a manuscript's receipt, and the tracking of manuscripts that have already been sent out to reviewers or associate editors.

9:30 A.M.

I leave the *JCD* office and travel to my official university office to carry out my official university duties (and earn a salary—an honorarium is paid by ACA to cover personal expenditures related to *JCD*) as a teaching professor and practicing counselor. While the University provides a graduate student to assist me in my

JCD-related work and the ACA provides funds for a second graduate assistant, the University has not provided me release time from any of my contracted duties. Once I arrive at this second location, I copy several handouts for my three classes (12 faculty members share one secretary), review my notes for the classes, and check to see if I am scheduled to meet any students for individual counseling.

11:05 A.M.

I teach three classes back to back. This back-to-back time management technique enables me to avoid losing time between classes, that is, I learned early in my teaching career that if there is too much time between my classes I tend to use the *between time* inefficiently.

2:30 P.M.

After taking about fifteen minutes to travel back to my office, I break for a late lunch. I use this time to collect my thoughts and decide the work priorities for the remainder of the day (e.g., which manuscripts should I place in my briefcase?).

3:30 P.M.

I leave the university to pick up one of my sons from his elementary school, which is followed by picking up another son from his middle school. The next two to four hours frequently are devoted to activities related to family responsibilities. The amount of time spent on family responsibilities depends on my schedule and Jackie's schedule. Jackie and I share several responsibilities, and we alternate responsibilities depending on our schedules. Jackie is a registered nurse who works at a local hospital. After twenty-four years of marriage, I still never seem to get the hang of her variable schedule. Simply stated, who does what is largely dependent on who is free at certain times that particular day. When I am not fulfilling family responsibilities, the remainder of the afternoon will be tied up with faculty responsibilities, such as various Division or university-wide committees. Occasionally, my afternoon will be devoted to working with a graduate student on his or her dissertation.

6:30 P.M.

As a licensed professional counselor, I believe it is essential to work with clients in a clinical setting. I also believe an editor is more likely to select articles that are meaningful to practitioners when that editor is involved in private practice. Thus, I reserve a portion of my time to see clients at a clinic called Psych-Health Associates.

8:30 P.M.

Time spent with my children and Jackie—and having dinner with Jackie. This is the time spent that keeps me grounded in the real world.

10:30 P.M.

I read over two manuscripts and make decisions. One will be rejected and one is a revision that will require additional changes before I can accept it for publication. I also spend about 15 minutes looking through the package sent by ACA Publications (the ACA department responsible for producing journals) to my home address. The package contains 128 pages for the next issue, pages that have been typeset and ready for my review and approval. Typically, I am allotted five days by ACA to proof the 128 pages for corrections.

Tuesday—5:00 A.M.

The alarm goes off . . . Having limited space for this chapter prevents me from discussing many of the work-related activities that can alter the typical day-in-the-life description I have provided. For example, there are times I must devote attention to revising policies, calculating the amount of space and the sequence of articles for an issue, following up with authors who have not returned a final copy of the article accepted for publication or have failed to return the copyright form or some other form required before an article can be sent to ACA Publications, interviewing and hiring new editorial assistants, training new editorial assistants, determining and submitting a budget for *JCD*'s operation, recruiting new board members, and, above all, maintaining an awareness of important professional issues and the interest of *JCD* readers, so that issues and interests are reflected in articles accepted for publication.

IS THERE ENLIGHTENMENT AT THE JOURNEY'S END? YES—*SATORI* HAPPENS

According to Japanese Zen Buddhists, enlightenment or *satori* can occur for a number of reasons. It happens both as a result of becoming devoted to some activity that provides a regimen (an editor's work certainly provides this) or when *everything falls in place* and spontaneously a sudden awareness or knowledge occurs. Considering that serving as an editor provides ample opportunities for both, the following represents just four of the many things I have come to realize about being an editor.

1. *The Editor and the Journal Are Not One and the Same.* Regardless of what an editor thinks (or what others think), editors work *for* journals. While the editor from a surface perspective has considerable control over each published issue of a journal, there are many factors involved that are beyond an editor's control. For example, regardless of what topics are important and deserve coverage, authors must submit manuscripts pertaining to the topic if the journal is to bring scholarly attention to the topic. Even inviting an author to submit a manuscript on a topic is no guarantee a manuscript will be submitted. In relation to such restrictions, I have on occasion compared journals to large oil tankers on the ocean—making an immediate 90-degree turn in one direction is simply not possible.

2. *The Editor Will Never Satisfy Everyone.* This outcome of work can be very troublesome, since there is a very high probability that editors of counseling journals pursued training in counseling because of a strong interest in helping others. Being an editor forces one to develop the ability to identify and reject those manuscripts that should be rejected. This is not a pleasant experience for the author or editor who frequently realizes that even though the author has devoted a great deal of time and energy to a manuscript, the central idea or research approach is flawed. I have found that every time I forget this unpleasant aspect of serving as an editor, I receive a letter or e-mail clearly outlining, in emotional language, my failings as an editor. In such cases the only solace an editor sometimes receives is that the correspondence commonly reflects the same quality issues that resulted in rejection of the manuscript and thus reflect an indirect validation of the decision to reject.

3. *An Editor Can Dramatically Increase Her or His Competence by Surrounding Himself or Herself with People Who Voice Disagreements.* Serving as an editor can feed the belief that one is omniscient. After becoming an editor, one begins to notice that some colleagues at professional conferences (and during other types of encounters) treat her or him as if he or she is brighter or possesses an excess of some other human characteristic that is generally recognized as very desirable in one's culture. During my first tenure as an editor, I learned that I was not automatically brighter as a result of accepting the position of editor. If anything, I began to question my level of intelligence for agreeing to serve. I have selected some associate editors and board members because their views are different from mine. The end result is that a greater degree of diversity is injected into the whole process, which results in a journal that better meets the diverse needs of the professionals reading the journal.

4. *Journals Thrive When Approached from a Perspective of Simplicity.* This insight is not to be equated with publishing only articles that avoid complexity or controversy. Some of the most important articles—articles that had a beneficial effect on the whole of counseling—have been complex or controversial, or both. I am writing about a different kind of simplicity. A Chinese term for this is *p'u* which refers to an *unfinished* state or condition, such as a rough piece of wood before the carver shapes it into something recognizable. As with the other terms I have borrowed from Eastern philosophy, this one also has different meanings. For me it serves as a reminder to enter situations with as few preconceived notions as possible. For example, if I have the same expectations for all authors (novice and seasoned authors), I am likely to miss those opportunities to see the true potential of a rough manuscript—the potential for it to make a significant contribution to the field of counseling.

   In closing, I believe it is important to emphasize that this is just one version of what it means to work as an editor. If I were to distill everything down (both what was said in this chapter and what was not said) to one comment concerning work, it would be *follow the counseling "path" that energizes you the most in whatever set of activities you call work.*

Earl J. Ginter, Ph.D., LPC, LMFT earned a BA (Magna Cum Laude) with a major in psychology and a minor in philosophy and social studies from Nicholls State University in 1974, a MA degree with a major in psychology and counseling and a minor in guidance from Nicholls State University in 1977, and a Ph.D. in counseling and student personnel services with a minor area of focus in research from The University of Georgia in 1983. Currently, Ginter is a licensed professional counselor and a licensed marriage and family therapist affiliated with Psych-Health Associates in Athens, Georgia, and he is a professor at The University of Georgia. Prior to serving as editor for the *Journal of Counseling & Development,* he had obtained a number of experiences beginning in 1985 that were related to evaluating and editing publications. He served as an editorial board member for *Counselor Education and Supervision, The Professional Reader,* and *Record in Educational Administration and Supervision,* as a contributing editor for *National Association of Rehabilitation Professionals in the Private Sector,* and as an associate editor and editor for *Journal of Mental Health Counseling.*

SUGGESTED READINGS

American Psychological Association. (1994). *Publication manual of the American Psychological Association* (4th ed.). Washington, DC: Author.
>   Represents *the* style manual for writers and the editors evaluating writers' submissions. This work is an indispensable tool that covers topics such as content and organization of the manuscript, expression of ideas, APA editorial style manuscript preparation, and means to achieve specificity in reporting research as well as the appropriate manner to write about a study's participants so that information is both accurate and sensitive.

Lockwood, T., & Scott, K. (1999). *A writer's guide to the Internet.* London: Allison & Busby Ltd.
>   While the eventual impact of the Internet on the whole of publishing is impossible to predict with certainty, it is indisputable that creation of the Internet ranks in the same category as introduction of the printing press. Although this suggested reading does not focus specifically on writing journal articles, the work does serve as a useful guide for the novice who is not familiar with use of the Internet, e-mail, mailing lists and networking, researching topics electronically, and other aspects of what is now available due to advances in computer technologies.

McGowan, A. S. (1996). The research and publishing process: A rational approach. *The Journal for the Professional Counselor, 11,* 9–17.
>   A former chair of the American Counseling Association's Council of Editors wrote this overview, which covers how to write journal articles. This publication has relevant suggestions about conducting a thorough literature review, the importance of following the guidelines for a journal, tips on packaging a manuscript to create a good first impression, and the importance of realizing rejection is part of the process and that there are ways to effectively deal with rejection.

.